THE ELEMENTS OF PIZZA

THE
ELEMENTS
OF
PIZZA

Unlocking the Secrets to
World-Class Pies at Home

KEN FORKISH

Photography by Alan Weiner

Ten Speed Press
Berkeley

CONTENTS

INTRODUCTION

IT'S REALLY UP TO YOU.

The hidden reality of pizza is that you can easily make better pizza at home than you can buy at any but the best independently owned, quality-focused pizzerias. All you need are good ingredients—flour, canned tomatoes, and cheese—plus a few tools and a standard home kitchen oven. And some good instruction. Even if you live somewhere that has great pizzerias, imagine making your own—a pizza that you can be proud of and is exactly how you like it. Discover for yourself what different cheeses are like on pizza: splurge on water buffalo mozzarella, see what happens when you seek out caciocavallo cheese, or try adding freshly grated Pecorino Romano. Master thin-crust and Neapolitan-style pizza. Bang out a couple of killer pan pizzas to eat with Sunday football. Serve it with confidence to your family and friends. Making it yourself will give you a greater appreciation for the craft of the *pizzaiolos* at your favorite pizzeria: you will probably find yourself looking more closely at their shaping technique; the dough they use and its texture; and how it's topped, loaded into the oven, and baked. By making pizza yourself, you become more intimate with it. It's seductive. You are more informed, and that understanding leads to better pizza, great pleasure, and plenty of pride.

I grew up in Maryland, and I now live in Portland, Oregon, where I opened Ken's Artisan Bakery in 2001 after a Silicon Valley career, first as an engineer and then as a sales guy. In 2005 we started making pizza once a week in our big bread oven at the bakery and called it Monday Night Pizza. Then, in 2006, I opened Ken's Artisan Pizza, a wood-fired-oven pizzeria, with my head baker turned chef Alan Maniscalco. My third venture is a full-service restaurant called Trifecta Tavern & Bakery, open since 2013, where we include flatbreads on our dinner menu that are baked in yet another wood-fired oven. I've been to Italy about a dozen times. I wrote about pizza in my first book, *Flour Water Salt Yeast*. So, what did I know about pizza? Put it this way: the more you know, the more you know you don't know. As it turns out, I had plenty left to learn.

Researching pizza for this book took me to Naples for the first time to visit its pizzerias. Many of the lessons I learned there opened my eyes to another way of thinking about pizza—especially about how to make the dough. It took a while to realize what was right in front of my eyes: think like a *pizzaiolo*, not like a bread baker. Pizza dough and bread dough have different needs. Bread wants to expand to its maximum volume; pizza does not. Pizza dough has structural needs—to stretch without breaking and without being too elastic. I knew this before, but I was still

Pizzaiolos at Da Michele in Naples.

1

thinking of pizza as a kind of bread. The bread I like to make comes from wet doughs—made with a lot more water than you're probably used to—but pizza doughs that are equally wet don't work very well. And who knew that I should think about matching the hydration of the dough to the type of oven the pizza bakes in? At my pizzeria we long ago figured out the right dough for our oven. What I realized is that finding the perfect dough, *and* figuring out the perfect baking technique, is different when you're baking in a standard home oven. What's more, it depends on the style of pizza you want to make.

The best part of this little journey of mine was affirming that great pizza in the home kitchen is not complicated. It's really very simple. On the pages that follow I take you through the process—how to make it—and the reasoning behind it so you can learn the same lessons I learned.

Even in Italy, more than 25 percent of households make their own pizza from time to time. It's an easy meal that comforts—pizza baked in a pan in the home kitchen. I guarantee you can make better pizza at home than you would buy from any chain, and for less money, too. And it's going to have heart. A decent home oven (not necessarily an expensive one); a baking stone, or better yet, a baking steel; a few baking accessories; good ingredients; and simple-to-follow instructions will get you there. (Trust me, you can buy affordable ingredients that are far better than any chain pizza place will put on your pie.) Making pizza can be a solo effort, where you enjoy the process as much as the result (and get better every time you do it), or it can be a tradition you share with your family or housemates.

Great pizza as we know it has been happening in Italy for about 150 years, especially in the region surrounding the Bay of Naples. Great pizza is happening in America, too, with a dramatic growth in quality pies around the country in the twenty-first century. And this may not sound like news, but in the last several years a movement has grown that honors traditional techniques and ingredients, then goes beyond the standard to push the quality boundaries higher. It's in the air. People are traveling long distances to eat pizza made by Franco Pepe at Pepe in Grani in the small village of Caiazzo, about a 45 minute drive from Naples. The queues at Pizzeria Bianco in Phoenix are legendary. Nancy Silverton's ingredient-inspired Pizzeria Mozza in Los Angeles is known for brilliance on top of a great crust. The Salvo brothers in Naples select from seven different olive oils to match to their pizzas. Enzo Coccia at Pizzaria La Notizia in Naples is packing the house with a fantastic dough, perfectly baked and using the traditional ingredients of a TSG pizza (see page 41), and then going beyond to source specific flours and toppings. "There are two pillars of pizza: the ingredients and the *pizzaiolo*," according to one Neapolitan I met. Paulie Gee's, Roberta's, and Franny's are killing it in Brooklyn and making their own distinctly New York versions of Neapolitan pizza, and Pierre Luigi Roscioli in Rome lists the provenance of his ingredients on his menu using things like Piennolo and Datterini tomatoes, *culatello* from Podere Cadassa, and *mozzarella di bufala* from Paestum.

I find great inspiration from all of these people. The pizzas from each of these places are all distinctly their own and reflect a variety of pizza styles. Should the pizza crust be spotted with char on its rim and underneath? Should it be stiff when you hold it on its end, or should it sag? What's the best kind of cheese to use? Bread flour or Italian 00 flour? The answer to all of the questions is that it depends on what kind of pizza you are making, and even then there is plenty of wiggle room and individual variation. Let's get this out right now: *There is no one way to do it*, no one right

Pizzaiolos Franco Pepe (top left)
and Enzo Coccia (center right).

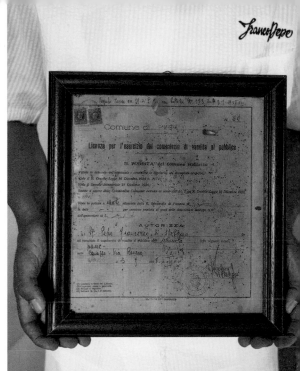

answer, no one platonic ideal of pizza that applies to everyone. Di Fara's pizza on Avenue J in Brooklyn is nothing like the pizza at La Notizia, Salvo, or Da Michele in Naples, which are nothing like Frank Pepe's in New Haven, Patsy's in Harlem, Buddy's in Detroit, Totonno's on Coney Island, Delancey in Seattle, Anthony Mangieri's Una Pizza Napoletana in San Francisco, or Pizzeria Bianco in Phoenix. All are terrific pizzas. That's one thing that's great about pizza, because depending on where you're from and what kind of pizza is iconic in your memory, there is usually just one right answer to these questions. Pizza is a very personal experience. And you're likely to forcefully defend your opinion, because in your mind this isn't even a matter of debate—it's a clear right and wrong and I'm stupid for suggesting otherwise.

This is a book that tells you how to make really great pizza at home in *many* styles—Neapolitan, Roman, American pan, New York, creative flatbread, gluten-free. In my first book I wrote how I high-fived my dog, Gomez, when I discovered how good pizza from my standard home kitchen oven could be. Great pizza at home can happen and it won't break your brain or your daily routine. It all starts with a good dough, and I've got you covered there.

The soul of pizza starts with Neapolitan pizza— the soul of pizza *is* Napoli. It started there and it's a defining cultural emblem. And after making pizza professionally for a short nine years, I was lucky enough to travel to Naples—to meet some of Italy's top *pizzaiolos*, go to a *mozzarella di bufala* farm and dairy, tour a tomato plant, and visit the flour mill that provides flour for most of Naples's pizzerias with the idea that I would gather inspiration and knowledge to inform the writing of this book. When I sat down with people whose families had been making pizza for the last hundred years, I kind of had my

ass handed to me—gently, for the most part—and I asked myself: Who am I to even think I could represent what pizza is all about? But you know what? I discovered that there is a deep tradition that defines this culture, these people, and their food, and we are lucky to have had it become part of our lives, too. Naples doesn't own pizza, but it lives and breathes it like no other place. It's kind of like I've been making some nice music for the last ten years, and then I meet Beethoven or Mozart. And these are beautiful people who are willing to share their knowledge and experience that came from generations of hard, hard work and attention to detail. Pizza is a way of life in Naples. It flows through the bloodline. But people everywhere get emotional about the pizza they love, be they from Rome, Detroit, New Jersey, St. Louis, Old Forge, Portland, or the five boroughs of New York City. My goal in this book is to honor the pizza makers everywhere, but to do that, I had to start in Naples. Naples is the root of all pizza that follows.

My first book, *Flour Water Salt Yeast*, was about bringing methods used in the best artisan bakeries into the home kitchen to make professional-quality bread (with a few pizzas included for good measure). This book has a similar aim, but this time I focus solely on pizza and draw inspiration from several of the best pizza makers in Italy and the United States. I have my own pizzeria too, of course, but instead of an insular "here's the pizza we make" approach to this book's recipes, I want to offer you something that's more representative of the range of pizza styles and traditions that inspire me. These are practitioners of the pizza craft for whom pizza is *the* principal expression of their lives, and in Naples it is a fundamental part of a regional identity. I'm a big fan of them all. I ask myself what I can learn from them, and how to make my version of whatever they do best. Replicating is not the point. What's theirs is theirs, and it is

of their time and place. But I can look at a Detroiter pizza and make a pan pizza my way that is inspired by it. So here in this book I give you my take on pizza styles I admire.

If you have already read and used my first book, *Flour Water Salt Yeast* (*FWSY*), you will find here the same methods for measuring ingredients using a scale, mixing dough by hand in a small dough tub, and making your own wild yeast leavening culture. I made some refinements too, with recipes for smaller batches of dough than those that were in my first book, and for using smaller amounts of flour to start and maintain a levain. This book's pizza dough recipes are streamlined, and they take less time to make than the pizza doughs in *FWSY*—but they make better pizza. I decided to abandon my bread baker's point of view and instead adopt pizza-dough-making methods I learned that are widely practiced in Italy.

Also, as in my first book, I've tried to write with the understanding that you need some recipes for dough that work within what I'm assuming to be a standard workweek, where you probably go to work in the morning, come home in the evening, and don't have a bunch of time to make dinner. My pizza doughs are long-fermented because that's how you get the best flavors and textures—good flavors build while you sleep. This is ideal. So, as with my first book, time is treated like an ingredient, and I've highlighted the dough-rising schedule up front in each recipe. Mix a dough in the evening, shape it into dough balls (5 minutes) a couple of hours later, put them into the fridge, and when you get home the next night you fire up the oven and not much more than an hour after that you have an amazing pizza for dinner that was a total of 30 to 40 minutes of work. Or, maybe it's a weekend, and you get up on Saturday

*"You always have pleasure in doing your thing well;
it must give you independence from the whole buffoonery
into which we have been born."*

—Albert Einstein

morning deciding you want to have pizza that night but you were too wacked Friday night to even think about the next night's dinner. Make a dough first thing in the morning, divide the dough into balls 2 hours later, fire up the oven in the evening, pop open a bottle of wine, put on *La Traviata,* and the world is yours. Do all your Saturday stuff in between. Be a hero.

All you have to do is learn the method, and after a few repetitions you won't even be looking at the instructions anymore; you'll maybe just double-check the recipe for ingredient quantities.

If you're feeling more ambitious, I have a dough recipe that uses a pre-fermented dough called biga. And if you really want to go the distance, I show you how to make a naturally leavened dough that uses your own starter and no commercial yeast. You can use any of these doughs—naturally leavened, made with pre-ferments, or straight—to make one of several styles of pizza: Neapolitan; Roman-style with a super-thin, crackery crust; American pan pizzas and bar pizzas; and New York–style classic hearth pies. You can integrate excellent pizza, made at home just

the way you like it, into a busy lifestyle. If you want to splurge on ingredients, go for it. If you want to do it on a budget, you can do that, too—and still spend less and make a better pie than you would buy out. Maybe for you pizza making is about engaging your family or housemates in the effort. Maybe it's a solo pursuit where you take pride in geeking out on the details. Pick your crust. Pick your toppings and sauce. It's showtime!

CHAPTER 1
THE SOUL OF PIZZA

In 2014, a trip to Italy changed my thinking about pizza forever. I was moved by the way the people I met in Naples relate to pizza: for them, it was a soulful connection, related to the bigger picture of who they are as a culture. And then I became interested in the stories of the immigrants from Naples and the south of Italy who began making pizza in the United States in the early 1900s. I wanted to learn how pizza evolved from its early days to the present, how it stayed true to its roots in Italy, and how it grew to be its own thing in America. The stories always came back to the pizza maker, and how his or her passion was as important as the quality of the tomatoes.

ITALY

Enzo Coccia, a globally celebrated Neapolitan *pizzaiolo*, altered my pizza reality when he made me stare at a naked truth I had not confronted directly before. "Pizza is not the same as bread," he said, and I'm glad he said it with force. Meaning I needed to adjust my thinking.

I set out to understand pizza's place in the culture, which means understanding its history and the role it plays in people's lives, and meeting the people making it today. During my visit, I focused on Naples and Rome. Naples, because it is where pizza began. Neapolitans bleed pizza—it is a defining element of who Neapolitans are and how they live. Rome, because it has two distinct styles of pizza that I admire: one a super-thin crusted wood-fired-oven style; the other called *al taglio*, served by the slice, which is found in bakeries. You will find pizza in both of these cities' styles, with plenty of hybrids of the two, throughout Italy and beyond. In Bologna you will find very thin crust pizza like in Rome, but as a much larger pie, and in Florence it's possible to find crust even thinner than in Bologna. In this book

I focus on the styles of pizza that both interest me most and that I believe can be successfully adapted for the home kitchen. It inspires me that pizza making is not a static craft in Naples and Rome. The best *pizzaiolos* are pushing their skill to new heights, making extremely high-quality pizzas that are in harmony with tradition but not constrained by it. In my mind, this is the best evolution possible. It's like jazz to me.

Naples

Naples is the birthplace of pizza, where by most accounts it took its modern form in the 1700s, without tomatoes—which, though they were first imported to southern Italy in the 1500s, probably didn't make it onto pizzas until the 1800s. Establishing firm timelines for specific evolutionary steps in pizza history (or for any other food that began as a street food) is difficult. One of the earliest Neapolitan pizzerias in the written record is Zi Ciccio, first written about in 1727, located in the Piazza Cavour. Others from that era include Port'alba and, in Porta San Gennaro, the pizzeria Capasso. According to one account, the most successful was called Ntuono, run by Antonio Testa near the church of Santa Teresa, where King Ferdinand I (1751 to 1825), the ruler of Naples, secretly went to eat. Did he wear a wig? (It wasn't the public he was hiding his pizza habit from; it was his wife, Queen Maria Carolina of Austria, Marie Antoinette's sister, who apparently dominated her unsophisticated husband and ruled the Kingdom of Naples in his name.)

Earlier forms of pizza described in the sparse historical record were made with eggs, sugar, almonds, and spices and were not food for the commoner but rather for the ruling classes. But the early modern Neapolitan pizzas of the 1700s were indeed for people on the street who were hungry and either had a little money or bought their pizza on credit using a Neapolitan pay-it-forward system that is still in use today. Toppings included inexpensive local ingredients like olive oil, garlic, oregano, grated cheese, lard, and salt. When tomatoes started appearing on pizzas in the 1800s, they would have only been used during their fresh season from late spring through summer and autumn (or, possibly, as a conserva during the winter and spring). By the early 1900s they were being commercially canned in southern Italy and thus were available year-round. Pizza has been called *il sole nel piatto*—the sun on a plate—and Naples is famously sunny, hot in the summer and temperate in the winter (perfect for out-the-window laundry drying). The climate, the sea air, and the volcanic soil make an excellent *terroir* for tomatoes, olives, and herbs. Tomato on pizza was magic waiting to happen.

Modern pizza started as a street food for the working classes (and the occasional disguised king), but became an obsession across Neapolitan society once Queen Margherita famously ate what became her namesake pizza at Pizzeria Brandi in 1889. Pizza was sold in outdoor stalls and was also vended by boys carrying pails, called *stufa*, full of baked, folded pizzas. "In Naples we call these *portafoglio*, folded like a packet," a taxi driver in Naples told me. Marinara pizza got its name because it was a favorite among fishermen (mariners), who would take it on board to eat during their workday, folded over upon itself to make it easily transportable. Nowadays we think of "marinara" as referring to an iconic red sauce, but in fact, in its early days the marinara pizza was just topped with garlic, oil, and oregano. Tomato sauce didn't enter the equation until later. According to a book published by the Molino Caputo flour company (*Teri, Oggi e . . . Domani, la Pizza tra passato e future*),

DA MICHELE

Today, Da Michele might be the most popular of the traditional, old-school pizzerias in Naples. It's often just called "Michele" by locals, who queue up for one of the eight hundred pizzas (!) made daily at this iconic spot in the middle of the city. Da Michele, founded in 1870 and in its present location since 1930, makes two kinds of pizza: marinara and margherita, costing 4 euros each, 5 euros if you want double cheese on your margherita. There is an old framed poster on the wall at Da Michele; here is a rough translation:

With garlic, oil, and oregano
Or with tomato rather
It seems an easy thing
But making pizza is far from easy
You do not want a soft dough
You need to know how to bake
The flavor comes from he who prepares it
And it's something wholesome and good
Pizza was born in Naples
But few in the trade
Can enable you to fully enjoy
The pleasure of eating it
Only Don Michele
A pastry chef of refined skill
Makes a pizza so splendid
It will comfort you and make you happy

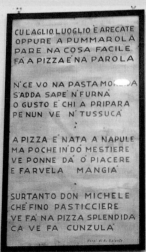

Salvatore Salvo (left); pizza margherita, Pepe in Grani *(right).*

the first pizza to have a proper name was called the mastunicola, made by the wife of a mason, Mastro Nicola, to fortify him for a hard day's work. According to sources, it was topped with cheese and lard. I take most of these recorded "facts" with a grain of salt—the research is scanty and one author's assertion becomes another's fact. Still, I like imagining Mastro Nicola going to work with his namesake pizza in his satchel, clueless to his future fame. But didn't his wife have a name, too?! She made the pizza!

The original pizzas were made from simple, local ingredients. The flour was from nearby wheat fields and mills; the small, pear-shaped tomatoes that ended up as pizza sauce stared at Mount Vesuvius from the valley floor as they ripened in the ever-present sunshine. Olive oil, oregano, garlic, and mozzarella cheese were all from Campania too. Neapolitans get emotional about the pizza they love. "Pizza isn't just a food, it's a way of *being* Neapolitan," Enzo Coccia once said in an interview with video journalist Sky Dylan-Robbins.

Pizzeria Brandi, Starita, Di Matteo, Gino Sorbillo, and Pizzeria Port'Alba are but a handful of the classic, old-school Neapolitan pizzerias that serve the platonic form of Neapolitan pizza, a cheap food for all walks that is primal sustenance for the people of Naples. "They are selling an emotion," said Costantino Cutolo from the tomato processor Compagnia Mercantile d'Oltremare, who grew up just outside of Naples. Other pizzerias, like La Notizia, Salvo, and Pepe in Grani, are still firmly based in tradition, yet focus extra attention on the quality of the dough. They also push the boundaries of what goes on top of the pizzas, thinking more freely but still intent on using the bounty of Campania's land and sea.

The craft of the *pizzaiolo* has been handed down from generation to generation. They are not chefs, nor bakers—they are *pizzaiolos*. It is a very proud and respected profession. Naples is awash in *pizzaiolos* today who are third- or fourth-generation pizza makers. One said his grandfather, a *pizzaiuolo* (Neapolitan spelling), had twenty-one grandchildren and every one is a *pizzaiuolo*. It is a pride of Naples that they have the history and culture that produces generation after generation of serious, dedicated pizza makers for whom this craft is the one profession they will have all their lives. Their work is often a measure of respect for their fathers and grandfathers (there are some, but very few female *pizzaiolos*; I hope this changes). "The soul of pizza is the pizza maker," Antimo Caputo, of the Molino Caputo flour mill in Naples, told me. Making pizza isn't just a mechanical act. "It has to be made with love to be good," Antimo continued. "He puts in the pizza his passion."

I asked most of the people I met in Naples how often in a week they eat pizza. The answer usually began with a "pfffff," as whomever I was talking with had to stop and think to answer this ridiculous question, which is apparently akin to, "How many times a week do you think about sex?" The answer ranged from once a week to too many times to count. Neapolitans are very social, and meeting up with friends at a pizzeria is a very common weekly thing.

Enzo Coccia is one of my pizza heroes, and I met him at his pizzeria, La Notizia. Enzo is a third-generation *pizzaiuolo* making some of the best pizza in Naples right now, and La Notizia won the Associazione Verace Pizza Napoletana (AVPN) Best Pizza award for 2014, a great honor. Enzo is making pizza with a strong respect for tradition, but he also pushes accepted Naples boundaries by going beyond margherita and marinara, using ingredients you would more likely find in a great *salumeria* or a top restaurant. This is a touchy, controversial subject for Neapolitans!

In a 2012 article, Sergio Miccu, head of the Neapolitan Association of Pizza Makers, is quoted as saying, "There is no such thing as gourmet pizza; we are not OK with this. Pizza was born as a food for the poor and any complicated pizza loses its identity." While I don't completely agree with Sergio—by his logic, anything other than margherita or marinara would be heresy—I appreciate his sentiment. There's something to be said for preserving traditional pizza, which at its heart was commoners' food. Putting expensive toppings on the pizza takes it out of that realm. This further explains something Enzo had said to me: "There are a thousand pizzerias in Naples. It's difficult to succeed with high quality." Many, maybe even most, Neapolitans aren't seeking creativity or "gourmet ingredients" on their pizza, and many are offended by pizza that aspires beyond its working-class origins—preservation of traditional pizza is important and is one of the goals of the Neapolitan Association of Pizza Makers. Enzo Coccia is one of Naples's most famous—and most controversial—*pizzaiolos* because he is creative and uses better-quality toppings than many of the traditional and more famous places, and charges more for it. Miccu might sneer at his "gourmet" approach, but for me, Enzo deserves admiration. And judging by the line on the sidewalk the last time I was there, he's got nothing to worry about.

Enzo seems to have a particular point of view about pizza that is grounded in tradition yet a little bit poetic. But it seems modern, too. Maybe he's a practical, yet very talented dreamer, willing and confident enough to take his own road, follow his own whim. As a craftsperson, what's wrong with doing what you are inspired to do? It means you can choose pizza at La Notizia that's traditional, or uniquely Enzo's own. Others may copy him someday, but he is copying no one; rather, he's building on two-hundred-some years of local pizza tradition and adding his own next step. For that, he has my admiration. And his pizzas are so good!

Enzo does not speak English, so when we sat down to talk pizza he brought one of his young cooks to sit with us and translate. I arrived at La Notizia with no particular agenda other than to meet him and see what I could find out about how he makes his dough. I was quickly schooled and quietly thrilled that my simple questions and honest curiosity were taken so seriously. Hopefully I'll be a better pizza man for it. The conversation began with a one-on-one, gentle but stern, 15-minute lecture on the history of pizza—or pizza dough, to be specific. Until about 1920, all pizza was made with a natural levain (also known as a wild yeast culture), *levitazione naturale* in Italian, and each day's batch was leavened with a piece of the previous day's dough. Then, when commercial monoculture yeast (*Saccharomyces cerevisiae*) became available in Naples around 1920, many pizzerias switched to this because it was less work and demanded less expertise, and was therefore sometimes more reliable. Commercial yeast, for all but the extremely talented *pizzaiolos,* produces a lighter, more delicate pizza crust, too. But they were still in the habit of using pre-fermented doughs, a portion of old dough to leaven

the next batch as they had done before (this is called *pâte fermentée* in French baking). In the 1950s, many but not all *pizzaiolos* began making direct doughs (I called direct dough "straight dough" in *FWSY*), making their jobs once again a little bit easier and producing reliable results. From this point to the present, only a small number use refrigeration to extend the fermentation and stabilize the dough.

Today, the exact fermentation method varies from one pizzeria to the next—many use either a direct dough or mix with old dough to leaven the next batch—but almost all of them use commercial yeast and long, slow fermentation. Most pizzerias tend not to use refrigeration (it takes up valuable space and is an extra expense); instead, they store the dough in the pizzeria at room temperature and mix multiple batches daily, if necessary, to meet demand. The busiest pizzerias sell four hundred to eight hundred pizzas every day. Each dough ball has a window of about 4 to 6 hours for optimum performance when held at room temperature; if left too long, the dough will be too gassy to make a good pizza. What these pizzerias need to do is meet the volume requirements of their business with good dough balls every time.

Enzo shared his dough-making process, which kind of turned my way of making pizza dough on its head (more on this later). He asked me what I am: a *pizzaiolo*? Enzo said being a baker and being a *pizzaiolo* are different, and don't assume because I know bread and croissants that I know pizza. His point wasn't just that pizza and bread are different, it was that being a *pizzaiolo* is different from being a baker. The life is different, the dough is different, the baking is different. The end product is different. The oven is different. And pizza is not the same as bread.

I felt humbled in Enzo's presence, and a little intimidated. He didn't crack a smile for ten, fifteen minutes. As he made his point that "making pizza is

not the same as making bread," he said it in a strong voice to communicate that this was inarguable, and to bring the point home, he showed me the palm of his hand. It was a strong hand, with the deeply creased palm of a longtime *pizzaiolo* who had shaped countless thousands of pizzas for decades. His pride was as strong as his hands. The classic Neapolitan *pizzaiolo* technique is to hand-cut dough balls out of a larger dough mass to make up hundreds of pizzas every day. It is a pincer motion, similar to how I hand-mix bread dough or cheese makers cut mozzarella (*mozza* means "to cut"). This repeated cutting motion works the palm creases over and over and over. Somehow, given enough time (decades) and enough dough balls (you do the math), dark gets in there. "Show me your palm" has some significance among *pizzaiolos*.

The Salvo brothers, Francesco and Salvatore (above); Cosacca Pizza from Pizzeria Salvo in Naples (below).

After a very serious conversation about pizza dough, Enzo's warm Neapolitan heart took over and we ended up smiling, and with a mutual respect. When I pulled out my pen and started taking notes, he looked at my notes, and could tell I know my dough, and then he opened up and really told me his exact dough recipe and process. He said pizza dough has just four ingredients, plus time. I added "and temperature," and showed him the part in Chapter Two of *FWSY* where it says to "think of time and temperature as ingredients." Enzo nodded his head and beamed at me. I asked if he would give me permission to include his way of making pizza dough in my new cookbook, and he agreed so long as I would say it's not the same as coming to his restaurant. (Duh, of course it's not.)

While I am a strong advocate for using traditional methods in bread, pizza, wine, *salumi*, agriculture, and so on, I also latched on to what, to me, seems like a new generation of *pizzaiolos* in Italy *and* in the U.S. They are (or more hopefully, *we are*) making great pizza by carefully respecting tradition yet topping the pizzas with rational creativity. Using artichokes and fresh goat cheese, smoked provolone and escarole, figs and honey, or the best *culatello* I've had in my life—this is a good thing. Yes, these pizzas cost more than the 4-euro pizza at Da Michele, but boy are they good to eat.

Pizzeria Salvo is another example of a great modern-day pizzeria in Naples. The brothers at Salvo, Francesco and Salvatore, use seven different olive oils to top their pizzas, depending on which olive oil goes best with which pizza. Their brother Ciro Salvo's place, Pizzeria 50 Kalò, is another example of a younger yet experienced *pizzaiolo* pushing pizza's quality boundaries. Neapolitan trash talking (in the press and in personal interviews) suggests that many of the old-school, classic pizzerias were using ingredients of low quality. Still, when you think of pizza as a humble food for commoners, it kind of makes sense that they would use cheap ingredients, but inexpensive doesn't always mean poor quality. I think this bad-quality-ingredients reputation is only a partial truth, knowing that most use good flour from Caputo, and how bad are the tomatoes and mozzarella from this region going to be? Maybe they use inexpensive oil. What is notable about the Salvo brothers and others that I'm writing about is that now a select group of *pizzaiolos* is making their reputation with the highest quality ingredients: specifically selected tomatoes, garlic, cheese, oregano, basil, and olive oil. A simple marinara pizza from these impeccable local ingredients becomes an exceptional thing, especially when married with an excellent dough and expertly baked. Take, for example, Ciro Salvo at 50 Kalò. He's certified by the Associazione Verace Pizza Napoletana (AVPN) but goes beyond that to specifically source garlic from Campania's Ufita valley, oregano from the Alburni mountain villages near Salerno, and olive oil from Don Alfonso 1890 on the Amalfi coast.

What strikes me as funny is that a classic, old-school pizzeria in Naples—Starita—has sixty-eight different pizzas on its menu, with toppings as varied as mortadella on pistachio cream, yet La Notizia is controversial for making "gourmet pizza." Familial slings and arrows is all this hubbub amounts to, but it's a great indicator of how seriously they take their pizza.

Caiazzo

About 50 kilometers (30 miles) outside of Naples, the small, old village of Caiazzo has a beautiful church built around the ancient tomb of Santo Stefano, narrow alleyways, all-stone buildings, a courtyard, and atmospheric lamplit cobblestone streets. The surrounding valleys of Caserta, one of the regions where *mozzarella di bufala* is made, are fertile with volcanic soil, painted with gentle hills and farmland. This region is a mecca for produce. Outside of the church, the other landmark of Caiazzo is Pepe in Grani, a new pizzeria in a very old stone building that fashions a modern-day pizza built on the foundation of pizza history. Opened in 2012, Pepe in Grani was constructed in a restored circa 700 AD stone building as a place for pizza, research, and hospitality. Franco Pepe is a third-generation *pizzaiolo*. In 2014, Jonathan Gold pronounced it the Best Pizza in the World in *Travel & Leisure* magazine. On this trip I brought April, one of the managers from my pizzeria, and we visited Franco and had an epic dinner, two of us eating a crazy six pizzas. "Are you sure?" Franco kept asking, repeatedly checking on us with an amused grin while we ate. I couldn't travel all this way just to have one margherita, and the menu offered a "tasting menu" of five pizzas for three or four people. It would have been rude to sample each and send back the bones waiting for the next pie, so we just dove in. No regrets, either! Dough-wise, Franco follows the traditional methods of the nineteenth and early twentieth centuries: naturally leavened pizza dough, hand-mixed, no refrigeration. His ingredients are all from his area, seasonal (for example, figs, artichokes, sweet onions, cherry tomatoes, and fresh anchovies from the nearby coast), and of stunning quality. Best pizza in the world? Let's just say, at Pepe in Grani the dough is mixed perfectly, fermented perfectly,

shaped perfectly. The toppings are in perfectly complementary proportions. And, naturally, the pizza is baked perfectly. These were flawless pizzas. His reputation is well deserved. The crust had a very thin layer of crisp on the outside and the bottom, and a feathery light crumb inside the rim. It was almost weightless. The inner base of the crust was very thin and perfectly leopard-spotted on its bottom from the oven's floor. On this, our fifth consecutive day of eating pizza, April said, "I've never had anything like that, ever." I can't print the rest of what she said, but it was definitely complimentary.

Our tasting menu at Pepe in Grani was preceded by a folded-over *libretto* pizza filled simply with tomato sauce, garlic, and fresh oregano, wrapped in brown paper. The *libretto*, aka *portafoglio*, remains Naples's street food, and while later pizzas went in the gourmet direction, Franco started us with this basic pie—where pizza began. I love this respect for tradition. Franco's crust tasted of lactic fermentation—a flavor that's sometimes described as milky and fruity, and similar to what you get with a ripe liquid levain (or, for anyone who's baked out of my first book, from my White Flour Warm Spot Levain Bread). His is a very well-fermented dough, with a beautiful balance of flavors, and as they might say in Italy, it is highly digestible ("digestibility" is loosely defined, but widely regarded as being a benefit of long-fermented, naturally leavened pizza and bread). We put that to the supreme test by eating five more pizzas: a traditional margherita pizza with *mozzarella di bufala*; a pizza with white fresh anchovies, olives, split Vesuvio tomatoes, and oregano; a folded-over pizza with escarole, ham, and smoked *provola* (the crust was so soft, so delicate, so delicious); artichoke with melted mozzarella and a light fresh ricotta piped on after the pie was baked; then the fig jam pizza with Conciato cheese grated over

after baking. The pizzas looked bready and doughy, but they were ethereally light. Tender. Delicate. Sexy.

I mention that Franco Pepe makes his dough the old-fashioned way, by hand—but this is a point worth reiterating, because it's ridiculously hard work. Imagine mixing 80 kilos (175 pounds) of dough by hand for 20 or 30 minutes. *At the end of the day*, so it has time to rise before the next day's service. Franco said to us, "My pizza is slow food." He is fond of saying his pizza is "wireless," meaning no electricity is used anywhere to make it. He mixes it in wooden boxes, and it never sees refrigeration. He uses thin, symmetrical pieces of wood to fire his gold-tiled Stefano Ferrara oven, ensuring even performance.

Pepe in Grani wants to communicate and promote the area's bounty through its pizzas. Franco has worked with local farms and a local agronomist, Vincenzo Coppola, in one case to revive an ancient indigenous variety of wheat, and in other cases to showcase the local tomatoes, garlic, onions, chickpeas, fruits, and so on. This work and his growing fame have helped revive a declining local economy.

Not content to simply make pizza the same way every day, Franco Pepe continues to experiment with different flours and adjustments to the fermentation of his dough. I get this, and I find inspiration from others like Franco, who are driven to experiment and look for the new in themselves and the world around them. It's one thing to experiment; it's entirely another thing to experiment and make it something we all swoon over. Franco Pepe's gift is combining ingredients that serve as a window on the region that he is proud of, and making them into pizza that stands at the pinnacle of pizzadom. He recognizes that many of the old ways are still the best, even if they mean harder work and more time. My thinking is that by doing something over and over with an open mind, not just repeating but learning,

and respecting tradition but building on it with your own inspiration—that's when new realities, new beautiful things, can happen. Learning from each experiment and applying it the next time is what leads to greatness.

To return to the schooling I received at La Notizia, when Enzo Coccia said, "Pizza is not the same as bread," he wrote down pizza dough's ingredients in the following order, to demonstrate how the dough is made: (1) *acqua* (water); (2) *sale* (salt) plus *impasto* (stir to dissolve); (3) *lievito* (fresh yeast) plus *impasto* (stir to dissolve); and, finally, (4) *farine* (flour). In Naples they base their ingredient quantities on one liter of water, whereas in French baking we base ingredients on 1 kilogram (2.2 pounds) of flour. This turned on its head my French baker's method (and my mind-set) of mixing flour and water, letting it rest for 15 to 20 minutes (what we call the *autolyse* period), then adding salt and yeast, then mixing the final dough. I later confirmed with Mauro Caputo at the Caputo flour company that the water-salt-yeast-flour approach is the typical Neapolitan way to mix pizza dough.

The second big shift in my thinking was to come from everyone in Naples: rather than mixing the dough and letting it rest for several hours to rise (what we call *bulk fermentation*), it is customary to mix the dough and then divide and shape it into dough balls early on in the fermentation timeline, often just 2 hours later. Enzo makes up his dough balls *just 10 to 20 minutes after mixing.* This was crazy to me. A bread baker thinks the bulk fermentation period is critical to allowing complex flavors from

Clockwise from top left: Enzo Coccia; Caiazzo street scene; waiting for a table at La Notizia; Franco Pepe mixing dough by hand; pizza at La Notizia.

fermentation to develop, so it's important to give your dough enough time for that to happen. And a bread baker is also driven to make a loaf that has its maximum possible expansion without collapsing. A *pizzaiolo* only thinks of managing the dough's ability to expand in the context of the rim, the *corni-cione,* of a pizza, and knows that a long fermentation at the second stage, in the dough ball, is sufficient to give that complexity of flavors from the dough's fermentation (the superb, mellow flavor of Enzo's crust is a testament to his methods and the flour he chooses). Most of the fermentation takes place *in* the dough balls, called *panetti* in Naples, which rest for 10 hours before Enzo's pizzeria, La Notizia, opens at 7:30 p.m. This change in pizza dough management and its timelines was really intriguing to me. I soon learned from other Neapolitan *pizzaiolos* and the folks at Caputo that a 2-hour first fermentation is the norm in Naples, with no refrigeration and the dough balls all being made into pizza the same night. Enzo takes the timeline to the extreme.

One of Enzo's kitchen staff brought out a tray of *panetti* for us to look at just 30 minutes before the restaurant was to open. They were gorgeous; perfectly rounded, with no hint of collapse; inflated and strong from the rise, beautifully smooth, and boasting a lovely, slightly lactic aroma. The resulting pizzas that we enjoyed not long after were delicate, light, savory, and delicious, with just the right slightly crisp exterior and soft crumb on the rim, the bottoms thin and spotted underneath. There was a very nice aftertaste that only comes from good flour and excellent fermentation. I had read about La Notizia's dessert calzone, and had to try it. We finished with a chocolate lava calzone that took pizza dessert to new heights. When we said our goodbyes and left the pizzeria, there was a lively, stylish crowd on the sidewalk waiting their turn to eat.

Pizza bianca, Forno Campo de' Fiori.

Rome

Pizza occupies an important place in Roman life, too, even if it doesn't have the deep cultural identity and history that it has in Naples. There are flatbreads in Roman history going back to the day of Caesar. One, called *pinza*, is a plain baked flatbread that is topped with fresh ingredients and olive oil after baking. Today there are two kinds of Roman pizza: bakery pizza, called *al taglio* (by the slice); and *tonda*, or round pizzas, also generically called pizza romana, served for dinner at pizzerias that are open only in the evenings. The beauty of Roman pizza in either form is its lightness; it can be a lunch, a snack, or dinner.

Al taglio pizza is a cheap and easy Roman street food. In the States we might call these sheet pizzas.

The most common version is quite long—about 4 or 5 feet—and about 10 to 12 inches wide. It's baked directly on the hearth or in a large rectangular pan inside of a bread oven, then cut into pieces in a size negotiated at the counter. Typically, as at Antico Forno Urbani, the person behind the counter will position a knife at a spot on the rectangular pizza and look to you to say yes, or smaller or bigger. When you give the nod, he or she cuts the pizza, weighs it, folds it in half, and wraps it up with a ticket that you take to the cash register to pay by the gram. Eat it on the go.

Al taglio always has a thin crust—about ⅛ of an inch thick—if it is a basic pizza rossa or bianca; sometimes it's thicker if the toppings demand a stronger base. This is not a heavy pizza. Very often the *al taglio* is made without cheese. The toppings are light and

Gabriele Bonci and his al taglio *pizzas.*

flavorful, and the portion sizes are up to you (but not large). Often the pizza is heated and, usually, served folded in half (it's a pizza sandwich!) and wrapped in paper with a logo. During the lunch rush, around 1:00 p.m. in Rome, the bakery is pulling fresh pizzas out of the oven and thus they don't need to be delayed with reheating. They are best at this point, with the most moisture and most tender crust.

The basic *al taglio* pizza is either a rossa—tomato sauce, oregano, and olive oil (my favorite)—or a bianca, baked with a very thin film of olive oil and a light sprinkling of sea salt. "It's just bread" is what the guy at Pizzarium's counter said to me when I ordered the bianca. The bianca is baked in rectangular sheets and it's like a thin focaccia, the same as the rossa but without the tomato. Good *al taglio* pizza

has an airiness to its crumb and the character of a long-fermented dough, texturally and flavor-wise, with that *retrogusto*, the mellow, fermented, wheaty aftertaste you get when you exhale. The top features a bubbly crust from a gassy dough. The pizza is shaped by hand into long, thin stretches of supple, soft dough and stretched on a floured board that is a little bit wider than the pizza, and about 4 to 5 feet in length. It's just a thin, light board. The dough is stretched from both sides to elongate, and allowed to rest for a bit. Then it's stretched lengthwise again, lightly oiled with a wide paintbrush, and pressed (docked) with fingertips, like focaccia. At Roscioli they let it rest and then repeat, stretching it out a third time to get the full length and proper thickness of dough. The board can be used as a peel to load the dough into the oven.

Later, the baker will use thin wooden peels about 3 feet in length to remove the pizza when it's finished. It's fun to watch these come out of the oven, with the baker's arms stretched sideways holding 5 feet of pizza as it is transferred to a cooling rack. Things really start to get interesting when the bakery goes beyond the rossa and the bianca to more creative toppings. Shredded potato is very common, as are zucchini and eggplant. Cured meats like prosciutto work well as a topping. Then, more recently, some have been going for more expensive toppings like the terrific pesto-and-*burrata* pizza I had at Roscioli in the Centro Storico, near the Campo de' Fiori. Gabriele Bonci has found his own personal stratosphere at Pizzarium, with *al taglio* pizzas done his unique way: naturally leavened dough made up with whole grain flour and using toppings that push the imagination, from mortadella with a chickpea puree to eggplant with red peppers and arugula to wild mushrooms and garlic on top of shredded potatoes. It's nice to see a baker go beyond the rules to make a very traditional food his own unique offering.

Al taglio pizzas are baked in bread ovens at temperatures between 520° to 590°F (270° to 310°C). This is several hundred degrees cooler than the wood-fired ovens of Naples. Some are baked directly on the hearth of a deck oven, the same kind also used to bake bread, and others are baked in the same oven but in special baking pans instead of on the hearth. Thicker doughs, like focaccia from Genoa, do well baked in pans that are lined with oil beneath the dough. Thin-dough *al taglio* pizzas, like the rossa and the bianca, bake beautifully directly on the hearth (only the panned pizzas need oil—or very well seasoned pans—to keep them from sticking).

Rome is also known for its pizzerias open for dinner only, baking super-thin-crusted pizzas in wood-fired ovens. To me, Roman *al taglio* pizza makers are bakers. Roman pizza makers doing the thin, round pizzas are *pizzaiolos*. I think they'd agree. The *pizza romana* differs from Neapolitan pizza primarily in the crust. It is a very thin crust with little to no poof in the rims. When I make these—and I love them—I use half the amount of dough I would use to make the same-size Neapolitan pizza, and I use a rolling pin to make the dough as thin as possible. These pizzas are still baked with a little bit of char on the edges, and a nice black spottiness on the bottoms is the best, coming from a very hot wood-fired oven. Excellent examples can be found at Da Remo in the Testaccio neighborhood, La Rioni near the Colosseum, and Pizzeria Emma in the Centro Storico. And while Rome may not be saturated with great pizzerias the way Naples is, it is the style of this super-thin crust that intrigues me and that led me to create a set of recipes in this book modeled after my ideal Roman pies. The thin, crisp crust is satisfyingly light. I can eat an entire pizza of this style without a heavy feeling in my belly for a somewhat light dinner, or have a fried starter beforehand (common in Rome and Naples), like the fried rice balls called *suppli*, artichokes, or fried zucchini flowers.

I so love these beautiful pizzas for their crisp, practically crackery outer rim. If they're topped with sauce and cheese, the moisture will put some sag in the middle. If the toppings are more minimal, the entire pizza might retain its crispness all the way through, depending on the pizzeria and how it's baked. One of my favorite Roman *tondo* pizzas has no cheese: it's topped with tomato sauce and a little oregano, and after it comes out of the oven, cured anchovies and a drizzle of good aromatic olive oil.

Clockwise from top left: Bonci; Pizza Romana at Da Remo in Rome; Da Remo patio scene.

THE UNITED STATES

What is American pizza? What did we do to it after it hit our shores?

In the beginning . . .

New York

In the late nineteenth century, pizza existed only in Naples and the surrounding region, Campania, in southern Italy. It was food for the working class. Between 1880 and 1920, over four million Italians escaped poverty and famine in southern Italy and came to America, a land of hopes and dreams, of plenty and opportunity. Their flight was literally a survival mission. Our nations are forever linked by this event. Our American pizza tradition began with Italian immigrants in New York who brought their gastronomic culture—and their love of pizza, a defining component of their diet—with them.

Lombardi's became America's first full-fledged pizzeria in 1905, when Gennaro Lombardi abandoned the grocery business at his store on Mulberry Street in New York City's Little Italy to meet the demand for his popular pizza. Pizza historian Scott Wiener pointed out to me that pizza was actually sold in bakeries all over Little Italy in 1900. Lombardi's was the first to sell *only* pizza, and most likely the first with the word *pizzeria* on the window. The early pizzas from bakeries in Little Italy were baked in coal-fired bread ovens and the pizzas served to cool down the hearth of the hot preheated ovens, preparing them for bread baking. The first pizzas were different from today, according to Scott's research: the toppings were Romano cheese, lard, tomato, and oregano, resembling the pizzas of Naples. Mozzarella came later. As in Naples, the emphasis was on cheap, affordable ingredients. The pizzas were, according to Scott, breadlike and soft.

Lombardi's popularity spawned more pizzerias, established by former employees: Totonno's Pizzeria Napolitana on Coney Island (1924), John's Pizza of Bleecker Street (1929), and Patsy's Pizzeria in Harlem (1933). These places marked the birth of the family-style pizza restaurant in America, at a time when it was still a street food in Naples. Italian immigrants longed for the staple food of their homeland, and for their own businesses, and New Yorkers outside of the immigrant community slowly learned that this ethnic food, a thing new to them called "pizza," was really good to eat. These immigrants told the world who they were through their pizza. But it was going to take some time. These early-twentieth-century New York pizzerias were mostly serving their own Italian communities. Pizza didn't really catch on in a big way in New York until after World War II.

Trenton Tomato Pies

Maybe there was a time when the word *pizza* might have sounded too exotic to draw a crowd. Across the Hudson River from New York City, Trenton, New Jersey, is its own pizza vortex, where they call it tomato pie. First there was Joe's Tomato Pies, opened in 1910. Then Joe Papa opened Papa's Tomato Pies in 1912. De Lorenzo's Tomato Pies opened in 1936. All were run by the families of immigrants from Naples. What's different about tomato pie? The sauce goes on top of the cheese and toppings. The crust is very thin.

New Haven

Not far from New York City, New Haven, Connecticut, is another place where, in the early 1900s, coal- and coke-fired (hot!) bread ovens were used to bake pizza (coke is converted coal and burns very hot, and is cleaner than coal). But the stories of these historic places go well beyond the pizza itself. It always comes back to the pizza maker. I like this story of Frank Pepe of Frank Pepe Pizzeria Napoletana in New Haven, Connecticut (1925), that romanticizes his heritage and underprivileged beginnings (from their website): "Born in the town of Maiori, on the Amalfi coast southwest of Naples, Frank Pepe was the quintessential Italian immigrant. Poor and illiterate, he immigrated to the United States in 1909 at age sixteen with little more than his health and a strong work ethic. In 1925, with his wife, Filomena, they started making a simple and humble product from their homeland, pizza—or as they would say in their dialect, 'apizza' (*ah-beets*). They baked their pizzas offering two types, tomatoes with grated cheese, garlic, oregano, and olive oil, and the other with anchovy."

Frank Pepe's, now run by his five grandchildren, is still iconic today. The neon sign above Pepe's kitchen reads "The Original Tomato Pies," and every pizza on the menu is called a "tomato pie." This makes sense when you think like they do at Pepe's: that cheese is an optional topping. If you want *muzz* (see sidebar), you need to ask for it. The Original Tomato Pie has tomato, garlic, oregano, and olive oil and is—as it ever was—topped with grated cheese (grated cheeses as toppings are almost always either Romano or Grana Padano) or anchovy.

Frank Pepe's was the first of three famous, and now historic, pizzerias in New Haven. Pepe's was followed by Modern Apizza in 1934 (moved to its present location just two years later, in 1936, when

> *Mozz* or *muzz* on the pie? The affectionate slang moniker was adopted from the Neapolitan dialect that remains in use today in corners of New York, New Jersey, and Connecticut. If you listen to Rosemary Clooney singing "Mambo Italiano," you'll hear, "Hey Mambo, no more-a *muzzarella*. All you Calabrese do the mambo like-a crazy." Thanks, Rosemary.

it was called Tony's Apizza), and Sally's Apizza in 1938. The style of these New Haven pizzerias, while similar, is not exactly the same. Today Pepe's and Sally's still have their super-hot coal-fired brick bread ovens, with the firebox underneath the hearth, while Modern Apizza converted their coke- or coal-fueled brick bread oven to oil-fueled in 1967. Until pizza became more widespread in the United States, there were no ovens that were designed for pizza, because pizza wasn't a thing yet. All these early pizzerias were making pizza in ovens designed for bread.

Each of these three historic New Haven pizzerias makes pizza from a very thin crust, not poofy on the rims, and charred on its edges. Clam pizza, which was born at Frank Pepe's, has been widely adopted by other pizzerias, for good reason. Fresh-shucked clams, garlic, olive oil, herbs, and bacon make a beautiful combo. Bobby and Rick Consiglio, two sons of Sally's Apizza founder Salvatore Consiglio (himself a nephew of Frank Pepe, whose restaurant is where he got his start in the pizza business), continue to make the pizzas at Sally's to this day.

Frank Pepe clam pizza (above), Modern Apizza (below)

American Pizza: Doing It Our Way

Family-owned pizzerias, run by moms and pops usually of Italian-American heritage, slowly spread around the country, but without the informational interconnectedness we have today, distinct regional styles evolved. GIs returning to the States after World War II who wanted more tastes of the pizza they had in Italy? Many say they were the catalyst for pizza's spread beyond Italian-American communities. I asked my dad, born in 1929 and raised in a suburb of Washington, D.C., when he ate his first pizza, and he said it was in the early 1950s and it was called tomato pie. The ubiquity of pizzerias that we see today did not begin for another two to three decades.

The distinct American regional styles fascinate me—like Detroit pan pizza (for example, Buddy's), the New Jersey thin-crust tomato pie (like De Lorenzo's), Philadelphia tomato pie (no cheese), New Haven tomato pie, and bar pizzas from the Midwest and East Coast. Then there are the unique pies of Old Forge, Pennsylvania, population 8,300, with about twenty pizzerias all making "trays" of Old Forge pizza in the same style—pan pizza made crisp underneath because of a layer of fat or oil under the dough, with onions in the sauce, and no rules about the cheese, though if you go there they will tell you what's different about each one. In the next chapter, I'll go into greater detail about the different pizza styles—but their origin stories are fascinating.

A lot of us grew up eating pan pizza. It's a very different thing than hearth pizza (for example, New York, New Haven, Roman, and Neapolitan-style pizzas, where the pizzas bake directly on the floor of the oven). There's a reason pan pizzas are often called grandma pies: it's a commercial version of the pan pizza Nonna would bake at home. Pan pizzas need some fat to keep the crust from sticking, for one thing. The pan gets a thin film of olive oil, lard, shortening, or some other fat so the pizza can come off it after it's baked. Some will even remove the pizza from the pan near the end of the bake and finish it directly on the oven's hearth. But if too much oil or fat is on the pan, then the pizza will leach excess oil or fat onto the oven floor if that's where it goes to finish the bake, and that's not good. The oil or fat will smoke and somebody's gonna be mad. When it's properly baked, the fat gives the crust a nice little bit of crisp and a flavorful browning, too. In Maryland, where I grew up, there were some pizzerias that had slightly flaky crusts, which can only come from fat or shortening *in the dough*.

The cheese and the ovens are big differentiators for what makes American, or New York–style, pizza distinct. The low-moisture, full-fat mozzarella cheese used on a good American pizza retains its soft, gooey, stretchy texture and its heat for a long time. You can take it home in a box and it's good to eat later, whether or not you warm it up. (Neapolitan, by contrast, has a shorter lifespan.) Typical American pizza ovens, modeled after bread ovens, bake at temperatures between 550° and 650°F (290° and 345°C) depending on the pizzeria. The longer baking time at a lower temperature than the Neapolitan wood-fired ovens produces a crisper pizza crust. (For comparison, most of the breads we make at my bakery bake at temperatures from 440°F/225°C—for baguettes—to 500°F/260°C—for levain breads.)

The ubiquitous pepperoni, unheard of in Italy, is a truly great American creation, perfect for crisping up on top of a pizza. Yet it's hard to pin down exactly what pepperoni is—some is made with beef, some with pork, often it's a blend of the two—even though it is always characterized by a reddish pigment and a mild spice. It should also be lightly smoky, fine-grained, and semisoft. I don't care that pepperoni is not Italian. I think it's a perfect topping for pizza: its meaty, smoky spiciness—with maybe a little puddle of grease in its cup as it curls from baking—goes so perfectly with a good crust, sauce, and cheese.

Pepperoni is a perfect symbol of American pizza evolution: it's Italian-*ish*, sure, but more important, it just tastes good on a pie. Today, we have an ever-increasing mash-up of styles and toppings that are all American by virtue of their place and their sense of freedom about what pizza can be. And we continue to innovate and evolve. Some pizzerias, like mine in Oregon, aren't making pizza to the specific style of other pizzerias so much as we are making pizza that we like, and making it in our own way—although in our case we have a strong Italian influence. Many pizzerias are getting creative with toppings, with some using classic Italian pasta combinations—*arrabiata*, *amatriciana*, or *cacio e pepe*—and others looking to their larder, the season, and their imaginations to see what might go together.

As interesting as the national evolution of pizza in America is, in a way, it all kind of circles back to the original birthplace, New York City. Just like a few of their creative counterparts in Italy, some leading New York *pizzaiolos* have taken a strong, century-old tradition and really run with it. You want rock 'n' roll pizza? Roberta's in Brooklyn once made a pizza they called Def Aleppo, topped with mozzarella, Parmesan, ricotta, Aleppo pepper, and spring garlic. Or get crazy (and very happy) with Paulie Gee's (also in

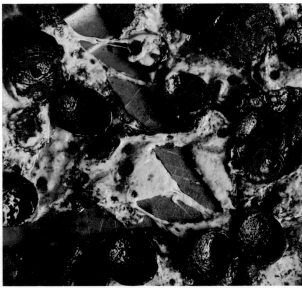

Brooklyn) Hellboy, topped with spicy *capicola* and Mike's Hot Honey. Oh God, it's good. Emily, in the Clinton Hill neighborhood of Brooklyn, slings terrific pies with classic, quality ingredients like *mozzarella di bufala* and Benton's ham, yet their most popular pie, the Colony, is topped with pickled jalapeño peppers, pepperoni, fresh house-made mozzarella, and a squeeze of honey, post-oven. What's cool about Emily, Roberta's, and Paulie Gee's is they start with Italian methods and boffo Italian wood-fired ovens, then take it their own way with their own inspirations and quality toppings. But the bones are still based on Neapolitan tradition.

Then there are a growing number of Neapolitan pizzerias in Manhattan and Brooklyn—Don Antonio, Kesté, and Motorino—and then, also in Brooklyn, at the aforementioned Paulie Gee's, Emily, and Roberta's, plus Franny's, that are Neapolitan in style but often creatively topped. This Brooklyn family of wood-fired-oven pizzerias is not just an interesting niche; it now represents its own branch on the pizza tree. New York also has thin-crusted bar pizzas, pan pizzas from Adrienne's, square pies from GG's, and the particular thin-crust pizza of places like Rubirosa and Joe & Pat's in Staten Island.

The fact is, even an average crust with sauce and melted cheese still tastes pretty good. For that reason, there are a lot of average pizzas that plenty of people happily eat—and plenty of people for whom pizza is more of a business proposition than a passion for quality. Please ignore them. Then there are purists who have hand-built wood-fired ovens and are using ingredients from Campania as well as their own region, like we do at Ken's Artisan Pizza and like Mark Hopper, who gets local *mozzarella di bufala* the day after it is made and imports tomatoes from southern Italy, does at Vignette Pizzeria in Sebastapol, California.

As Americans, we distinguish ourselves with our variety, abundance, and freedom to experiment. And, countering the Pizza Huts of the world, there is now a well-established movement, a rebirth of independent pizzerias committed to artisanal skill and ingredients—not just pizza that sells, but pizza that aspires to greatness. Independent mom-and-pops that have been making quality pies the same way for decades have an important place in American pizza culture. Anything but soulless chain pizza for me, please.

Let's talk about pizza styles and then cut to the chase and make some pizza.

A Slice of Poetry.
By: Cubs The Poet.

Slices sold to society,
  crust crushing the
    dough . .

Profit passed for passion,
  pepperonies, and
    cheese, melting the mind.

Stuffed with shines and
  cycles of circles,
  we toss the taste of
    time towards
      the dominos of
          r
          e
          a
          m
          s.

Pizzas & Poetry, purposing
          perfect portions
          of pieces
          fit to fill the
          mouth of the masses.

CHAPTER 2
PIZZA STYLES

Do you want to eat the same kind of pizza all the time? Maybe. You could make the same thing again and again, and hopefully get very good at it. But perhaps you'll wake up one morning craving something new. Or you traveled and had a different kind of pizza that you liked and decided you want to try your own home version of it. The pizza styles represented in this book will give you enough range that you can successfully make a variety of pies and can switch up your repertoire depending on your mood and who you are serving. These styles are a representation of what many great pizzerias are producing in Italy and in the United States.

Many independent pizzerias are making their own style of pizza and don't want to be pigeonholed into somebody else's style or concept. In America, we are maybe not quite as rules-bound as other countries. I still have a hard time saying exactly what style pizza we make at Ken's Artisan Pizza here in Portland: call it wood-fired-oven pizza inspired by Italian pizzas that our chef, Alan Maniscalco, and I have enjoyed. Ours bake in 2 ½ minutes, compared with Naples's 60 to 90 seconds, so I can't call it Neapolitan, but our influences draw more from Italy than, say, New York. Many American pizza styles have their own defining characteristics—a form that is further adapted

by each individual pizzeria into something it calls its own. Sometimes the style is something you know when you see (or eat it), but codifying it—putting it into words—is challenging.

The classic New York pizza is thin-crust, mostly crisp, not poofy on the rims, baked on the hearth of a deck oven, and topped with tomato sauce and with cheese that holds its soft texture for a long time after it's out of the oven. Look around at any Best-of New York list and you will find a glorious combination ranging from coal-oven thin-crust pizzas from places like Totonno's and the original Patsy's to slices at joints like NY Pizza Suprema to square pie slices

at Prince Street Pizza. And the conversation always comes around to the legendary Di Fara, which stands in a unique place of its own.

There is only one place in the world where the language of pizza *has* been codified—and even written into law. The Associazione Verace Pizza Napoletana (AVPN) and the Italian government went to great lengths to protect their cultural treasure, the Neapolitan pizza. They registered with the European Union and, in 2009, gained approval to classify the specific things that are required to make Neapolitan pizza truly *pizza Napolitana*, even if it's made in Phoenix, Arizona. You can be TSG (Traditional Specialties Guaranteed, or *Specialita' Tradizionale Garantita*; an Italian-speaking American might say either TSG or STG—it's the same thing) certified anywhere in the world so long as you follow a set of strict rules, have the right kind of wood-burning oven, and use the right ingredients. Neapolitan pizza is the only pizza with specific definitions and instructions dictating its creation: a dough with just flour, water, salt, and yeast in defined ratios, mixed in a particular way for 20 minutes without raising the temperature of the dough, and then fermented for 2 hours, divided by hand into dough balls (*panetti*), and fermented for another 4 to 6 hours, with the dough balls to be used any time during the next 6 hours, and baked in an oven averaging 905°F (485°C). There's much more, but this gives you an idea. These rules and actual certification ensure that a TSG-certified pizza is consistently a very specific pizza, and properly representative of the pride of Naples. I've been at a restaurant serving pizza labeled "TSG" and discovered they used a gas-fired oven and their pizza takes several minutes to bake. That just isn't right.

I love that about the AVPN—that the point was to protect a cultural icon in a region where pizza is part of what it means *to be* Neapolitan.

Other pizza styles don't involve government-approved certification. However, there are reference points for each pizza style outside of Naples. A New York pizza is often characterized by a stiff, crisp crust and cheesy toppings and by the facts that it's eaten by the slice, that there's not too much poof in the rim, and that the sauce and cheese go almost to the edge of the crust, which is baked golden but not often with a char. In contrast, Rome has its own common examples of simple bakery pizzas: pizza bianca and pizza rossa, crisp but with a nice bit of delicate chew, baked only to golden and cut to order in slices about ⅛ inch thick. And then there are the Roman super-thin, crisp-crust, wood-fired-oven pizzas that I love and think fit a platonic pizza ideal.

This book is about being inspired by regional Italian and American pizza styles to make really good versions at home. We'll never be able to replicate the pizza that comes from a specific pizzeria. That said, the more you know about the history, style, and tradition of a pizza, and the deeper your affection and respect for that tradition, the better your home version of it will be.

This book is not a comprehensive guide to every style of pizza under the sun. But there are a lot of different types of pizzas in these pages; this chapter introduces the styles and their key characteristics.

NEAPOLITAN PIZZA

In Naples, pizzas are baked in 60 to 90 seconds in wood-fired ovens at around 905°F (485°C) directly on the hearth. At the table they are eaten with a knife and fork. The sauce is nothing more than canned tomatoes—whole peeled tomatoes from southern Italy—pureed with salt. Toppings are simpler and less cheesy than a New York pizza, and the cheese is one of two kinds of fresh mozzarella, either *fior di latte*, from cow's milk, or *mozzarella di bufala*, from water buffalo milk, often with the addition of a small amount of grated hard cheese such as pecorino or Grana Padano sprinkled underneath.

The Neapolitan-style pizza recipes in this book are baked on a preheated pizza steel or pizza stone (see page 77) in a standard home kitchen oven at 550°F (290°C), and finished with the broiler, taking a total of about 7 minutes. Because the home oven is so different from a 905°F (485°C) wood-fired oven, the pizzas you make using this book are going to be different from a real *pizza Napolitana*, but they're still great pizzas inspired by the real deal, so why not? At home you get the same size pizza with a poofy rim; the flavorful crust will be crisper than that in Naples (you get a really nice light, crisp, chewy texture in the crust from the home kitchen oven); and you get the bright and savory flavors of tomato and baked cheese on top of it. My recipe has you adding the cheese 4 minutes into the bake so its finished texture resembles the texture of the cheese on a real Neapolitan pizza.

You cannot exactly replicate the methods of Neapolitan *pizzaiolos* and expect to get their same results if you are baking in a home oven. That may seem obvious, but it's significant. The AVPN rules state that the allowed hydration in a true Neapolitan pizza is between 55 and 59 percent of the flour weight. This makes a dough that is perfect for baking in 60 seconds in a 905°F (485°C) oven. It is not perfect for baking in a home oven at 550°F (290°C)! The result would be a very stiff crust, crisp and dry, and nothing at all like a tender Neapolitan pizza that you eat with a knife and fork. The bottom of a Naples pizza needs to set very quickly in the hot oven so it can be turned before the side closest to the fire gets burned. A dough above 70 percent hydration

is a disaster when baked at 905°F (485°C)—if you try to slide a peel under the pizza once the back of it is getting charred, it turns to soup in the middle because the base isn't yet set. But a well made 70-percent-hydration pizza dough works great for making a Neapolitan-style pizza in a home oven at 550°F (290°C). With the 7-minute baking time, this dough retains its softness in the middle, although the *cornicione* (the outer rim of the crust) in the home oven version will be crisper than that of a true Neapolitan pizza. So I make an adjustment to the dough for home oven baking compared with how it's made in Naples, adding over 10 percent more water to the dough than in the AVPN formula, though I recommend the same 00 flour they use. It's not to the AVPN's code, but I maintain you end up with a pizza that's as close to the Neapolitan spirit as possible.

The desired results for a Neapolitan-style home kitchen pizza are:

- When fully stretched, the dough is 10 to 12 inches across.

- The underside of the crust has dark brown (and occasionally black) leopard spots.

- The crust at the center of the pizza is soft but fully baked; each slice should flop from rim to tip when held up.

- The rim is poofy with visible air bubbles on the inside and splotches of dark brown or black where the crust has charred.

- The cheese is fully melted but not burned, and not completely liquefied.

- All the elements—crust (underside, interior, and rim), toppings, and cheese—reach their perfect point of baking at the same time. In the home oven, finding the ideal rack position helps make this happen.

PIZZA ROMANA, OR
ROMAN DINNER PIZZA

With its ultra-thin, crisp crust, Roman pizza is a study in lightness. Like their Neapolitan cousins, these pizzas also bake quickly in very hot wood-fired ovens. The sauce and toppings are also similar. What differentiates the Roman style, though, is the thinness of the crust. The Roman pizza is the same diameter as the Neapolitan pizza, but uses about half the dough. In Rome, some pizzas are crisp all the way through, while some have cracker-crisp outer edges and a soft interior with a little bit of flop to it. This interior texture is determined by the dough hydration (the less water in the dough, the crisper the whole crust will be), the thinness of the dough, the way it's baked, the amount of sauce the pizza is topped with, and how much moisture is released from the cheese as it bakes. Crispness will vary from one Roman pizzeria to the next. This pizza in its home kitchen incarnation, baking at 550°F (290°C), is going to be pretty crisp all the way through. One of my favorite versions of this style is called a pomodoro (see my version on page 158): crust baked with nothing but tomato sauce and a bit of olive oil, then topped with freshly grated pecorino, caciocavallo (a fantastic stretched curd cheese from Campania), or other cheese right after it comes out of the oven.

If you sit down for dinner at a Roman pizzeria in the evening—and they usually open at 7:30 p.m.—you are likely to be served a pizza that has a very thin, light, crackery crust, with just a little give when you bite into it. These are delightful pizzas and are the exact opposite of a doughier, softer Neapolitan pizza. There are also true Neapolitan-style pizzerias in Rome, and some are excellent, but the pizza *tonda* style (round, wood-oven pizzas) Rome is known for is this thin, almost crackery crust. Toppings are not heavy, but they should be of excellent quality, and not much different from their neighbors to the south: good tomatoes, olive oil, anchovies, perhaps some dried oregano, *fior di latte* mozzarella, or for an extra 2 or 3 euros, *mozzarella di bufala*. In season, fresh and semidried cherry tomatoes are a popular topping.

The desired results for a Roman dinner–style home kitchen pizza are:

- When fully stretched, the dough is 12 inches or more across.

- The sauce is spread pretty close to the edge, say a ¼-inch.

- The crust is medium brown with darker spots, very thin and crisp but bubbled at the rim.

- It's very light to pick up.

- The underside of the crust is spotted dark brown or even black.

- The interior crust is soft to crisp. Slices might not flop from rim to tip when fully baked, depending on the moisture content of the toppings.

- The cheese is fully melted but not burned, with no oil separation.

- All the elements—crust (underside, interior, and rim), toppings, and cheese—reach their perfect point of baking at the same time. In the home oven, finding the ideal rack position helps make this happen.

ROMAN AL TAGLIO BAKERY PIZZAS

In Rome, *al taglio* (by the slice) pizzas are rectangles of very simply topped pizza, usually wrapped in paper, that one takes away to eat as a light lunch or a snack. The bianca and rossa are classics; topped *al taglio* pizzas get a bit more creative (see page 26).

These pizzas bake one of two ways in Rome: in rectangular steel or other metal pans; or directly on the hearth in oblong stretches of dough, maybe 12 inches wide by 4 to 6 feet in length. (Fun to watch!) The bakeries use mostly electric deck ovens that can also be used to bake bread, and I've observed baking temperatures at a few of these bakeries ranging from 520° to 595°F (270° to 312°C).

These baking temperatures are happily very close to what we can get from our home kitchen ovens. What we can't replicate is the depth of the

Roman deck ovens, which often go 10 to 12 feet deep. To load the pizza the dough is set up on a long, narrow floured board or peel, then lightly stretched until it is the proper length and thickness, oiled, and dimpled. Then, with a well-trained motion, it is quickly and completely loaded onto the deck of the oven. Imagine holding the peel from the back of its handle, placing the entire peel all the way into the oven, and scootching the peel out with a series of rapid jerks while the pizza remains inside. Easy, right? Now imagine doing it while some idiot American (looking exactly like me and wearing a ridiculous grin) is staring at you, taking photo after photo.

Because of the rectangular shape of *al taglio* pizza, I can't recommend baking the oil- or tomato-topped dough right on your home kitchen oven's pizza steel or stone. Our ovens are too shallow, only about 18 inches deep, and trying to load a rectangle of dough sideways onto a hot pizza stone is a bad idea. I do the home versions of *al taglio* pizza on parchment-lined sheet pans, moving the pizza at the very end of the bake to finish it on the pizza stone for a couple of minutes to get an extra degree of crisp on the crust.

The desired results for a Roman al taglio–style home kitchen pizza are:

- The crust is golden brown with only a little poof in the rim.
- There's a small amount of bubbliness in the dough and in the finished pizza, but not much rise.
- The crust is about an 1/8 inch thick after baking and is crisp and delicate, not dry.
- The underside of the crust is golden.
- It's coated with brushstrokes of olive oil after baking.

AMERICAN PIZZA, NEW YORK STYLE

This is probably the easiest style to replicate in a home kitchen. The biggest difference between what you'll get from a pizzeria and what you'll make at home is the size of the pizza: a New York slice pizza from a pizzeria is usually about 18 inches in diameter, whereas the home version is smaller, about 12 inches, because of the oven depth. For the New York–style pizza recipes in this book, I recommend using a higher protein flour (like King Arthur bread flour) and aiming for less poofy rims than with a Neapolitan pizza. The dough is stiffer too, with less water in it, and it's good for tossing, if that's your bag. The goal is for the crust of this pizza to be crisp but not dry. As far as cheese is concerned, I recommend a combination of grated pecorino or Parmesan underneath grated low-moisture mozzarella.

The desired results for a New York–style home kitchen pizza are:

- The crust is golden brown with only modest poof in the rim, which is thin and crisp.
- Unless it's heavily sauced, there should only be a little bit of "tip sag" when you pick up a slice.
- The underside of the crust is medium to dark brown.
- The sauce and cheese reach almost to the edge of the pizza, leaving a very narrow outer layer of just crust.
- The cheese is fully melted but not burned, with no oil separation.
- All the elements—crust (underside, interior, and rim), toppings, and cheese—reach their perfect point of baking at the same time. In the home oven, finding the ideal rack position helps make this happen.

AMERICAN PAN PIZZAS, AKA THE SQUARE SLICE, AKA GRANDMA PIZZA

This is the kind of pizza I grew up eating in Hyattsville, Maryland. My brother had a job at a place called The Pizza Pan, but I was a Ledo's fan, which is why my birthday dinner was always there. Ledo's was not a thick-crust pizza, but it was definitely greasy, and the dough was flaky, as if it had fat in it—probably lard or shortening (Ledo's ain't talking). The pepperoni was thick cut, and the pizza was sliced into squares. As another example, Buddy's in Detroit tops their dough with cheese, sauce, and then cheese again. Their cheese lines the edge of the pizza, where it gets crisp like a *frico* and frames the rectangular pie. Quality examples of the New York square slice, another gooey, cheesy pan-pizza classic, can be found at Adrienne's, Prince Street Pizza, and GG's (where it's called the Grandma Square). You might call any of these pan pizzas Nonna's pizza, Grandma pizza, or square pizza. The crust is not as thick as an American "Sicilian" pizza, which is almost as thick as most focaccia. Old Forge pan pizza from Pennsylvania is its own thing; the sauce contains onions and it's called "fried pizza" by some because fat underneath the dough fries the bottom of the pie. Oh Daddy-o.

The pan pizza recipes in this book suggest you use a half sheet pan and bake the pizza on top of a preheated pizza steel or stone, or on a rack in the lower third of the oven. The most critical thing about making this style of pizza is keeping the crust from sticking to the pan as it bakes. You have two options: line the pan with parchment (see page 81), or coat the pan with a film of olive oil or clean animal fat like duck fat, bacon fat, or lard. I like the latter option because the oil or fat cooks the dough from underneath and gives it both flavor and a crisp texture.

Pan pizzas allow for more sauce and more cheese, and fresh mozzarella can hold onto its heat and gooeyness much longer when topped with sauce, as on a Detroit pizza. The sauce-on-top configuration keeps the cheese from cooling quickly, and it holds its heat much longer than a Neapolitan- or New York–style pizza does.

I love pan pizza for its ease in the home kitchen, its versatility, and its ability to be a sexy, gooey flavor bomb on top of a crisp yet tender crust. If you've never made pizza before, pan pizza is a great intro, as it has fewer creation failure points than hearth pizzas like Neapolitan or Roman style. When you're making hearth pies, it takes a few tries to learn how to reliably load the pizza from a wooden peel onto a preheated baking stone that's sitting inside a 550°F (290°C) oven. When you make pan pizza, you use your hands to spread the dough out on a room-temperature pan on your countertop, and parbake it (see page 190), or top and bake it in a single stage. Easy cheesy.

Strip Pizza

You could call the strip pizza a subgenre of the pan pizza. It's a strip of dough rolled out with a rolling pin and baked on a pan lined with parchment. Nothing fancy here. It's just another shape, but the race-track-like, oblong oval has an aesthetic quality that I like. It is another fun way to make pizza. For the other pan pizzas in this book, I suggest you stretch an entire batch of dough to fit inside a half sheet pan. But for strip pizza, use one of the normal dough balls (roughly 280 grams) if you divide your dough into three. When the dough is ready and it's time to make pizza, use your hands to decompress and stretch it out. Then use a rolling pin to roll it out to size, as thin or as thick as you like it. I prefer thin crust for strip

pizza; I finish it off the pan, directly on the pizza steel, for the last couple of minutes of baking so it's nice and crisp.

The desired results for an American pan pizza and a strip pizza are:

- Once baked, the crust is about a ¼-inch thick, slightly thicker around the perimeter.

- It has a golden- to medium-brown crust on the edges.

- It has a crisp, golden crust bottom, not soft or saggy.

- The sauce and cheese reach almost to the edge of the pizza, leaving a very narrow outer layer of just crust. Some variations apply cheese all the way to the edge and it crisps up very nicely there.

- The cheese is fully melted but not burned, with no oil separation.

- All the elements—crust (underside, interior, and rim), toppings, and cheese—reach their perfect point of baking at the same time. In the home oven, finding the ideal rack position helps make this happen.

AMERICAN BAR PIZZA

Adam Kuban, the founder of *Slice*, a popular blog about pizza, is a bar pizza aficionado. As of this writing, Adam is running his own bar-pizza pop-up, Margot's Pizza, from the Brooklyn pizzeria and restaurant Emily and is planning to open a brick-and-mortar version of Margot's in New York. Here is Adam's take on what bar pizza is all about:

"They're all round, very thin, decidedly crisp pizzas that are usually loaded with toppings and cheese. It's very much a 1950s/1960s notion of pizza as interpreted by—or for—people who were not necessarily of Italian descent. I don't think anyone who was making them was historically that concerned with hole structure, rise, fermentation times, etc. That's not to say the crust is an afterthought or inconsequential, but I would say that at least in the case of bar pizza, I get the feeling that it was something bars started putting on the menu as 'bar food'—eventually the bars morphed into venues better known for the pizza. Which is to say I don't think these folks were putting that much thought into all this stuff the way we do in the Internet/blog/online forum era.

"The other notion, too, is that there is even a genre called 'bar pizza' or 'bar pies.' I mean, there is, but since it's (as of yet) not super well known and because they're all a little different, it's not as easy to point to it the way there are certain hallmarks of Neapolitan or deep-dish or even New York–style. Very few places that make it actually refer to it as 'bar pizza.' Only really Eddie's in New Hyde Park, New York, which bills itself as 'Home of the Bar Pie,' really seems to acknowledge it. It seems like a thing that was sort of thrust on the style from the outside. And heck, as the guy who did Slice, I'm as guilty of doing it as anyone. You see the same thing with 'Detroit-style' pizza. Whenever I used to write about Detroit-style pizza on Slice, I'd get comments from Detroiters saying, 'There's no such thing as "Detroit-style" pizza! That's just pizza!' Similar to how a Philly cheesesteak is just a 'cheesesteak' in Philly."

You can make a rendition of Adam's pie at home if you buy the necessary pan (see page 81), and follow the recipes for dough and pizza that Adam offered for this book. It's a round pizza that you bake mostly in a round deep-dish nonstick pan set on a pizza steel or stone, then remove and finish it directly on the preheated surface if the bottom needs to crisp up. It should be served sliced, in a round pan of the same dimensions. (I bake and serve in different pans, because the baking pan has a rim that makes it hard to eat from.) Cheese melts into the pan on this pizza, so nonstick is highly recommended (I use Lloyd deep-dish nonstick pans; see page 81). Stretch the dough by hand and then use a rolling pin to finish, making it very thin but not as paper-thin as the Roman style. The dough is less gassy than the other pizza doughs, and is made from high-protein bread flour. It bakes crisp and doesn't poof at all. These pizzas are topped with a blend of cheeses that includes anything that melts: fontina or provolone are not uncommon; cheddar won't offend the clientele; low-moisture mozzarella and a hard cheese like pecorino or Grana Padano work, too. Experiment to find the blend you like best, but be sure to use good cheese and grate your own. A box grater is easy to use.

The desired results for an American bar pizza are:

- It has a very thin, crisp dough and is moderately sauced.

- It has golden- to medium-brown crust on the edges.

- The bottom of the crust is crisp and golden, not soft or saggy.

- The sauce and cheese reach to the edge of the pizza—there's zero outer layer of just crust.

- The cheese is fully melted but not burned, with no oil separation.

- All the elements—crust (underside, interior, and rim), toppings, and cheese—reach their perfect point of baking at the same time. In the home oven, finding the ideal rack position helps make this happen.

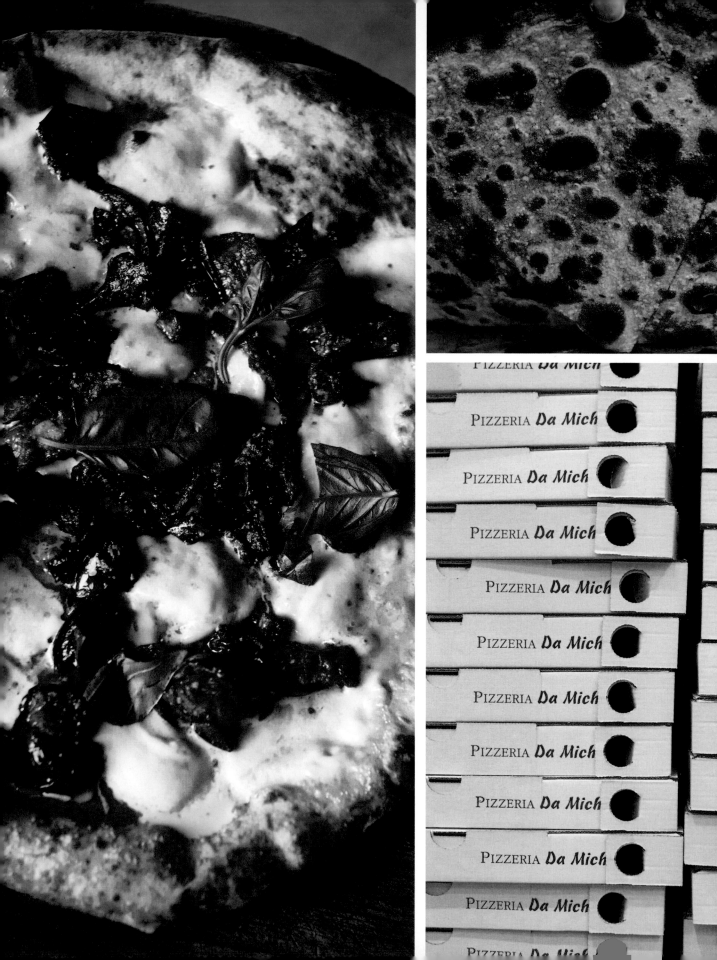

CHAPTER 3
EIGHT DETAILS FOR GREAT PIZZA CRUST

No matter the style, great pizza is not just about the recipe. It's also about the pizza maker. It's caring and taking the time. This is true in a pizzeria and it's true in the home kitchen. It's also about the quality of the ingredients; the skill, knowledge, experience, and dedication of the pizza maker; and the way the ingredients balance and complement each other. There's another, slightly less intuitive key to great pizza, too: the type of oven you use, and how you match the dough and baking technique to the oven. No matter what style you're aiming for, or what your platonic ideal of "the very best pizza" is, there are principles that guide quality. And the best way to ensure the best pizza is to start with the foundation of it all: the crust.

In this chapter I'll outline eight details that will help make your crust as good as it possibly can be. When you read them, they may feel intuitive to you, but if you think about them and stay engaged while you're baking, you'll see a difference. Think of these eight details like the roots, trunk, and major branches of a beautiful tree.

What is the best pizza crust you can remember? Imagine being able to make a home version of it. It's not complicated, but there are subtleties. If you allow yourself to make a simple dough often enough, you will learn to understand it, and know just when it's perfect, or when it needs a little more time. Take the time to consider the following details and put them into action, and you will be rewarded.

DETAIL 1: MATCH THE DOUGH AND ITS HYDRATION TO THE OVEN AND ITS BAKING TEMPERATURE

You might do some research and learn that the pizza dough they make at your favorite Neapolitan pizzeria on Via Tribunali, where the pies bake in 60 seconds in a 905°F (485°C) wood-fired oven, follows the guidelines of the Associazione Verace Pizza Napoletana (AVPN) formula for dough: 1 liter of water, 1.7 to 1.8 kilos of flour, 50 to 55 grams of salt, and 3 grams of fresh yeast. (See page 108 for my adapted AVPN recipe, the Saturday Pizza Dough.) The percentages work out to a dough hydration between 55 and 58 percent. So you decide this is the pizza you want to make at home and you mix this dough, but your oven only heats up to 550°F (290°C) and it takes 7 minutes for your pizza to bake. Don't be surprised that this pizza crust will be nothing like the pizza crust at your favorite pizzeria in Naples—AVPN pizza dough comes out as a great Neapolitan pizza only when it is baked in the 905°F (485°C) oven. Yours will be crisp all the way through and a little dry, not soft and delicate. But don't just blame your oven and give up: you can make an adjustment. To come close to that ideal of a delicate, slightly-crisp-on-the-*cornicione*, yet soft, pliable, and foldable pizza, you need to match the hydration of your pizza dough to your oven.

What's going on here? The pizza crust, while baking, loses moisture rapidly through evaporation. Seven or 8 minutes of baking at 550°F (290°C) will take much more moisture out of the pizza dough than 60 seconds of baking at 905°F (485°C). The longer it's in the oven, the more moisture the crust loses. If your goal is to bake a Neapolitan-style pizza in your home kitchen oven, by making a wetter dough, at 70 percent hydration, you can make a terrific pizza that, while not the same as at Da Michele, is firmly

in that style. It will be delicate and lightly crisp—way more delicate than if you had followed the strict AVPN guidelines and baked the pizza in your home kitchen oven with a 58 percent dough. In short, there is an inverse relationship between ideal dough hydration (lower) and your oven temperature (higher).

But let's say you do have a wood-fired oven to bake in, fired for several hours before starting. It's got a lovely bed of coals glowing in the left half of the oven, with a perfect 905°F (485°C) on the floor and 800°F (425°C) at the dome, and you know this because you bought an infrared thermometer. Then you *do* need the 58 percent pizza dough. In this baking chamber, the crust has to set very quickly so you can turn the pizza within its first 30 seconds—otherwise, the crust facing the fire burns. If the dough is too soft, like it would be when hydrated to 70 percent or more, you are likely to tear through the dough when you run the metal peel underneath to turn it. Wood-fired-oven baking is a balance between avoidance and achievement: avoid burning while achieving a perfectly baked crust (bottom and rim) and toppings.

DETAIL 2: THINK OF TIME AND TEMPERATURE AS PIZZA DOUGH INGREDIENTS

For readers of my first book, *Flour Water Salt Yeast*, this detail should be familiar. It applies to pizza dough like it applies to bread dough: in every recipe, time and temperature have target values—the same as salt or water. You could use top-quality flour, measure all your ingredients perfectly, knead with A-plus technique, and still end up with crappy dough that tastes bland and is stiff and dense because you didn't give it enough time to ferment. Give time its due. The temperature of the dough, the temperature of the room, and the amount of leavening in the dough all need to be in balance to get the proper amount of rise and flavor development. Temperature affects the rate of the dough's fermentation. Warmer dough and dough in warmer rooms will develop faster. I give specific guidance in each recipe, and I assume an ambient room temperature of 70°F (21°C), but you might want to make seasonal or climatic temperature adjustments to allow the timelines of each recipe to deliver the best results in your kitchen.

Here's an example of how this plays out in a recipe:

Let's say the recipe tells you to mix a dough with 90°F (32°C) water and room temperature flour so the dough temperature right after mixing is about 80°F (27°C). Then, it tells you to let the dough ferment for 2 hours at room temperature, then form dough balls and refrigerate them to make pizza with the next day. See Detail 5 for how to make adjustments in your own kitchen according to climate or season.

Keep in mind that yeast dies at around 114°F (46°C), so hot hot water is not a good idea. To help you get consistent, dependable results, I ask you to use a digital probe thermometer to measure water temperature for mixing dough, and to get the dough temperature after the dough is mixed. (A probe thermometer has multiple uses in the kitchen, especially for making sure meats are properly cooked.) My ideal bread dough temperature, for maximum volume and flavor development, is 78°F (26°C) after it is mixed. However, most of the direct pizza doughs in this book use very tiny amounts of yeast, and I have gotten the best results mixing dough that ends up between 80° and 82°F (27° and 28°C), creating a warm, productive environment for the yeast to feed, replicate, and ferment. This is all easy if you keep your flour at room temperature. I'll tell you what water temperature to use when you mix the dough; pay attention,

and adjust it warmer or cooler the next time until you know, in your environment, just what water temperature gets you the dough mixed to the temperatures I advise. All you need is a thermometer that works, plus memory or a notepad. (A little bit of obsessiveness doesn't hurt, either.)

Use your common sense and adjust if your room temperature is different from my norm of about 70°F (21°C). If your house is colder than mine, consider starting with warmer water and dough, or let the dough rise in a sunny corner of the room, or just take into account the fact that it may take longer for the fermentation to take place.

DETAIL 3: MEASURE YOUR INGREDIENTS BY WEIGHT, NOT VOLUME

Here's another classic rule that also appeared in *Flour Water Salt Yeast*. Quality digital home kitchen scales are inexpensive and widely available, and they allow you to accurately and confidently measure ingredients with consistent results. By weight, a cup of flour can vary dramatically depending on how it's packed into the cup. My cup might be 120 grams, while your cup might be 160 grams—a big difference! The same rationale applies to the measurement of water, salt, and yeast: small differences of weight in ingredients that are the same by volume can make a significant difference in the dough. With a scale, accuracy's not hard, and will give you a better pizza.

I do give guidelines for making volume measurements for yeast that approximate the weight in a recipe, so you'll be able to use this book while awaiting the arrival of the scale you just ordered. Some of my recipes use as little as 0.1 gram of dry yeast, which is about ⅒ of a ¼ teaspoon. I was thrilled

when I learned there is now an affordable scale on the market (around $13) that can measure these tiny amounts (see page 79).

DETAIL 4: MIX YOUR PIZZA DOUGH BY HAND, NOT IN A MACHINE

Mixing most of my pizza doughs by hand is easier than using a mixer and involves less cleanup, plus you get to learn a feel for the dough, which has benefits for the rest of your life as a pizza maker. Hand-mixing also makes dough that creates the most delicate pizza

crust. What is delicacy? It's the opposite of chewiness, an ethereal weightlessness—the experience of picking up a pizza and its feeling lighter than you were expecting it to. It has crispness in its texture, but your teeth go right through it like there's magic inside. The first time, it's a surprise. It's the pizza of your dreams.

Machine-mixing pizza dough works fine, and on one or two occasions I recommend it (more on that later), but only with the minimum amount of mixing needed to incorporate all the ingredients and bring the dough ball together. Machine-mixing the dough for too long puts too much organization into the

GLUTEN'S ROLE IN PIZZA DOUGH

Strong flours are high in protein, up to 14 percent as measured by flour weight, and have long been thought of as ideal for bread making. In fact, they're really ideal for industrial bread baking, but not so much for high-quality breads. The high protein level works best with the intensive mixing and fast rising production of industrial baking. Yet, an American style of pizza grew from using bread flour in bread ovens to make pizza whose crust has chew and crispness. High-gluten flour is part of what makes a New York pizza what it is. Softer, low-gluten flours that are still suitable for making bread or pizza have 11 percent protein or even a little less, which is about how much protein there is in all-purpose flour. We use low-gluten flour (even this is a nonspecific term, with no standard definition) for making bread at my bakery, and for making wood-fired pizza at Ken's Artisan Pizza. The protein percentage in a wheat crop depends on the genetics of the wheat, the climate, and the specifics of a year's growing season. (Wheat farmers usually measure the protein content before harvesting, as protein in wheat increases as it matures on the stalk. Many wheat farmers get a higher price for higher protein wheat, too, because it's what their biggest customers want.)

The words *protein* and *gluten* are often used interchangeably. When water is added to flour and mixed into dough, gluten is created: a web of interlaced strands of glutenin and gliadin, two proteins that are in wheat flour (and also rye and barley).

Adding water to flour lubricates the protein strands, allowing them to stretch. Mixing the dough, either by hand or by machine, organizes the gluten, and folding organizes the dough further. I like to imagine dough as a web of gluten and starch, which holds onto the gas that comes from the dough's fermentation. Gluten, then, has this specific role of being the backbone of pizza dough. Higher protein flours form a stronger gluten web and can give the dough greater strength than dough made with low-protein flours. High-protein flours can also make dough that is elastic and difficult to form into a pizza—it needs longer fermentation to break down the gluten a bit. In time, the gluten network in dough degrades. Enzymes eat it up, literally. *Elastic* is not a happy word in the pizza maker's lexicon, because you need the dough to expand to pizza diameter, not snap back. However, you do want enough strength for the dough to support its toppings, keep its shape as you slide it into the oven, and hold onto the fermentation gases that make it taste good and give open holes in the rim.

CHAPTER 4
INGREDIENTS
AND EQUIPMENT

What do you need to be your own *pizzaiolo?* A handful of items for baking pizza, a standard home kitchen oven, and a few good ingredients: this chapter is where I'll talk about those. (You maybe need some good instructions too: we'll get to those next.)

INGREDIENTS

Quality rules here. Try your farmers' market for vegetables and your butcher for cured meats. Support your independently owned food purveyors—they know and care about what they are selling you. If you have access to a good cheesemonger, take advantage of it—because, man, theirs is a hard business. You should feel lucky they're there for you, and I'm sure they would appreciate seeing you more.

Above all else, you need quality flour, tomatoes, and cheese. Here's what you should know about these essential pizza ingredients, with some added recommendations regarding salt and yeast.

Flour

In Naples and the surrounding areas, the overwhelming majority of pizzerias—about 90 percent—use flour from a single mill in Naples: Molino Caputo. The Caputo family has been making flour for pizza for three generations, since 1924. It is the only example I know of a mill making flour designed specifically for pizza. Most mills are making flour as a general-purpose product in a variety of types, each suitable for many uses.

Caputo pizza flours blend several kinds of wheat selected to produce flours with good flavors and the right physical characteristics for pizza baking. The milling meets a specification called "oo" (*doppio zero* in Italian, commonly called "double

This man has worked at the Caputo mill for seventy years.

zero" in the United States), and it gives the flour a refined, almost powdery consistency. (The 00 designation is a reference to how fine the flour is, and in Caputo's case it takes twenty-five passes through the roller mill before it becomes 00—this does *not* refer to the protein content, which in Caputo's 00 ranges from 12.5 to 13.5 percent.) Today the wheat in Caputo flours is all from Europe (they once imported North American wheat) and is blended to meet strict specifications that give it just the right properties for water absorption, dough formation, fermentation, stretchability, and the baking qualities that work best for Neapolitan pizza. In the U.S., Caputo flour is available in both a blue bag and a red bag. The blue bag, while labeled "Pizzeria" rather than "00," is still a 00 flour. As Antimo Caputo himself said to me when I visited the mill, "The soul of pizza is the pizza maker. That is why the blue bag says '*Pizzeria*,' not the kind of flour." The blue-bag flour is about 12.5 percent protein, and it's the bag I've seen the most in Neapolitan pizzerias. The red bag is labeled "00" or "Chef's Flour" and has about 13.5 percent protein, giving more elasticity to the dough. This flour works better for very long rising times, like in a biga or an overnight levain starter that gets mixed into the final dough after 10 or 12 hours. (The 48- or 72-hour pizza doughs require refrigeration or the dough just breaks down.) Some pizzerias blend these two flours. Of the two, the blue-bag flour produces more extensible (less elastic) gluten. Antimo Caputo cited the example of Da Michele pizzeria, which makes eight hundred (!) pizzas each day—the *pizzaiolos* need to be able to finish the stretching of the dough with just three turns in order to keep up the pace. If the dough were too elastic, it would slow them down. They wouldn't be able to meet the demands of the fast-paced production, meaning you would have to wait even longer to get your Da Michele pizza!

Although these Caputo flours are designed for pizza that bakes in a 905°F (485°C) oven, I really like the results in my home kitchen oven, too. On U.S. store shelves, I've more often seen Caputo's red-bag 00 than the blue bag. But both work great for making home kitchen pizza, and if you can't find it locally, it is easy to order online. The pizza dough recipes in this book, when made with Caputo flour (either the red bag or the blue bag), are wonderfully soft and make up dough balls that are smooth, and supple. It makes a light, delicate, tasty pizza crust.

Naturally, there are many other flour choices for making good pizza. Know that different flours can have very different water-absorption characteristics, so with one flour you might get a much looser or stiffer dough than with another flour if the water amount is the same. Usually, the higher the protein content in the flour, the more water it will absorb. But high-protein flours make dough that is more elastic, with a less delicate texture once baked. There is a kind of Goldilocks middle ground for protein content. Too little, like in pastry or biscuit flour, and the dough will not hold its gas well enough to give the open and light *cornicione*, the outer rim of the crust that should be eaten, not set aside on your plate.

At Ken's Artisan Pizza, we have been using the low-gluten flour from Shepherd's Grain, a product of the Pacific Northwest, since we opened in 2006. The results are excellent. Dough made with Shepherd's Grain flour stretches well, has excellent flavor, and has a protein content between 10.5 and 11.5 percent, depending on the previous year's wheat-growing conditions. A single harvest of spring and winter wheats takes place over a 3- to 4-week span in August every year. That's the crop until next year. It then goes into storage silos for milling throughout the year. Some characteristics of the wheat, like its protein content, remain constant during storage, while others—starch damage and moisture content, for example—can vary from one milling to the next.

While testing the recipes for this book, I alternated between Shepherd's Grain and Caputo flours, and each worked well (the Shepherd's Grain flour is a little more absorbent, meaning a little bit stiffer dough, so I would add a touch more water to soften it up). Other good options include King Arthur flours, which are also of generally high quality, and searching out small mills near you, such as Hayden Flour Mills in Tempe, Arizona. Flour labeled all-purpose, which has a medium protein content (usually between 10 and 12 percent), is worth trying for pizza, too.

Be forewarned, though: the protein content is rarely labeled on the bag; you may have to do some sleuthing online to find out.

Many styles of American pizza, like New York and bar pizza, are made with a higher protein bread flour, in the 14 percent range. If you think of an American pizza as sliced, and heavy with toppings, or even as a cheese-and-tomato slice pizza that has a crisp yet foldable crust, then you need more structure, and higher protein flour helps with that. I think the reasons for using high-protein flour in American pizza dough are more historical than intentional. Big American flour mills have long paid a premium for high-protein wheat, so that's what the wheat farmers grow. American pizzerias used this flour, and the resulting style of pizza became what we were all accustomed to. In this book's recipes for American pizza dough, I recommend using high-protein bread flour.

When it comes to pizza, I depart from the current bread trend of using whole grain flours. I adore these in bread, but I do not use whole grain flours in hearth-baked pizzas because the crispness and delicate lightness of texture in the crust go away. When making pan pizzas, however, I do sometimes like a blend of white flour with whole wheat, whole emmer, einkorn, or whole spelt flours (I order from Bluebird Grain Farms online).

Because temperature is such an important element of the equation when making pizza dough, and because I calibrated water temperatures for the dough using unrefrigerated flour when writing these recipes, you should use flour at room temperature for all of the recipes in this book.

Tomatoes

While the myth of Neapolitan pizza is that they all use San Marzano tomatoes, the fact is that *true* San Marzano tomatoes are a Denominazione di Origine Protetta (DOP) product (see sidebar on page 65) and only represent 30,000 tons of a total of 2.5 million tons of tomatoes harvested each year in the south of Italy. In my first book, describing the secret to a good and authentic tomato sauce for Neapolitan pizza, I wrote "use San Marzano tomatoes." I have since learned that was an oversimplification, and even looked at my own pizzeria, where we are making a very good pizza sauce using tomatoes that are from *near* San Marzano, but are not DOP San Marzano tomatoes. This ideal *terroir* for tomatoes—the climate and volcanic soil—exists throughout the region. No offense intended, but writing "use San Marzano tomatoes" would be like saying "only drink wine from Barolo." DOP San Marzano tomatoes are wonderful, but they are not the only good tomatoes for pizza.

According to Costantino Cutolo of Compagnia Mercantile d'Oltremare, a Campania tomato processor, "[San Marzano] is a huge ground for fraud.

Naples pizzerias don't even know what they are using . . . Here they call 'San Marzano' what is not San Marzano." Still, he said, "Quality is almost the same; you don't realize." The San Marzano DOP controls the seed bank for these tomatoes. You can grow tomatoes from these seeds outside of the DOP zone and call them San Marzano, but to be DOP San Marzano they have to be grown within its very small, defined territory, in and around the village named San Marzano, located between Mount Vesuvius and Naples (not on the slopes of Mount Vesuvius, as many have written—the slopes are covered in trees and rock). When I asked Cutolo what the accurate description is for good-quality canned tomatoes from around Naples that are not San Marzano, he replied, "Small, pear shaped tomatoes. Whole peeled tomatoes from the south."

I asked Cutolo the very important question of how they control for consistent moisture content in each can, because from the pizzeria's perspective, you can't have one day's sauce be thick and the next day's sauce be thin. Cutolo replied: "You have to control the Brix of the tomato to get consistency from one can to the next. This is the average ripeness of the crop at harvest and before processing."

DOP

Denominazione di Origine Protetta, or DOP, translates as "Protected Designation of Origin" and is a certification for many Italian heritage food products intended to discourage fakes from using a heritage product name without merit. DOP products include balsamic vinegar from Modena; Parmigiano-Reggiano cheese from near Parma; Prosciutto di San Daniele and Prosciutto di Parma; *mozzarella di bufala* from Campania and Lazio; and of course, San Marzano tomatoes from the village of San Marzano and a defined area around the village. The DOP does not just protect consumers; it also protects the producer, who uses time-honored methods to make traditional products of quality that characterize the pride of a town or a region and ultimately the pride of Italy. To get DOP designation, a producer needs to meet strict standards for each product, all the way through packaging and labeling. So if you want to buy real DOP San Marzano tomatoes, look for the sunburst "DOP" logo on the can.

Cutolo's average desired post-production Brix level (see sidebar on page 67) is 7.0, but the tomatoes have an average of about 4.5 at harvest. During production, the juice is concentrated to a degree that will result in the final can of juice and tomatoes reaching the desired Brix of about 7.0. This is Cutolo's target (as of this writing), and their Ciao brand canned tomatoes are indeed a little bit sweeter and also thicker than others I've tried. The industry in general has a target of 6 Brix in the can, and these are very good tomatoes, too. Lower Brix means a thinner, more watery sauce that is also less sweet, and sometimes a pizzeria will drain some of the cans to obtain a thicker sauce. More often they do not—they just have a thinner sauce. Cooking the sauce to thicken it before making pizza removes the freshness of flavor and is rarely done in Italy, although it is not uncommon in New York pizzerias.

At harvest, about two-thirds of the crop is collected when the vines are shaken by hand over low truck beds filled with metal containers. Then, in a second pass, mechanical harvesters pick up the rest of the crop.

We took a fun tour of Cutolo's processing plant and watched how the tomatoes go from delivery to can. Shifts of women (all women; it's a village tradition) sort the tomatoes on a very rapid manual sorting line after they are steamed just long enough to loosen their skins, which are then removed by blasts of air in a machine. Then the underripe and imperfect tomatoes are removed to a secondary channel. Only the best tomatoes move on to be canned whole. It's difficult work, fascinating to watch. The women start their shifts at 4 a.m. While we stood on a platform above them, observing, with me taking pictures while they were focused on their sorting, not one of them had the time to notice us staring at them. They were absorbed in their work as

tomatoes on the sorting line flowed past at a steady pace, endlessly.

Why use whole peeled tomatoes? There are also cans of crushed tomatoes or tomato puree on supermarket shelves, but the highest-quality tomatoes are reserved for canning whole. Others are sorted out to make into juice or into cans of other tomato products, like tomato paste.

Many Americans prefer canned whole peeled tomatoes from the U.S. or Canada. I've read reviews on *Serious Eats* and in *Cook's Illustrated* that rate North American brands, such as Whole Foods' 365 and Trader Joe's, higher than Italian canned

WHAT'S A BRIX?

Here's an explanation of Brix, courtesy of Teri Wadsworth at Cameron Winery in Dundee, Oregon:

The Brix scale is named after nineteenth-century German scientist Adolf Brix, who invented the hydrometer, an instrument that could measure the sugar content of grape juice for wine. Before this, ripeness could only be determined subjectively, by taste. The Brix scale can also be used to measure ripeness in the juice of other fruits, like tomatoes. In winemaking, 1 degree Brix is equivalent to 1 gram of soluble solids (the sum of sucrose, fructose, vitamins, proteins, and so on) per 100 grams of grape juice. In winemaking, an effort is made to harvest at a particular Brix level, and this measure of ripeness and its corresponding sugar content in the fruit directly relates to the fermentation potential in the wine, its flavor, and ultimately the conversion to alcohol. In theory, alcohol is produced at a rate of approximately 51 percent of fermentable sugar. Variables such as exposure to oxygen and temperature, the amount of yeast, and yeast diversity determine the actual conversion rate from fermentable sugars to alcohol and carbon dioxide.

Tomatoes go through the same seasonal harvest variability as grapes and other fruits of the earth do. There is a right time to harvest, and measuring Brix in tomatoes is as important to timing harvest as it is for grapes, when the desire is to produce canned tomatoes that have consistent flavor, acidity, texture, and water content (think of it as thickness or thinness of tomato sauce from one can to the next, from one day to the next). Fruit ripening involves a series of related and complex enzyme-catalyzed transformations. When starches are converted into simple sugars by natural enzymes, the fruit sweetens. A tomato changes from green to red as chlorophyll breaks down to reveal underlying pigmented compounds such as anthocyanins and lycopenes. It becomes less tart as organic acids are converted into less acidic molecules; softer as pectin is broken down; and more fragrant as volatile aromatic compounds are synthesized. Brix is an extremely useful objective marker for ripeness.

tomatoes. Bianco DiNapoli is an American brand that I like. We have tried several options at Ken's Artisan Pizza, including Alta Cucina brand California tomatoes, which we substitute when there is an interruption in the supply line from Italy. However, we always end up returning to our preference: Italian whole peeled tomatoes. The richness of their flavor and their balanced acidity—perfect for pizza. Right now we are blending Rega and Ciao brand tomatoes to get the flavor and consistency that work for us.

Some Italian *pizzaiolos* are seeking out tomatoes that are not from San Marzano. Roscioli's Emma

of the pie, which helps retain the moisture of the sauce underneath. Some places tear off pieces of the balls of fresh mozzarella by hand for an organic look. These are stylistic differences and I encourage you to experiment with the size and shape of your sliced or torn cheese to find your own pizza cheese sweet spot.

USING LOW-MOISTURE MOZZARELLA

I like low-moisture mozzarella for the texture of the cheese after the pizza bakes. It's really *the* cheese for that iconic American pizza flavor and texture. Low-moisture mozzarella cheese holds its semiliquid, melted, hot-and-stretchy state for a very long time, often with more browning than its fresh, brine-packed counterpart. It's why an American pizza in a box with this cheese is good to eat long after the pizza is baked—unlike a pizza with fresh mozzarella, which really needs to be eaten within 10 minutes of baking.

Texture is as important as taste with low-moisture mozzarella. It is nothing if it doesn't deliver an oozing, elastic, stringy pull when you bite into it. Low-moisture mozz is shredded before topping the pizza, and it melts evenly to cover the pizza in a gooey cheese lava halfway between liquid and solid. Whole-milk low-moisture mozzarella gives the sexiest mouthfeel and the richest flavor compared to low-fat or skim-milk mozzarella (imposters!). The yellower the mozzarella, the more age and saltiness it is likely to have. Try different kinds of low-moisture mozzarella to find the one you like best. As a rule, I prefer whiter, fresh brands like Calabro and Losurdo for American pizzas.

If you're using low-moisture mozzarella, shred your own cheese. It takes just a minute with a decent box grater. Grate over the large holes. The shredded cheese you find at the store has a coating of starch and other stuff over each strand to prevent clumping, and it costs more. You don't want to eat that, do you?

Aged Hard Cheeses

Hard grating cheeses such as Parmigiano-Reggiano, Grana Padano, and pecorino are very commonly used in both Neapolitan- and New York–style pizzas. The AVPN definition of pizza margherita includes two cheeses: grated hard cheese and fresh mozzarella. One treatment I'm very fond of is to top a pizza with grated hard cheese immediately after it comes out of the oven. For recipes in this book that call for Parmigiano-Reggiano cheese, feel free to substitute Grana Padano. These two cheeses are made in the same places using the same techniques and have a very similar character, but Parmigiano-Reggiano is finer—made from a higher quality milk—and is aged longer.

Salt

Please use fine sea salt in this book's pizza dough recipes. Do not use iodized salt, because it tastes like iodine. I recommend fine sea salt as opposed to coarse because it dissolves quickly in water. You can use whatever grind or texture of salt you want for topping your pizza—enjoy the variety of textures and mineral flavors of finishing salts from Hawaii, Oregon, Portugal, and wherever else you find them. I'm a big fan of my neighbor Jacobsen Salt, down the street from Trifecta Tavern here in Portland, which specializes in hand-harvested salt from Netarts Bay, Oregon. Jacobsen's flake salt has a beautiful texture and appearance with a very clean taste.

Consider the salt content in the pizza's toppings, too, and balance the saltiness of them all on the baked pizza. Most of the salt on the pizza is going to be in the cheese and in the toppings—especially cured meats. Low-moisture mozzarella will have more salt than fresh *fior di latte* mozzarella. Hard

Clockwise from bottom right: mozzerella di bufala; burrata di bufala; *Pecorino Romano;* caciocavallo; pecorino tartufo.

TALKING CHEESE WITH STEVE JONES

I sat down with my friend Steve Jones to talk cheese and pizza. Steve is a Portland cheesemonger who owns Cheese Bar; Cheese Annex in The Commons Brewery down the street from my Trifecta Tavern & Bakery; and Chizu, a sushi-inspired cheese bar downtown.

Turn to page 240 for a recipe for raclette pizza from Steve Jones. You can thank him later. It has beer-braised leeks, raclette cheese, and roasted potatoes. Yes, please.

Ken: *You have had a series of pizza nights at Cheese Bar. What were your favorite cheeses on the pizzas you made?*

Steve: Taleggio, raclette, and washed-rind stinky cheeses. These are really good with spicy cured-pork products like *soppressata* or spicy *capicola*. Taleggio I like with tomato sauce. Raclette is great with potatoes and leeks, no tomato sauce, and we've even served it with chopped cornichons.

Brebis, a fresh sheep's milk cheese, is great and we look forward to its season every year. We treat it like *fromage blanc*. It comes in the spring when the sheep have just finished lambing, so the milk is at its richest and tastes a little grassy. We pair it with other springtime ingredients: peas, spring onions, even mint. Crescenza, also called stracchino, is another favorite: it's yeasty, gooey, and spreadable. This cheese is good paired with speck and arugula. Bellwether Farms in California makes it.

K: *What do you consider when choosing a cheese to pair with other pizza toppings?*

S: Meltability first. Flavor offsets that are compatible as well, of course. Some cheeses just don't melt well, including most sheep's milk cheeses that are not fresh; same goes for aged goat cheeses. As far as flavor offsets, we don't want to marry powerful cheese with another strong-flavored ingredient, so raclette goes great with potato, and if we add a pork component it is in small pieces. We always find the happiest combinations of toppings when we stay within a geographic region or within a season, so Taleggio and speck, raclette and potatoes, spring cheeses with springtime crops.

K: *What are your favorite melting cheeses?*

S: The list could begin and end with raclette. It is inexpensive and loaded with flavor, and it melts beautifully.

K: *What about acidity in cheese?*

S: Goat cheese when it's young and fresh has a nice tang to it, kind of a citric tang, quite often lemon, whereas an aged goat cheese goes tropical, more sweet than bright. Time produces more complex flavors in cheese as it ages.

K: *I love topping a pizza with* burrata *after the pizza is baked. Do you know how it's made? I just know that it's mozzarella on the outside and cream in the middle.*

S: I'm sure the first *burrata* that was made was at the end of a batch, using up remnants of a mozzarella batch, including the stringy ribbons that are formed. *Burrata* is made by hand, making a purse of stretched mozzarella, and as they pull it together they are putting cream and the ribbons in the middle. It's yet another example of a great thing to eat coming from a "waste nothing" mind-set.

K: *I'm having a hard time finding an American aged mozzarella for melting that doesn't brown too fast, or isn't too salty in flavor. Any recommendations or ideas?*

S: Try Polly-O brand. That's a big delivery pizza cheese. It's a national brand.

K: *Why is it that the more age a cheese has, and the harder it becomes, the saltier it gets? Is this entirely from moisture loss, or are aged cheeses made with more salt to preserve them?*

S: It's both. For preservation for sure. Most people nowadays don't think of cheese as what it was originally: preserved milk. The cows, the sheep, the goats don't naturally produce milk year-round; they produce milk after birthing, in the spring and summer months. Today we artificially inseminate cows to get milk year-round. You still can't trick sheep—they make milk on their own schedule. Tradition guides a lot when it comes to salt content in cheese and aging it. Cheese traditionally was made to be consumed in the late winter when other food supplies—grains and storage crops—were running low. You were left with cheese and beer, and that's what would get you through until spring.

K: *When is salt introduced to the cheese as it's being made?*

S: The salt comes from a brine bath for many cheeses, like Parmigiano-Reggiano (which is in the brine bath for many days) and mozzarella (in a short brine bath, for minutes). In other cheeses salt is added to the milk before the break happens, or after the whey is drained.

grating cheeses like pecorino and Parmigiano-Reggiano are aged 12 to 24 months typically, and sometimes more. They are saltier. If you generously top a pizza with grated pecorino and then an aged low-moisture mozzarella (like Grande brand), you might get a pizza that is very salty. You can combine cheeses, a practice common in good pizzerias everywhere, but be careful not to overdo it with the amount of aged or hard cheese. As in cooking generally, if one ingredient is salty, balance it with other ingredients that are not.

Yeast

Considering there are about fifteen billion viable yeast cells in one teaspoon of instant dried yeast (yes, I checked—they are *really small*), accurate measurement is helpful for getting consistent results. A ¼-teaspoon of instant dry yeast conveniently weighs very close to 1 gram. Since some people will not have a digital scale that measures accurately to the small weights I sometimes call for—as little as 0.1 gram of dry yeast—I use fractions of a ¼ teaspoon to approximate the measurement, and the recipes will work fine with some wiggle room. (However, see page 79 for information about an affordable scale that accurately measures from 0.1 to 100 grams.) Another option is to measure ¼ teaspoon of yeast (about 1 gram), spread it out in a line, and then divide the line into tenths. Then you can fairly easily measure out 0.1 gram, 0.3 gram, or however much is called for in the recipe.

The pizza dough recipes in this book call for instant dry yeast. You're likely to find three kinds of dry yeast at the store: active dry, rapid rise, and instant. All of these yeasts are the same species: *Saccharomyces cerevisiae*. What differentiates them is their coating, the way the yeast is manufactured,

and performance. At my bakery, we use SAF Red Instant Yeast. I recommend that you buy a 16-ounce (455 g) package, which is available from King Arthur Flour's website or other online stores. It will keep for 6 months if stored airtight in the refrigerator. Jeffrey Hamelman, King Arthur Flour's master baker, told me he has kept a package of yeast in his freezer, wrapped airtight, that has performed consistently for several years.

EQUIPMENT

A few of the equipment items listed here are essential—a baking steel or stone for hearth pizzas, a digital scale for measuring ingredients, and a probe thermometer to measure water and dough temperature (see page 53). Others have acceptable substitutes: a large kitchen bowl with a sealable cover can substitute for the 6-quart dough tub; a cookie sheet can fill in for a half sheet pan; a blender can work if you don't have a food mill for making sauce; and a Lloyd deep-dish pan is only for a single recipe in this book (bar pies, page 195).

I'm intentionally leaving the oven out of the equipment discussion. I've written this book with recipes tested in my standard, nothing-very-fancy home kitchen oven. Recipe testers using their own home kitchen ovens of different makes have had excellent results, mirroring my own. Most home kitchen ovens can heat on a bake setting up to 525° or 550°F (275° or 290°C) and have a broiler element or gas-fired broiler. That's all you need to make a good pizza. I do make a few comments about wood-fired-oven baking throughout this book, but every recipe is designed for a standard home kitchen oven.

Pizza Steel or Pizza Stone

A pizza stone in the home kitchen was once the only option for baking pizzas brick-oven style, on a hot, earthen surface. An improvement to the earthen pizza stone is now on the market: the pizza steel, made from ¼-inch-thick steel. Steel is more conductive than stone, and in all of my test baking I get superior results with the steel. The stone doesn't release its heat as fast as the steel does. A greater intensity of heat hits the bottom of the pizza crust, which is exactly what we want, and you see more of the leopard-spot pocks of dark color on the bottom of the crust, just like at a good pizzeria. Pizza steels are made to the same dimensions as a pizza stone, and the thick steel won't crack or break like some poorly made pizza stones will. It's a little more expensive than most stones, but it will last a lifetime and then some.

Andris Lagsdin of Stoughton Steel deserves credit for being the first to market a pizza steel—though he gives credit for the inspiration to Nathan Myhrvold's *Modernist Cuisine*. It works so well that he now has competitors. I bought my pizza steel online from Stoughton Steel. It came pre-seasoned

and shipping was included in the purchase price ($79). A good pizza stone is less expensive than a steel; before you buy either, I would encourage you to check user reviews: I have heard reports of some brands of pizza stones cracking under the high heat of pizza baking.

Wooden Pizza Peel

You want a wooden peel measuring about 14 inches wide with a short or medium length handle. I find the dough is more likely to stick to a metal peel.

Dough Tub

I recommend buying a 6-quart round plastic tub for mixing your dough by hand and holding the dough as it rises. I use Cambro brand translucent tubs (they call them "storage containers") with matching lids; they're available online and at most restaurant supply stores that sell to the public.

Whatever brand you choose, just be sure it's food-grade plastic. The size is important: it needs to be big enough to allow you to mix the dough by hand inside the container and to contain the dough as it expands (usually no more than double in size); the Cambro 4-quart tub, for example, is too narrow to allow for easy hand mixing. A round shape makes it easy to incorporate the ingredients; squared edges and corners make it harder. A clear container lets you see through it to chart the progress of the rise. And you need a lid to keep the dough from drying out during its rise.

Deli Containers

I use small plastic deli containers for weighing salt, yeast, cheese, sauce, and toppings on my digital scale. These containers are about the size of a single serving or two of to-go potato salad. Very handy. Quart-sized plastic deli containers with matching lids are what I use to store tomato sauce in the fridge. If you don't have any deli containers, use whatever normal storage containers you have on hand.

Digital Kitchen Scales

It is settled beyond debate that measuring ingredients by weight works better than measuring with cups and tablespoons. Your 350 grams of water will be the same as mine, but I'd be less confident that you and I would come up with exactly the same amount of water if I told you to measure out 1½ cups. A splash of water can make a big difference in the consistency of the dough. The same goes for a tablespoon more or less of flour, which can affect the texture of the finished dough. If you buy a kitchen scale, your baked goods will reliably turn out better, and I promise you'll find plenty of other uses for it.

I really recommend two inexpensive scales, though you can get by with just one for larger measurements—or, as the market evolves, look for one that can measure from 0.01 gram all the way up to 2000 grams (2 kilos). Almost all scales will convert from pounds and ounces to metric weights. I like OXO scales for their pull-out display. I use them at home and at work.

Another scale (inexpensive—around $13) that measures in the ⅟₁₀₀-gram increments is useful for measuring yeast. I like the American Weigh Scales ACP-200. It measures from 0.01 gram to 100 grams. Several dough recipes in this book call for very small

amounts of yeast—0.1 or 0.2 gram. Using volume measures, the closest I can come to describing these amounts is to say what percentage of a ¼ teaspoon to eyeball—one-fifth of a ¼ teaspoon, for example. Using weight measures, I can ask you to measure 0.2 gram of instant dry yeast and know both that the measurement is simple and straightforward, and that you are going to get dependable results. Still, since a ¼ teaspoon of instant dry yeast weighs very close to 1 gram, you can estimate fractions of that ¼ teaspoon to approximate the weight in each recipe (see page 76).

Food Service Film

There's something comically insufficient about a narrow box of plastic wrap you buy at the grocery store. Home-use consumer brands of plastic film are oddly much more difficult to use than food-safe commercial wrap. It's hard to remove from the box, it often doesn't stick well to what's it's supposed to stick to, and it just, it just . . . sucks. Meanwhile, in the sane world of things meant to be used without giving you a headache, you have a box of food service film, designed for restaurant kitchens where it is used many times each day to quickly and easily wrap anything that needs airtight storage.

In this book's dough recipes, once you have shaped dough balls, they need to be stored airtight. My recommendation in the recipes is to put the dough balls on one or more flour-dusted dinner plates, wrap it in plastic film, and let it rest until ready to use. Simple and done. While boxes of food service film are rarely, if ever, found in a supermarket, you can buy them online or at restaurant supply shops that sell to the public. One box will last you years, and I promise you'll never go back to that stuff made for the mass market. Buy in sizes between 12 and

CHAPTER 5
METHODS

Even if you have no pizza making experience, I can give you a start-to-finish method that is easy to learn and simple to execute, and it will last you a lifetime. The dough can be made up in five minutes without using a mixer. Another five minutes' work two hours later, and your dough balls are shaped. Sauce takes just a few minutes and requires no cooking time. Preheat your oven, cut up some cheese, tear the leaves off some fresh basil, slice a pepperoni, shape the dough into a round or spread it out on a pan, top it, and bake your pizza.

The trickiest part, until you've done it enough times for it to be familiar, is going to be stretching the ball of dough into a round disk and learning to load it from a wooden peel onto a preheated baking stone or steel. I recommend you practice loading an undressed pizza (just a stretched disk of dough), first on your countertop a few times so you learn the feel of it, and then into the oven from the peel once or twice. If there's an accident, there's no mess. It might take one or two tries to sense the feel of scootching the dough accurately off the peel onto the hot baking steel. If you get the transfer right, you can parbake that crust (see page 190), then top it and finish baking, so you're not sacrificing the dough ball. This is the easiest way to

learn with the least penalty for screwing up. Detailed instructions and photos follow in this chapter, and I also have a series of instructional videos that demonstrate each step on my website, kensartisan.com.

Enjoy it! Allow yourself a few errors as you learn. Consider doubling the recipe to make more dough balls than you know you'll need so that if you mess one up, you're not gonna kill dinner. For the cautious beginner, I'd suggest starting with the pan pizza recipes. This type of pizza is simpler to make—less error prone—and these "Grandma pizzas" are terrific.

In the following chapter, I offer several dough recipes, each with different schedule options, ranging from same-day to 24- or 48-hour dough. Most of the doughs are multipurpose and can work with 90 percent of this book's recipes (there are a few single- purpose doughs), so pick one whose schedule suits your lifestyle. Good pizza dough does not happen in just a couple of hours, so each dough recipe uses my "time as an ingredient" philosophy. Still, active time on your part consists of just a few minutes to mix the dough.

Once you get familiar with the techniques discussed here, including mixing the dough by hand, forming dough balls, stretching the dough into a round disk, or laying it out in a pan, making sauce, and baking the pizza, you can successfully make any pizza in this book.

WATER, SALT, YEAST, FLOUR

As I described in the introduction, my trip to Italy when I was researching this book absolutely changed my approach to making pizza at home and provided a few course corrections to some of the pizza-making techniques I offered in my first book. The biggest and most dramatic one (at least for the guy who named his first book *Flour Water Salt Yeast*) was the order in which the Italian *pizzaiolos* added the ingredients to make dough for pizza. I took their lessons to heart, which is why, in this book, I suggest you mix ingredients as follows:

1 Add water to the dough tub, then stir in the salt until dissolved.

2 Add the yeast. Stir until dissolved.

3 Add the flour and mix the dough by hand.

Readers of *Flour Water Salt Yeast* may pause and say, "But what about the autolyse?" That step takes around 20 minutes, and while very appropriate in

bread making, it is not necessary in pizza dough fabrication (see page 57), so I'm scratching it in this book. This is the way it's done in Naples, it works great, and it saves time.

Learning to think like a *pizzaiolo* instead of like a bread baker was also necessary for me to adopt the Neapolitan dough-making practice: allowing much or most of the dough fermentation to take place in the dough ball, not in the bulk dough. This was a dramatic change for me, a person who had always applied a bread baker's point of view to pizza dough, and it took me a while to fully embrace it. But embrace it I did, because the results are undeniably superior: the crust is more delicate and less chewy, while being crisp and light. So instead of making dough and letting it rise until it's doubled in size, in this book's recipes we mostly let the dough rise just a little, maybe about a 50 percent increase in size, and then make up dough balls, where the second stage of fermentation takes place, when they will about double in size as they expand (rather than rise).

GREAT PIZZA, STEP-BY-STEP

I recommend taking the time to read through this section and visualizing the process, and you will have less to think through when you are in the moment with your pizza making.

Step 1: Measure and Combine the Dough Ingredients

First set yourself up with your bag of flour, fine sea salt, and instant dried yeast or starter. Complete your dough making setup by having handy a container for water (quart-sized is plenty big, but whatever you have in your kitchen is fine so long as you can pour from it), your scale(s), your thermometer (if you have one; highly recommended), dough tub, a small container for measuring salt and yeast, and another quart (or so) container for measuring flour. (See Chapter 4 if you have questions about any of these things.)

MEASURE THE HOT WATER

Fill your water container from the tap with hot and cold water until you get it to 90° or 95°F (32° or 35°C). If you don't have a digital probe thermometer, guess at the temperature: water gets pretty hot to the touch at 105°F (41°C).

DIGITAL SCALE

Use a digital kitchen scale to measure your ingredients. Put your empty container on the scale and push the scale's "zero" button (sometimes labeled "tare"). After the scale zeroes out, carefully pour in the ingredient until you reach the desired weight.

ADAPTING DOUGH RECIPES TO MAKE PAN PIZZA

The dough in this book designed for pan pizzas, the Saturday Pan Pizza Dough (page 116), is a good place to start to learn the process. But you can go with any of the long-fermented dough recipes in this book to make a medium-thick pan pizza, like the Grandma Pie (page 192). Instead of dividing the dough into pieces to make up dough balls, shape the entire batch of dough into a single ball and then follow the remaining instructions for that dough.

a whim to try mixing a dough with cold water, know in advance that it's not going to work on the schedule I list. It will take much longer. Use warmer or cooler water next time if your mix temperature was below or above 80°F (27°C).

Step 3: Knead the Dough and Let It Rise

Fifteen to 20 minutes after you finish mixing the dough, knead it to help the mass of dough come together. I find it easiest to do this on a countertop lightly dusted with flour. Using floured hands, reach under the dough and remove it from the dough tub onto the floured surface. Fold the dough over itself and turn, fold over and turn repeatedly, for just about 30 seconds, until the dough is in a unified mass with a smooth surface. This doesn't really require one

fixed set of motions to work. A general kneading and folding will do the trick—whatever gentle hand action molds the dough into a ball with a smooth surface. Lightly oil the bottom of the dough tub and place the kneaded dough back in the tub, seam side down. Let the dough ferment according to its recipe.

Step 4: Divide the Dough and Shape the Dough Balls

Lightly flour a work surface that's about 2 feet wide. Set your digital scale nearby. Flour your hands and layer some flour inside the dough tub (it will help the sticky dough come out), around the back edge of the dough where it meets the tub. Don't just pull the dough out; help it out, using your working hand to loosen the dough from its container. Tip the tub toward your floured countertop and work the added flour around the edges of the dough, using that to help prevent the dough from sticking too much to the tub as you very gently release it onto your countertop. All this care is to keep the gluten strands in the dough from tearing.

Spread a very thin film of flour over the top of the dough. Cut the dough into equal-sized pieces with a metal dough scraper, a rigid plastic bowl scraper, or a chef's knife to weigh on the scale; eyeball it if you don't have a scale. It's best not to have a bunch of small pieces of leftover dough stuck together to make up a single dough ball. If you need to add a piece of dough to one you've already cut to bring up the weight, fold the additional dough into the middle as you shape the dough into a ball.

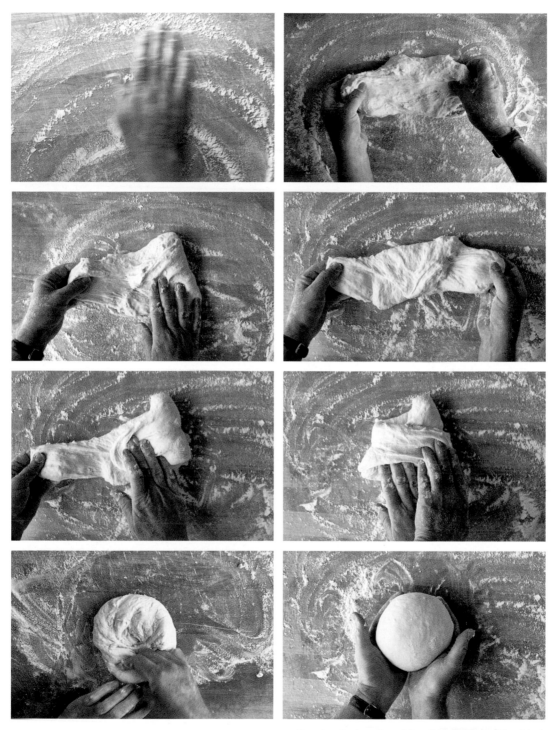

*Twenty minutes after mixing, fold and knead the dough
to create a ball with a smooth surface.*

HOW MANY DOUGH BALLS?

The Neapolitan and New York–style pizza recipes in this book tell you to divide the dough into three equal pieces between 260 and 285 grams each.

For Roman pizzas, you should divide the dough into five pieces of 150 grams each. If you don't want that many dough balls, just cut the recipe in half.

For bar pizzas, the Bar Pizza Dough recipe (page 136) yields four dough balls of 190 grams each.

To shape the dough balls:

1   Take a piece of dough and stretch one-third of it sideways until it resists, then fold it back over the main piece of dough. Repeat, working your way around the dough and forming it into a round. The emerging dough ball will develop tension and form a smooth outer skin as you repeat this folding action. Stop when the dough ball is in a roughly circular shape.

2   Then flip it over and put the seam on the work surface in an area cleared of flour (the clean, less-floured surface will provide more friction, or grip, so you can add tension to the dough ball in the next step).

3   Cup your hands around the back of the dough ball as you face it, and with the pinky fingers of both hands make contact with the dough ball where it meets the surface of your countertop. Pull the entire dough ball 4 or 5 inches toward you on the clean, unfloured surface, leading with your pinkies and applying enough downward pressure as you pull so the dough ball grips your work surface and doesn't just slide across it. As you pull, the ball will tighten up.

4   Give the dough a turn and repeat this tightening step one or two more times until the dough ball is rounded. The dough doesn't need to be super tight, but you don't want it to be loose, either. You want to avoid any visible tears on the outer skin of the dough. Maximum dough tension is not necessary; all that's needed is just a medium amount of tension in the skin of the dough ball.

5   Repeat the process with the remaining pieces of dough.

Step 5: Let the Dough Balls Ferment

In bread baking, vital flavor development and expansion happen during the bulk fermentation stage—after the dough is mixed but before it is shaped into individual rounds or oblongs. The best breads have a lengthy bulk fermentation—as long as 6 hours or even overnight.

The pizza recipes in this book are different, because the majority of the dough expansion and flavor development happen during the second stage of fermentation, after the pizza dough balls are shaped. Two things happen at this stage:

1   The dough balls *completely relax* after being cut off the main dough and shaped. Ultimately, the gluten will relax and the dough should be easy to stretch while remaining cohesive and retaining its tensile strength.

2   This is the second fermentation of the dough. Additional gas builds up, the balls expand, and the good flavors of fermentation build. This can happen at room temperature in some recipes or in the refrigerator in other recipes. Time does

the work for you in this step. Every dough has its own arc for being at its prime point for making pizza. Recipe notes indicate the timelines for each dough.

3 After making up dough balls, lightly dust a baking sheet or a couple of dinner plates with flour. I can often find room for plates in my refrigerator more easily than a larger sheet pan. Put the dough balls on the pan or plates with a few inches between them to accommodate their expansion. Dust the tops with flour and cover with plastic wrap. I expect the dough balls to grow together a bit by the time they are mature. To separate, dust with a bit of flour at the seam between the dough balls and cut with a bench knife or the edge of a spatula through the seam to separate. Don't tear them apart.

4 When and how to use refrigeration depends on the dough and its schedule. That's why you will see some variation in my recipe instructions from one to another. The refrigerator is a great tool for slowing down dough when you need more time.

Step 6: Set Up Your Pizza Station

There's no substitute for an organized workplace in the kitchen. It makes you feel more in control and therefore more confident. The pizza will be better as a result. Good organization will also give you an efficient timeline for dinner. So while your oven is preheating, set up your pizza assembly station. Prepare your toppings, such as cut-up and grated cheeses, salami, and basil leaves. If you haven't made pizza sauce yet, do it now; it takes just a few minutes (see pages 145 to 148). Have the sauce with a large spoon next to where you'll top your dough, along with the prepped toppings. Give yourself about 2 feet of width on the countertop to work with the dough, plus enough space for the pizza peel right next to the work area.

Shaping the dough balls.

A QUICK NOTE ABOUT HEARTH PIZZAS

For hearth pizzas, shape the dough and place it on a lightly flour-dusted wooden peel (not metal; the dough sometimes sticks to metal peels), dress it, and then put it in the oven. In American and Italian pizzerias you will frequently see *pizzaiolos* dress the raw dough on their countertop, then use their hands to pick up the dressed pizza and drag it onto the peel, which is held slightly below countertop level to ease the transfer. At other pizzerias they slide the peel deftly under the dough. There are Italian metal pizza peels that have perforations in them to make this work better, so there is less surface area for the dough to stick to.

But transferring a dressed pizza from a countertop to a peel is really difficult to do without a lot of practice in a professional kitchen. This method also doesn't work well with the softer pizza doughs I use in many of the recipes designed for home kitchen ovens. All in all, I find it easiest to dress the pizza *after* the dough has been transferred to a very lightly floured wooden peel. We use this technique at Ken's Artisan Pizza and for flatbreads at Trifecta Tavern & Bakery.

Step 7: Stretch the Dough to Make Pizza

Pan pizza, Neapolitan pizza, New York pizza, and Roman pizza each have dough-stretching techniques that are ideally suited for their style. Use a rolling pin for thin, crackery, Roman pizza crust and for American bar pizza. Spread and stretch the dough out on an oiled pan for pan pizzas. Neapolitan pizzas and New York–style American pizzas are shaped by hand.

FOR NEAPOLITAN AND NEW YORK–STYLE
The traditional dough-stretching method used in Naples is fun to watch—check out some videos online. It is designed, I think, for both speed and quality. And because it looks really cool. Neapolitan pizza is thin in the middle but not too thin. If you look at pictures of pizza from some of Naples's most famous pizzerias, you'll see that many of them are saucy pies. The cheese is moist, too. If the crust is too thin, you risk a perforation in the dough, with the sauce and molten cheese leaking through it onto the baking stone or the floor of the oven, and that's not a happy moment.

For this book, I've modified the traditional Neapolitan method (see sidebar on page 95) a bit, to better suit the doughs of this book, and to make it easier. This is the same dough-stretching method I used in my first book, and it's a very common method I've seen used in pizzerias across the U.S.: stretching the dough out with fists balled up inside the dough. It works well with the soft doughs I use, and I continue to get my best results with this technique, whether I'm making New York– or Neapolitan-style pizza. Be careful not to leave the rim of the dough too thick; as the rim expands during baking it pushes all the toppings toward the middle. For stylistic purposes I compress the dough to create a narrow rim

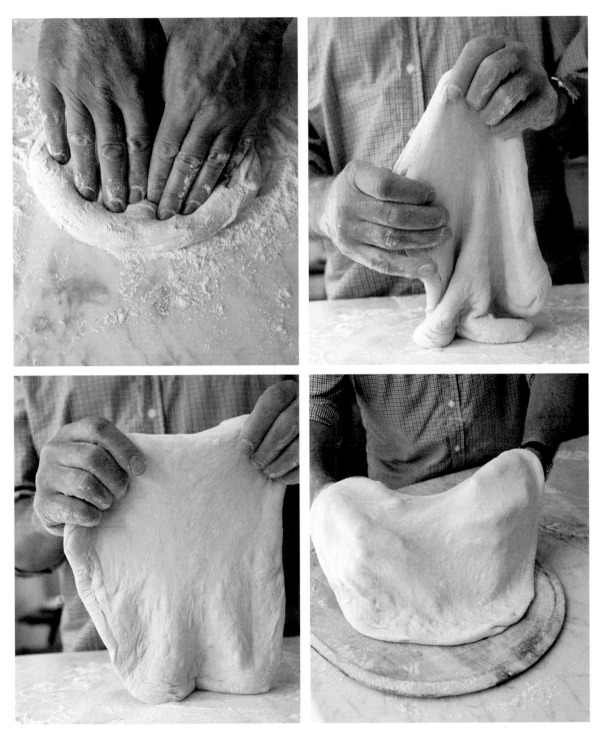

Stretching the dough.

for New York–style pizzas, where toppings go almost to the edge, and I leave a slightly thicker rim, about ½ inch, for Neapolitan-style pizzas.

Set your pizza peel on the work surface next to where you are working your dough. A wooden peel is definitely best because the moist, unbaked pizza slides easier off a wood surface than a metal one. Lightly dust the peel with the same flour you used to make your pizza dough. Don't use cornmeal or other coarse grains, as they interfere with the delicacy of the pizza. Very finely ground semolina flour is often used at good Neapolitan pizzerias, but it's not necessary to seek it out just for the purpose of dusting your peel.

Make sure you are working with a mature dough ball, according to each recipe's instructions. It should take very little effort for it to stretch out to the dimensions of a pizza. If it's too elastic, the dough needs more time.

When working with the pizza doughs in this book, flour is your friend. Generously flour your work surface, then leaving about a ½ inch of the outer rim un-deflated, punch down the middle with your fingertips, pushing the air toward the rim of the disk, then flip the dough over and repeat. (The diameter of the rim of the pizza is determined here—if you want a more bready pizza with big, poofy rims, or if you want a narrow rim, this is the point where you make that happen.)

Using floured hands, grab the rim at about the 10 o'clock and 2 o'clock positions and lift so the crust hangs down vertically; preserve the outer rim by placing your thumbs about a ½-inch from the edge for a Neapolitan-style pizza, or a ¼-inch from the edge for a New York–style pie. Let gravity pull the rest of the dough down to stretch it. If the dough is stretching easily I let the bottom of the dough rest on the counter while I'm turning it so I can control the speed

Stretching the dough while preserving the rim.

and evenness of its expansion. Run the rim between your hands, working all the way around the circumference of the dough a couple of times. You can work as slowly as you want. If the dough gets sticky, set it down and give both the top and the bottom another dusting of flour. The easiest way to do this is to keep a floured area on your work surface and just plop the dough down onto the flour, then turn it over to dust the other side.

Next, make two fists and position them just inside the rim, with the crust still hanging vertically. Gently stretch and turn the dough repeatedly, letting the bottom of the dough pull down, expanding the surface. Keep a close eye on the thickness of the dough. There is no benefit to overstretching it—when it's done, it's done, and then you lay it onto the flour-dusted peel. You want the dough thin, but you don't want it so thin that it tears or can't support the weight of the toppings. If you end up with a small tear, don't panic—it's okay to patch it by folding a small bit of dough over the hole. The dough balls in this book are designed to give a proper thickness when shaped to a diameter of 12 inches for a New York–style pie, and a bit smaller (closer to 11 inches) for a Neapolitan-style pizza.

Note that at a good pizzeria, they might stretch the dough to where it is hanging over the edge of the loading peel before lifting the edges to fit it back on. This removes any elasticity from the dough, for predictable baking without shrinkage.

THE NEAPOLITAN SLAP

In Italy, *pizzaiolos* traditionally shape the dough on a floured countertop, first compressing the dough ball before following it up with a "Neapolitan slap." The dough is pushed gently with all the fingers, from the middle to the rim, then flipped, then the dough is flattened from the middle to the rim again. The goal is to move the gas to the perimeter of the crust. As Enzo Coccia of La Notizia put it, "The hands are essential. You have to push the air out and create that really high, fluffy outer crust." Then the dough is stretched in a rapid two-handed motion that expands the dough with one hand while the palm of the other hand holds down the other half and the dough makes a light slapping sound. There is a slight turn each time the dough is passed from hand to hand to stretch the dough gently with each motion. With each turn it grows a bit in width and the pizza becomes fully formed. Three to five slaps of the dough from hand to hand is all it takes for these folks. I think there is a special gene in Naples for this.

PAN AND PARCHMENT METHOD FOR ROMAN AL TAGLIO AND PAN PIZZAS

Roman bakery pizzas bake on the hearth of deep deck ovens that are also used to bake bread. The tops of these pizzas have oil and salt (and tomato for the rossa), but the bottoms remain dry. Thus, the design challenge for home baking is to create a hearth pizza with no oil or fat underneath the dough while also using a pan. How, then, do we prevent the dough from sticking to the pan? Easy. Use parchment paper, and, to keep it in place, a trick we sometimes use for pastry in my bakery; water acts like a temporary glue for the parchment. Here's how:

1 Spray a very thin film of water on the sheet pan; if you don't have a sprayer, spread a thin layer of water on the pan with your hands.

2 Cut a piece of parchment to size, place it on the watered sheet pan, and seal it with your palms, moving from the center of the pan to the edges. It works!

3 Remove the plastic film from the dough and spread a medium dusting of white flour over the top of the dough to keep it from sticking to the parchment.

4 Invert the plate of dough onto the middle of the sheet pan.

5 With floured hands and fingers, reach underneath the dough and gently pull it to the edges of the pan in each direction. Only stretch the dough to its point of resistance. Let it relax for five minutes, and repeat until the dough is shaped to the dimensions of the sheet pan.

ROLLING PIN METHOD FOR ROMAN-STYLE AND AMERICAN BAR PIZZAS

We use this method at Trifecta Tavern & Bakery and I like how thin we get the dough. To make the same size pizza as the Neapolitan and New York pizzas, about 12 inches in diameter, we use half the amount of dough you would use to make Neapolitan or American pizza crust. Flour is essential to keep the dough from sticking to the work surface or to the rolling pin. Use a wooden rolling pin (the dough is less likely to stick compared to rolling pins made of stone or metal), ideally without handles, between 1 and 2 inches in diameter. Any rolling pin will do, but I prefer the feel and closer connection to the dough when my hands are on the pin itself rather than on the handles.

Dip both sides of the dough ball in flour and place it on a lightly floured surface, dusting the top of the dough ball moderately with more flour. Using a rolling pin, press down from the middle to the outer edges, rolling over the edges in each direction, turning the dough as you go. Do not try to preserve the rim; go over it with the pin, pressing down.

Flour is your friend here. Do not be shy about using it to prevent the dough from sticking to the surface or the pin from sticking to the dough.

If the dough is elastic and doesn't stretch as far as you want it to, just let it rest for a few minutes and then go back to it. This is the normal situation in my kitchen.

Work the dough with the pin until it is very, very thin—like a piece of paper for Roman-style pizza or like a piece of cloth for bar pizza.

Step 8: Top the Pizza and Load It into the Oven

Spread the dough onto the lightly floured peel, running your hands around the perimeter to shape it into a round and work out any kinks. Before topping the pie, give the peel a test shake to make sure the dough slides without sticking. If it does stick, remove the dough, dust the peel a little more generously, and give it another go.

Once you've shaped the dough, spread your sauce over it—not too thickly—using a small ladle or a large serving spoon, smoothing and spreading the sauce with the back of the utensil. Scatter the toppings over the surface, using only moderate amounts (all the toppings in this book's recipes were carefully measured, so you can use the ingredient amounts by weight with confidence) so as not to add more weight than the dough can handle. Dressing the pizza should take into consideration how much crust you want to remain free of sauce and toppings. A typical New York pizza is dressed almost to the edge, while a Neapolitan pizza preserves more of the rim.

Before sliding the pie into the oven, do another test to confirm that the pizza will slide off the peel: give the peel a quick shake, but not too aggressively. If any part of the dough sticks, first try working it out with a few more quick back-and-forth shakes. If that doesn't do the trick, you'll need to gently lift the dough up and toss a bit of flour underneath. Yes, this is a pain, but it's better to find out in advance and deal with it than to have your pizza do a belly flop into a super-hot oven.

Loading the pizza from the peel onto the baking steel or stone takes a little practice, but it shouldn't be out of your reach, and again, try the first couple

times loading an untopped pizza into your oven, or parbake it with just a bit of sauce. It takes the pressure off. Have an extra ball of dough on hand—the recipes make three dough balls, and you can view your first pizza as a test pie, so you can get the feel of the peel and how to transfer the pie to the pizza steel or stone, and also see what happens after you put it in the oven. After a minute or so, you can remove the test pizza crust, top it, and place it back into the oven to finish. If it's plain and unsauced, the middle will bubble up, so pull it out after just 45 to 60 seconds in the oven.

There are two techniques for loading the pizza onto the steel or stone. With both, as you are reaching into the oven with the peel, the dough will come off much more easily and predictably if the handle of the peel is held a few inches higher than its front.

One technique is to place the peel with the pizza on top all the way into the oven, with its leading edge at the back of the stone. Then in a series of stuttered shakes, slowly work the peel back toward you, releasing the raw pizza onto the preheated surface. You need confidence to make this technique work—this is a good one to practice the first time or two with an undressed disk of stretched dough for a quick parbake. With the practice pies, you might learn that you can actually nudge it around a bit if needed, or that it's okay if a lip of the dough overhangs the baking steel by a ½-inch.

The second technique is the one that probably works best, once you've done it a few times and get the knack. Give the peel a couple of quick, easy back-and-forth shakes before loading it, so you can get a sense of control over the sliding of the pizza. Then reach the loaded peel, slightly tilted, into the oven to the point where the front edge of the peel is aligned with the very back of the baking steel. At that moment, and without hesitation, quickly pull the

peel back toward yourself in a controlled jerk. You have to commit to this completely—it reminds me of Julia Child's "confidence-is-required" instructions for flipping an omelet: a half-effort might not work. Once you master this with raw, undressed dough, you will be able to load a fully dressed pizza this way.

Step 9: Bake the Pizza

Here's the basic drill for the five categories of pizza in this book.

NEAPOLITAN, ROMAN THIN CRUST, AND NEW YORK PIZZAS

Preheat the oven to its maximum temperature—550°F (290°C) is very common—with the pizza steel or stone set on an upper rack about 8 inches below the broiler coil, for 45 minutes total. This timeline allows the oven to be fully saturated with heat, and it will bake the pizza better than if you just preheat it to reach the temperature.

Switch the oven to broil about 10 minutes before loading the pizza. Meanwhile, shape the pizza and top it. After 10 minutes on broil, turn the oven off and load the pizza onto the pizza steel or stone. (See Note, below.) Close the oven door and return the oven to its maximum bake temperature. Set the timer to 5 minutes (usually, but check the specific recipe instructions). If one side of the pizza is baking faster than the other side, use a pair of tongs to rotate the pizza, turning the front to the rear.

If the recipe specifies it, switch the oven back to broil and set the timer to 2 minutes, but check after 1 minute and remove the pizza when it's finished.

If you are going to make more than one pizza, pull the oven rack out (so you don't risk burning yourself on the broiler element) and use an oven mitt or folded-over thick kitchen towel to quickly but very carefully wipe the left-behind, burned flour from the pizza steel or stone onto a plate; discard it.

Set the oven to broil to reheat the steel or stone for a few minutes while you prep the next pizza. Bake as before, turning off the broiler to load the pizza, then returning the oven to bake at its highest temperature once you've closed the door.

Remember the goal: The toppings, bottom of the crust, and rim should all reach their point of perfect baking at the same instant. You may need to play with the position of the baking stone or steel; try it at the topmost rack spot or the second down from the top, to get the best results. Every oven is different.

Note: Some ovens, like mine, will wig out if you switch from an extended broil cycle to bake, because they sense a higher temperature than their maximum baking temperature, and then a safety shut-off throws the breaker. So I wait until I have opened the oven to load the pizza before returning the oven setting to bake at 550°F (290°C). Having the door open for the brief period of loading the pizza releases enough heat to keep my oven's high temperature limit switch from kicking in.

ROMAN AL TAGLIO AND PAN PIZZAS

Bake it in the middle rack, with the pan sitting on top of the pizza steel or stone, for about 15 minutes or until it is golden brown (check progress at 10 minutes and turn the pan). It should be lightly bubbled. You always have the option of finishing the pizza out of the pan, directly on the steel or stone if the bottom of the pizza needs more color, as long as the pan wasn't coated with oil (smoke alarm!). Your kitchen's going to have a beautiful yeasty aroma and your housemates are going to love you.

GETTING TO KNOW YOUR OVEN

Ovens have their own personalities, and it often takes a little bit of experimentation to learn how to perfectly bake a pizza in each one. The timelines for baking pizza using this book's recipes work in the standard home kitchen oven I have in my kitchen, a Frigidaire (I love the irony of that brand name). When I define a bake time of 5 minutes at 550°F (290°C), then 2 minutes on broil, you might need 5 minutes of bake time followed by 3 minutes on broil if your broiler takes longer to heat up than mine does. The final stage of baking moves very fast at the broil stage, and if you pay attention, you'll be on top of it and will pull it out when it's ready. I used a baking steel to test all of my recipes, positioned on a rack 8 inches below my oven's broiler coil. You might need to adjust the rack position differently in your oven to get exactly the pizza you want. The best bake my oven allows might be a little different than the best bake your oven allows.

I don't have one checklist for proper baking that applies to all pizza styles. I go for more spots of dark color on the crust of a Neapolitan-style pizza than for a New York pizza, for example. For a pan pizza I want to make sure the crust is fully baked and that the bottom has enough color and crispness to keep it from being too soft. I frequently finish baking a pan pizza directly on the pizza steel or stone to crisp it up.

The bottom of the oven will usually have the most heat applied to the bottom of a pan, so a pan loaded on a bottom rack might scorch the underside of the crust before the rest of the pizza is fully baked. Or, if you are baking two pans at once, one above the other, you might want to switch rack positions halfway through baking.

If you have the mind-set to go through a little bit of trial and error as you bake pizza, you will quickly figure out exactly how to bake good pizza consistently in your unique environment. When the pizza's bottom, toppings, cheese, and rim all reach their perfect finish point at the exact same instant, you have a perfectly baked pizza.

EXTRA DOUGH BALLS

Most of the dough recipes in this book are based on 500 grams of flour and make enough dough for three Neapolitan or New York–style pizzas, or for five Roman-style thin-crust pizzas. You may not want to make this much pizza in one night. What to do with the extra dough balls?

You could refrigerate the dough and make pizza again the next day or night.

You can freeze extra dough balls, floured and tightly wrapped in plastic. Give them 24 hours to thaw in the refrigerator before using, and then remove them from the refrigerator a couple of hours before making pizza. It's a good idea to date the frozen dough balls (use tape and a Sharpie) and use them within a week or two from freezing—too long in

the freezer will kill the yeast and your dough will be fairly lifeless.

Another option is to make your own pizza shells that you store for next time: parbake the dough with just sauce and then freeze it, wrapped airtight in plastic. (If you want to see a recipe for parbaked crust and how to make pizza with it, check out the Pepperoni, Mushroom, and Onion pizza recipe on page 189.)

Storing parbaked pizza shells is a good option to prepare for impromptu meals or snacks. You can parbake the crust and immediately top it while it's still warm, then bake it to finish (you can parbake an hour ahead of time), or you can parbake unused dough balls, then wrap and freeze for later use somtime in the next week or two. The frozen shell can thaw while your oven is preheating. Top the pizza dough with 50 to 60 grams (¼ cup) of pizza sauce. Slide the pizza onto a preheated pizza steel or stone, bake for 3 minutes, change the oven setting to broil, and remove the parbaked crust after 2 minutes more.

> ### JUST ONE PIZZA
>
> If you just want enough dough to make a single pizza, use the Single Dough Ball recipe (page 112). If you just want two pizzas, double that recipe. All of the recipes in this book will scale up or down; just retain the ratios and do the simple math to get you there.

CHAPTER 6
PIZZA DOUGH
RECIPES

I could present you with instructions for just one or two simple pizza doughs and then give you a bunch of recipes for pizzas to make, but the fun of this book is that it includes a wide variety of doughs to match different pizza styles, skill levels, and life schedules.

There are many styles of pizza and many ways to make pizza dough. The same basic dough-making techniques apply to all the dough types in this book, so moving from one dough recipe to another uses experience you've already gained. The only variance is that a couple of the stiffer doughs are most easily made with a stand mixer or food processor.

People have asked what doughs I used the most and liked the most as I was recipe testing for this book. I found the 24- to 48-hour refrigerated dough to be the most convenient for my own life schedule. I'd mix the dough after coming home midevening from my restaurants, and 2 hours later, just before going to bed, I would make up dough balls and refrigerate them to make pizza the next evening or the evening after. The results were excellent and it seemed effortless. The first time I tried the Saturday Pizza Dough (page 108), I was wowed by how delicate the crust was, and friends I shared that dough recipe with had the same comment. My favorite dough overall for texture and flavor is the Overnight Levain Pizza Dough (page 130), and I make this on my weekend, as it wants me home around lunchtime to make up dough balls. Every dough here makes excellent pizza. Small amounts of yeast and long fermentation make great contributions to texture, color, and flavor. I'm expecting you'll choose your dough based on the

and let it rise on a covered dinner plate or large bowl in the refrigerator as you would for regular dough balls. Then move the dough to an oiled pan as a final step, instead of going for the entire second rise on the pan. These long doughs will have more flavor from fermentation and will be a little more delicately textured than the same-day dough, but you'll need to give them time to warm up so they can stretch out easily to the shape of the pan and not contract while baking (see instructions below).

The fat under the dough, whether it's olive oil, bacon fat, lard, or duck fat, flavors and crisps (some in the pizza business may even say fries) the underside of the dough while it bakes.

The dough recipes in this book make enough dough for a 13 by 18-inch half sheet pan, which fits comfortably in a standard home kitchen oven. Using pans of different sizes will yield thicker or thinner crusts, so you might want to adjust the amount of dough you use depending on the pan.

First-timers should start with the Saturday Pan Pizza Dough recipe (page 116), which has a 4-hour first rise and then just 30 to 45 minutes on an oiled or greased pan before baking. This is easy and good.

The possibilities for pan pizzas are endless. You can use a 275- to 300-gram dough ball from one of the hearth pizza recipes and roll it out very thin with a rolling pin to get a thin-crust pan pizza (see the Simple Tomato Pie recipe, page 177). These are great! Or, I like to riff and make what I call a strip pizza, taking a 275-gram dough ball and rolling it out into an oval shape—bake that on a pan lined with parchment.

Adapting Dough Recipes for Pan Pizza

You can adapt any of the refrigerated non-Saturday dough recipes in this book for pan pizzas. Here's how:

1 Increase the total amount of water in the dough to 75 percent of the flour weight: 375 grams of water for 500 grams of flour (most of these dough recipes use 350 grams of water).

2 Instead of dividing the dough into dough balls after its first rise, take the entire mass of dough, form it into one large dough ball, place it on a lightly oiled dinner plate, and cover it in plastic.

3 Follow the rest of the schedule for that dough, up to the point when you are preparing to make pizza.

4 Ninety minutes ahead of time, spread the cold dough out onto an oiled or greased pan, cover with a very light film of olive oil to prevent it from drying, and let it sit out in a warm spot (cold tightens up the gluten in the dough, so it needs a little time and warmth to relax). The dough will need two or three stretches to reach the size of the pan. Give it at least 10 minutes between each stretch and don't push it beyond what it's willing to give. There's time.

5 Forty-five minutes before baking, preheat the oven and baking steel or stone to 550°F (290°C).

6 Top the pizza with a very thin layer of sauce and parbake (see page 190), or top it completely, with the cheese under the sauce, and bake, with the pan set on the steel or stone, until done.

SATURDAY PIZZA DOUGH

This same-day dough is the answer when you wake up in the morning and decide you want pizza for dinner. Good call. Me too.

This dough was inspired by the Associazione Verace Pizza Napoletana (AVPN) pizza dough rules, with my adaptations for the home kitchen. It uses the same salt and yeast percentages as the AVPN specification (they require fresh yeast, and here we use instant dry yeast at one-third the weight of fresh yeast) and a similar timeline. After mixing, the dough rests for 2 hours. Then dough balls (*panetti*) are made and set aside, covered, and held at room temperature in their second stage of fermentation for 4 to 6 hours in Naples; Neapolitan pizzerias are warmer than a lot of American home kitchens, so I'm suggesting a 6-hour development in this recipe. The dough balls are ready to make pizza anytime following the second fermentation and hold for 4 hours at room temperature. The dough will be a little gassy, very easily stretched, and a little delicate near the end of its 4-hour hold time. To extend the dough balls' life span, you can refrigerate them once they get to a soft, malleable state after the end of the second fermentation. Let cold dough balls warm up at room temperature for the 45 minutes you spend preheating the oven.

This formula is a good example of how a high amount of salt in the dough—at 3 percent of the flour's weight (versus the standard 2 percent in many pizza dough and bread dough recipes)—slows down the fermentation and allows the dough balls to hold without refrigeration, which is the normal situation at a Naples pizzeria.

I adjusted the hydration up to 70 percent of the flour weight (from the AVPN standard 55 to 58 percent) to compensate for baking in a cooler home oven rather than a 905°F (485°C) wood-fired oven. The result is impressive. The crust is very delicate and light.

MAKES 3 regular or 5 thin-crust dough balls

BULK FERMENTATION 2 hours

DIVIDE, SHAPE, AND COVER DOUGH 10 minutes

SECOND FERMENTATION 6 hours

HOLD TIME FOR USE AT ROOM TEMPERATURE 4 hours, or refrigerate to extend the use until the next evening

SAMPLE SCHEDULE Mix the dough at 9 a.m., knead it at 9:20 a.m., shape it into dough balls at 11:00 a.m., make pizza between 5:00 p.m. and 9:00 p.m. For next-day pizza, refrigerate the dough balls 4 hours after they are made up, then leave them out at room temperature for 1 hour before making pizza.

INGREDIENT	QUANTITY		BAKER'S %
Water	350g	1½ cups	70%
Fine sea salt	15g	2¾ tsp	3.0%
Instant dried yeast	0.3g	⅓ of ¼ tsp	0.6%
White flour, preferably 00	500g	Scant 4 cups	100%

1   **Measure and Combine the Ingredients.** Using your digital scale, measure 350 grams of 90° to 95°F (32° to 35°C) water into your 6-quart dough tub. Measure 15 grams of fine sea salt, add it to the water, and stir or swish it around in the tub until it is dissolved. Measure 0.3 gram (about ⅓ of ¼ teaspoon) of instant dried yeast. Add the yeast to the water, let it rest there for a minute to hydrate, then swish it around until it's dissolved. Add 500 grams of flour (preferably 00) to the water-salt-yeast mixture.

2   **Mix the Dough.** Mix by hand, first by stirring your hand around inside the dough tub to integrate the flour, water, salt, and yeast into a single mass of dough. Then use the pincer method (see page 86) to cut the dough in sections with your hand, alternating with folding the dough to develop it back into a unified mass. Continue for just 30 seconds to 1 minute. The target dough temperature at the end of the mix is 80°F (27°C); use your probe thermometer to check it.

3   **Knead and Rise.** Let the dough rest for 20 minutes, then knead it on a work surface with a very light dusting of flour for about 30 seconds to 1 minute. The skin of the dough should be very smooth. Place the dough ball seam side down in the lightly oiled dough tub. Cover with a tight-fitting lid. Hold the dough for 2 hours at room temperature (assuming 70° to 74°F/21° to 23°C) for the first rise. This timeline is flexible, so if you need to do this after

1 hour or 1½ hours, don't stress, just make up your dough balls a little early and add the difference in time to the next stage.

4   **Shape.** Divide the dough and shape it into dough balls. Moderately flour a work surface about 2 feet wide. With floured hands, gently ease the dough out of the tub. With your hands still floured, pick up the dough and ease it back down onto the work surface in a somewhat even shape. Dust the entire top of the dough with flour, then cut it into 3 or 5 equal-sized pieces, depending on the style of pizza. Use your scale to get evenly sized dough balls. Shape each piece of dough into a medium-tight round following the instructions on pages 88 to 90, working gently and being careful not to tear the dough.

5   **Second Fermentation.** Place the dough balls on lightly floured dinner plates or a baking sheet, leaving space between them to allow for expansion. Lightly flour the tops and cover airtight with plastic wrap, and let rest at room temperature for 6 hours for the second fermentation. Alternatively, you can rest the dough balls for 4 hours at room temperature, and then refrigerate to hold for up to the next evening.

6   **Make Pizza.** Without refrigeration, the dough balls can be used anytime in the 4 hours following the second fermentation. If you refrigerated the dough balls, let them come to room temperature for an hour while you preheat the oven and prepare your toppings.

"I SLEPT IN BUT I WANT PIZZA TONIGHT" DOUGH

This same-day dough is yet another method for making dough the same day you want to make pizza. The best doughs take a little more time; for example, the Saturday Pizza Dough recipe (page 108) calls for a minimum of 8 hours after mixing the dough before you make pizza. If you have time and can plan for it, try one of the longer doughs. But say it's 11 on Sunday morning, you just finished reading the paper, and you decide you want pizza for dinner. This dough is the answer.

To accelerate the initial activity of the small amount of yeast in this recipe, you'll mix the dough with hotter water—100°F (38°C) in winter, maybe a little cooler in summer—so the temperature of the dough at the end of the mix is about 82°F (28°C). Then, about 1½ hours after the dough is mixed, make up your dough balls and let them rise in their second fermentation over the course of the afternoon, at least 4 hours, before making pizza.

MAKES 3 regular or 5 thin-crust dough balls

BULK FERMENTATION 1½ hours

DIVIDE, SHAPE, AND COVER DOUGH 10 minutes

SECOND FERMENTATION 4 hours

SAMPLE SCHEDULE Mix the dough at 11:30 a.m., shape into dough balls at 1 p.m., make pizza that evening anytime between 5 and 7. Refrigerate if you need the dough balls to hold a bit longer; let them come to room temperature before making pizza.

INGREDIENT	QUANTITY		BAKER'S %
Water	350g	1½ cups	70%
Fine sea salt	10g	Scant 2 tsp	2.0%
Instant dried yeast	0.5g	½ of ¼ tsp	0.1%
White flour, preferably 00	500g	Scant 4 cups	100%

1   **Measure and Combine the Ingredients.** Using your digital scale, measure 350 grams of 100°F (38°C) water into into your 6-quart dough tub. Measure 10 grams of fine sea salt, add it to the water, and stir or swish it around in the tub until it is dissolved. Measure 0.5 gram (½ of ¼ teaspoon) of instant dried yeast. Add the yeast to the water, let it rest there for a minute to hydrate, then swish it around until it's dissolved. Add 500 grams of flour (preferably 00) to the water-salt-yeast mixture.

2   **Mix the Dough.** Mix by hand, first by stirring your hand around inside the dough tub to integrate the flour, water, salt, and yeast into a single mass of dough. Then use the pincer method (see page 86) to cut the dough in sections with your hand, alternating with folding the dough to develop it back into a unified mass. Continue for just 30 seconds to 1 minute. The target dough temperature at the end of the mix is 82°F (28°C); use your probe thermometer to check it.

3   **Knead and First Rise.** Let the dough rest for 20 minutes, then knead it on a work surface with a very light dusting of flour for about 30 seconds to 1 minute. The skin of the dough should be very smooth. Place the dough ball seam side down in the lightly oiled dough tub. Cover with a tight-fitting lid. Hold the dough for about 1½ hours at room temperature for the first rise.

4   **Shape.** Divide and shape the dough into dough balls. Moderately flour a work surface about 2 feet wide. With floured hands, gently ease the dough out of the tub. With your hands still floured, pick up the dough and ease it back down onto the work surface in a somewhat even shape. Dust the entire top of the dough with flour, then cut it into 3 or 5 equal-sized pieces, depending on the style of pizza. Use your scale here to get evenly sized dough balls. Shape each piece of dough into a medium-tight round following the instructions on pages 88 to 91, working gently and being careful not to tear the dough.

5   **Second Fermentation.** Place the dough balls on a lightly floured baking sheet or dinner plate, leaving space between them to allow for expansion. Lightly flour the tops, cover airtight with plastic wrap, and let rest at room temperature for 4 to 6 hours.

6   **Make Pizza.** After the second fermentation, make pizza. Refrigerate if you need the dough balls to hold a bit longer; let them come to room temperature before making pizza. Have fun.

SINGLE DOUGH BALL

If you only want to make a single dough ball, you should know that all the recipes in this book work on scalable ratios. Each recipe that is based on 500 grams (a scant 4 cups) of flour makes enough pizza dough for three Neapolitan or New York–style pizzas for the home oven. You can adjust any dough recipe to make just a single dough ball and expect good results: just divide the weight of each ingredient by three. The process and timing remain the same. The biggest challenge may be in accurately measuring the yeast, as the recipes already use a very small amount. To do this right you will want to use the scale that measures accurately to the hundredth of a gram (see page 79), or you'll need to estimate 10 percent of a ¼ teaspoon visually.

MAKES 1 dough ball

FIRST FERMENTATION 2 hours

SHAPE AND COVER DOUGH 10 minutes

SECOND FERMENTATION 6 hours

HOLD TIME FOR USE AT ROOM TEMPERATURE 4 hours, or refrigerate to extend the use until the next evening

SAMPLE SCHEDULE Mix the dough at 9 a.m., knead it at 9:20 a.m., shape into dough balls at 11 a.m., make pizza between 5 p.m. and 9 p.m. or the next day; for next-day pizza, refrigerate the dough ball 4 hours after it is shaped, then let sit out at room temperature for 1 hour before making pizza.

INGREDIENT	QUANTITY		BAKER'S %
Water	116g	Scant ½ cup	70%
Fine sea salt	5g	Scant 1 tsp	3.0%
Instant dried yeast	0.1g	¹⁄₁₀ of ¼ tsp	0.6%
White flour, preferably 00	166g	1⅓ cups	100%

1 Measure and Combine the Ingredients. Using your digital scale, measure 116 grams of 90° to 95°F (32° to 35°C) water into a container. For a recipe this small, a large bowl will be fine—you don't need to pull out the dough tub. Measure 5 grams of fine sea salt, add it to the water, and stir until it's dissolved. Measure 0.1 gram (¹⁄₁₀ of ¼ teaspoon) of instant dried yeast. Add the yeast to the water and stir or swish it around until dissolved. This takes a couple of minutes. Continuous stirring is not required. Add 166 grams of flour (preferably 00) to the water-salt-yeast mixture.

2 Mix the Dough. Mix by hand, first by stirring your hand around inside the dough tub to integrate the flour, water, salt, and yeast into a single mass of dough. Then use the pincer method (see page 86) to cut the dough in sections with your hand, alternating with folding the dough to develop it back into a unified mass. Continue for just 30 seconds to 1 minute. The target dough temperature at the end of the mix is 80°F (27°C); use your probe thermometer to check it.

3 Knead and First Rise. Let the dough rest for 20 minutes, then knead it on a work surface with a moderate dusting of flour for about 30 seconds to 1 minute. The skin of the dough should be very smooth. Place the dough ball seam side down in a lightly oiled container. Cover with a tight-fitting lid or plastic wrap. Hold the dough for 2 hours at room temperature (I'm assuming 70° to 75°F/21° to 24°C) for the first rise.

4 Shape. Shape the dough into a medium-tight round following the instructions on pages 88 to 91, working gently and being careful not to tear the dough.

5 Second Fermentation. Place the dough ball on lightly floured plate, flour the top, cover with plastic wrap, and let rest at room temperature for 6 hours for the second fermentation. Alternatively, you can rest the dough ball for 4 hours at room temperature, and then refrigerate to hold for up to the next evening.

6 Make Pizza. Make pizza anytime in the 4 hours following the second stage of fermentation. If you refrigerated the dough ball, let it come to room temperature for an hour while you preheat the oven and prepare your toppings.

ENZO'S PIZZA DOUGH

Enzo Coccia is a third-generation *pizzaiolo* whose Naples pizzeria, La Notizia, won the AVPN Best Pizza award in 2014. His *mano e mano* lesson about the history of pizza dough (the best moment of my year) concluded with an explanation of his own evolution in dough making, circa 2010, when he opened La Notizia. "We use a mechanical fermentation," he said, using a term I'd never heard before. The mechanical fermentation, or *levitazione*, is, in Enzo's thinking, the air incorporated into the dough during a very slow 20-minute mix. (I've seen him demonstrate this by triumphantly showing pockets of air in the dough, right after he cut off a slab, immediately after he mixed a batch by hand.) Then the dough rests for just 10 to 20 minutes before being cut into dough balls—it's this short rest, along with the very small amount of yeast used, that's the hallmark of Enzo's dough method. The balls then sit out for 10 hours at room temperature to ferment, a lengthy second fermentation. Enzo had one of his guys bring us out a tray of mature dough balls shortly before the pizzeria was to open for service on a Saturday night. They were perfect rounds of dough with beautifully smooth skins.

I was surprised to hear myself asking Enzo if I could use his dough recipe in this book. And I was further surprised to hear him say yes, so long as I didn't say it's going to make pizza as good as it is at La Notizia. Ha! No way, Enzo. You have one of the best pizzerias in Naples; all we can do is salute you and adapt your method for making a good pizza dough in our home kitchens. I think of this recipe as a learning experience, to see yet another way to make a great dough. But if you want to eat La Notizia pizza, book a ticket to Naples.

I made two big adjustments to La Notizia's method. We cannot replicate at home the slow, 20-minute mix action of the mechanical dough mixer used at most Naples pizzerias, but we can do an extended hand mix, folding the dough over itself repeatedly to perhaps incorporate extra air. And we need more water in the dough for the home kitchen so it doesn't get too dried out while baking (see page 52 for a discussion of dough hydration in relation to oven baking temperature). At La Notizia they average about 60 percent dough hydration, which is fairly typical for Naples. Here, I've adjusted to 70 percent dough hydration, but if you have a wood-fired oven, try 300 grams water (60 percent hydration) in your dough. I also increased the percentage of yeast in my adaptation here, since home kitchens are often not as warm as a pizzeria kitchen, nor are they as fertile. Even with these adaptations this pizza dough works great, with almost all of the fermentation happening in the dough balls after they have been formed, even if it ends up being nothing like a La Notizia pizza. Enzo's *method* is the point of this dough. I really like the pizza that comes from it; I hope you do, too. If you want to salute La Notizia, buy a nice *mozzarella di bufala* and make Pizza Margherita (page 153) or Escarole Pizza (page 221), and serve it folded.

INGREDIENT	QUANTITY		BAKER'S %
Water	350g	1½ cups	70%
Fine sea salt	13g	Scant 2½ tsp	2.6%
Instant dried yeast	0.1g	⅒ of ¼ tsp	0.02%
White flour, preferably 00	500g	Scant 4 cups	100%

MAKES 3 regular dough balls

BULK FERMENTATION 20 minutes

DIVIDE, SHAPE, AND COVER DOUGH 10 minutes

SECOND FERMENTATION 10 hours

SAMPLE SCHEDULE Mix the dough at 9 a.m., rest for 15 minutes, knead again for 5 minutes, divide and shape into dough balls at 9:40 a.m., make pizza that evening anytime after 8.

1 Measure and Combine the Ingredients. Using your digital scale, measure 350 grams of 90° to 95°F (32° to 35°C) water into your 6-quart dough tub. Measure 13 grams of fine sea salt, add it to the water, and stir or swish it around until the salt is dissolved. Measure 0.1 gram (⅒ of ¼ teaspoon) of instant dried yeast. Add the yeast to the water, let it rest there for a minute to hydrate, then swish it around until it's dissolved. Add 500 grams of flour (preferably 00) to the water-salt-yeast mixture.

2 Mix the Dough. Mix by hand, first by stirring your hand around inside the dough tub to integrate the flour, water, salt, and yeast into a single mass of dough. Then use the pincer method (see page 86) to cut the dough in sections with your hand, alternating with folding the dough to develop it back into a unified mass. Continue folding the dough over itself for another minute or two to incorporate air into the dough. The target dough temperature at the end of the mix is 80°F (27°C).

3 Knead and Rise. Let the dough rest for 15 minutes, then knead again on a lightly floured countertop with floured hands for 2 to 3 minutes, without adding more flour, incorporating air into the dough as you fold and knead it. The dough should be smooth all around. Place the dough ball seam side down in the lightly oiled dough tub and cover with a tight-fitting lid. Hold the dough for 20 minutes, covered, at room temperature for the first rise.

4 Shape. Divide the dough and shape it into dough balls. Moderately flour a work surface about 2 feet wide. With floured hands, gently ease the dough out of the tub. With your hands still floured, pick up the dough and ease it back down onto the work surface in a somewhat even shape. Dust the entire top of the dough with flour, then cut it into 3 equal-sized dough balls. (*Note:* Each of your dough balls will weigh about 275 grams; Enzo's dough balls at La Notizia weigh about 210 to 220 grams.) Shape each piece of dough into a medium-tight round following the instructions on pages 88 to 91, working gently and being careful not to tear the dough.

5 Second Fermentation. Place the dough balls on lightly floured dinner plates or a baking sheet, leaving space between them to allow for expansion. Lightly flour the tops, cover airtight with plastic wrap, and let rest at room temperature for 10 hours.

6 Make Pizza. These dough balls will be fine for making pizza anytime during the next 3 or 4 hours.

SATURDAY PAN PIZZA DOUGH

This recipe is an easy same-day dough for making pan pizza. Pan pizzas are crowd-pleasers and go by affectionate names like "Grandma pie" or "Nonna's pizza." You just need a half sheet pan and a good dough, plus olive oil, tomatoes, and cheese. Top your pie simply or go large, but be careful with your enthusiasm—it's easy to go overboard and build one of these into a bomb that weighs 5 pounds. Its size and shape make the pan pizza a good candidate for a half-and-half pizza, or for a green, white, and red pie that looks like the Italian flag.

It's very important to parbake pan pizzas lower in the oven than hearth pizzas, so that the pie gets enough bottom heat to crisp it up. I have the best results baking in the rack position just below middle in my home oven. Baking with the pan on a steel or stone is ideal if you have one, but this works fine on an open rack, too. Multiple pans of dough can be lightly sauced and parbaked and set aside for hours until the next step when you're ready to either serve or eat: top the dough with another layer of sauce and toppings, then bake again until the toppings and the crust are finished. Easy. Take the finished pizza off the pan, cut it into long strips, then slice into individual squares and serve.

This dough gets 4 hours of bulk fermentation time before it's placed on an oiled half sheet pan. If you want a thin-crust pan pizza, cut the dough batch in half and roll the dough out with a pin or make two pans of pizza. I prefer the two-stage bake: first, parbake the crust with

a film of olive oil and tomato sauce until the tomato has soaked into the dough and caramelized around the edges; then, either right away or hours later, top it with cheese, sauce, and toppings and finish baking. See the recipe for Grandma Pie on page 192.

MAKES enough for 1 Grandma pizza or 2 thin-crust pan pizzas in a half sheet pan

BULK FERMENTATION 4 hours

SPREAD OUT ON A SHEET PAN 5 minutes

SECOND FERMENTATION 30 minutes

SAMPLE SCHEDULE Mix the dough at noon, spread it into the pan at 4 p.m., parbake at 4:30 p.m., and make pizza that evening.

1   **Measure and Combine the Ingredients.** Using your digital scale, measure 375 grams of 90° to 95°F (32° to 35°C) water into a 6-quart dough tub. Measure 11 grams of fine sea salt, add it to the water, and stir or swish it around until the salt is dissolved. Measure 2 grams of instant dried yeast (½ teaspoon). Add the yeast to the water, let it rest there for a minute to hydrate, then swish it around until it's dissolved. Add 500 grams of bread or 00 flour to the water-salt-yeast mixture.

2   **Mix the Dough.** Mix by hand, first by stirring your hand around inside the dough tub to integrate the flour, water, salt, and yeast into a single mass of

INGREDIENT	QUANTITY		BAKER'S %
Water	375g	1½ cups + 4 tsp	75%
Fine sea salt	11g	Scant 2 tsp	2.2%
Instant dried yeast	2g	½ tsp	0.2%
White bread or 00 flour	500g	Scant 4 cups	100%
Olive oil	75g	5 tablespoons	
Tomato sauce (smooth)	200g	¾ cup	

dough. Then use the pincer method (see page 86) to cut the dough in sections with your hand, alternating with folding the dough to develop it back into a unified mass. Continue for just 30 seconds to 1 minute. The target dough temperature at the end of the mix is 80°F (27°C); use your probe thermometer to check it.

3   Knead and Rise. Let the dough rest for 20 minutes, then knead it on a work surface with a very light dusting of flour for about 30 seconds to 1 minute. The skin of the dough should be very smooth. Place the dough ball seam side down in the lightly oiled dough tub. Cover with a tight-fitting lid. Hold the dough for 4 hours at room temperature (assuming 70° to 74°F/21° to 23°C) for the first rise. After 4 hours, the dough should have doubled in size to about 1 inch below the tub's 2-quart line.

4   Preheat. Put your pizza steel or stone on a lower middle rack in your oven. Preheat the oven to 550°F (290°C) for 45 minutes.

5   Shape. Lightly flour a work surface about 2 feet wide. With floured hands, gently ease the dough out of the tub. Lightly stretch the dough into a rectangular shape (it won't go all the way to the edges of the pan at this stage). Spread 4 tablespoons (60 grams) of the olive oil on a half sheet pan, making sure to oil the inside of the rim as well. Lay the dough onto the pan, drizzle the remaining 1 tablespoon (15 grams) of olive oil on top of the dough, and spread it out evenly with your fingers and palms to the dimensions of the pan until the dough resists. Let it rest for 10 minutes, then finish spreading it out to the length and width of the pan (but don't try to push it up the rim). Let it rest for about 30 minutes while the oven is preheating.

6   Parbake. Spread the tomato sauce on top of the dough up to about ¼ inch from the edges. Bake for about 15 minutes, until the edges of the crust are very lightly golden and the sauce is lightly caramelized on the perimeter. The bottom of the crust should be a light golden color and crisp. The dough should be fully baked.

7   Make Pizza. The second stage of baking can be immediate or hours later. Please see the recipe for Grandma Pie (page 192).

24- TO 48-HOUR PIZZA DOUGH

This trouble-free dough makes a great pizza crust, delicate and flavorful. Mix the dough any time of day (I do mine in the evening), letting it bulk-ferment at room temperature for a couple of hours before shaping the dough balls. Let them rest, covered, in the refrigerator until the next evening or two days later.

There is no morning step. Just give your dough balls an air kiss before you go off to work and let them slowly do their thing in the fridge. When you get home from work, the dough balls are already made up. All you have to do is fire up the oven, make a quick sauce, slice some cheese, and presto, it's *apizza*.

But the thing is, it's not just pizza. I was surprised by how good the pizza made from this dough is. This is one of the best doughs in this book. The long fermentation helps give the pizza crust a very tender lightness, and the airiness of the *cornicione* is just . . . wow. I think you'll be impressed. In Italy, a long-fermented dough like this would be called "very digestible." I love Italy.

MAKES 3 regular or 5 thin-crust dough balls

BULK FERMENTATION 2 hours

DIVIDE, SHAPE, AND COVER DOUGH 10 minutes

SECOND FERMENTATION 16 to 48 hours, refrigerated

SAMPLE SCHEDULE Mix the dough at 7 p.m., shape it into dough balls at 9 p.m., cover and refrigerate, make pizza the next evening (optimal) or the day after that (still very good).

INGREDIENT	QUANTITY		BAKER'S %
Water	350g	1½ cups	70%
Fine sea salt	13g	Scant 2½ tsp	2.6%
Instant dried yeast	1.5g	¾ of ½ tsp	0.3%
White flour, preferably 00	500g	Scant 4 cups	100%

1 Measure and Combine the Ingredients. Using your digital scale, measure 350 grams of 90° to 95°F (32° to 35°C) water into a 6-quart dough tub. Measure 13 grams of fine sea salt, add it to the water, and stir or swish around in the tub until it's dissolved. Measure 1.5 grams (¾ of ½ teaspoon) of instant dried yeast. Add the yeast to the water, let it rest there for a minute to hydrate, then swish it around until dissolved. Add 500 grams of flour (preferably 00) to the water-salt-yeast mixture.

2 Mix the Dough. Mix by hand, first by stirring your hand around inside the dough tub to integrate the flour, water, salt, and yeast into a single mass of dough. Then use the pincer method (see page 86) to cut the dough in sections with your hand, alternating with folding the dough to develop it back into a unified mass. Continue for just 30 seconds to 1 minute. The target dough temperature at the end of the mix is 80°F (27°C); use your probe thermometer to check it.

3 Knead and Rise. Let the dough rest for 20 minutes, then knead it on a work surface with a very light dusting of flour for about 30 seconds to 1 minute. The skin of the dough should be very smooth. Place the dough ball seam side down in the lightly oiled dough tub. Cover with a tight-fitting lid. Hold the dough for 2 hours at room temperature (assuming 70° to 74°F/21° to 23°C) for the first rise.

4 Shape. Divide the dough and shape it into dough balls. Moderately flour a work surface about 2 feet wide. With floured hands, gently ease the dough out of the tub. With your hands still floured, pick up the dough and ease it back down onto the work surface in a somewhat even shape. Dust the entire top of the dough with flour, then cut it into 3 or 5 equal-sized pieces, depending on the style of pizza. Use your scale to get evenly sized dough balls. Shape each piece of dough into a medium-tight round following the instructions on pages 88 to 91, working gently and being careful not to tear the dough. There is no floor time for these dough balls before going into the refrigerator.

5 Second Fermentation. Put the dough balls on one or two lightly floured dinner plates, leaving space between them to allow for expansion. Lightly flour the tops, tightly cover with plastic wrap, and put them into the refrigerator. Refrigerate until ready to make pizza, either the next evening (ideal) or the day after (still good).

6 Make Pizza. Remove the dough balls from the fridge 60 to 90 minutes before making pizza.

the initial dough have different consistencies it takes longer than usual for the dough to unify. You will find it comes together more completely after a bit of a rest period. The target dough temperature at the end of the mix is 75°F (24°C).

4   Knead and Rise. Let the dough rest for 20 minutes, then knead it on a work surface with a very light dusting of flour for about 30 seconds to 1 minute. The skin of the dough should be very smooth. Place the dough ball seam side down in the lightly oiled dough tub. Cover with a tight-fitting lid. Let rise for 45 minutes.

5   Shape. Moderately flour a work surface about 2 feet wide. With floured hands, gently ease the dough out of the tub. With your hands still floured, pick up the dough and ease it back down onto the work surface in a somewhat even shape. Dust the entire top of the dough with flour, then cut it into 3 or 5 equal-sized pieces, depending on the style of pizza. Shape each piece of dough into a medium-tight round following the instructions on pages 88 to 91, working gently and being careful not to tear the dough.

6   Second Fermentation. Place the dough balls on one or two lightly floured dinner plates, leaving space between them to allow for expansion. Lightly flour the tops, cover with plastic wrap, and let them rest for 2 hours, then put them into the refrigerator. The dough balls will hold in the refrigerator for 2 to 3 days.

7   Make Pizza. Remove the dough balls from the refrigerator 60 to 90 minutes or so before shaping them into disks to make pizza.

48- TO 72-HOUR NEW YORK PIZZA DOUGH

This dough uses a long refrigeration period—a standard practice in good New York pizzerias (though it's rare in Naples). The long, cold fermentation in the fridge lets flavors and mild acidity build and allows the proteins in the dough to break down just enough. This nets a more delicate and more flavorful pizza crust.

Because the dough is not as actively fermented, the crust is not as poofy-rimmed as a Neapolitan pizza; it's flatter. The toppings also stay put close to the edge of the pizza rather than being pushed toward the middle by the puffy rim.

New York pizzas usually bake at a lower temperature for many minutes longer than Neapolitan pizzas do, resulting in more moisture loss in the crust. This means a crisper pizza. When you slice a pizza made with this dough, the tips of the slices won't sag very much. For more detail on the relationship between oven temperature and dough hydration, see page 52.

Because of the stiffer dough in this recipe, I recommend using a stand mixer fitted with the dough hook rather than mixing it by hand. It's just easier with a machine. If you don't have a stand mixer but you do have a food processor, you can use that with the metal blade to briefly mix the dough (it works!). (While you're at it, put the plastic dough blade in the recycling. Gluten develops best when it's cut, not torn by blunt plastic.)

If you want to convert other pizza doughs in this book, such as my Saturday Pizza Dough (page 108), to a New York–style dough, substitute high-protein bread flour for 00 flour and use the same amount of water in the dough as in this recipe.

MAKES 3 regular dough balls

BULK FERMENTATION 2 hours

DIVIDE, SHAPE, AND COVER DOUGH 10 minutes

DOUGH REFRIGERATION 48 to 72 hours

SAMPLE SCHEDULE Mix dough at 7 p.m., shape into dough balls at 9 p.m., and make pizza two days later (optimal) or on the third day (still pretty good).

INGREDIENT	QUANTITY		BAKER'S %
Water	320g	1⅓ cups + 1 tsp	64%
Fine sea salt	14g	2½ tsp	2.8%
Instant dried yeast	1.2g	¼ tsp + ¹⁄₁₆ tsp	0.3%
High-protein bread flour	500g	4 cups	100%

1 Measure and Combine the Ingredients. Using your digital scale, measure 320 grams of 90°F (32°C) water into the bowl of your stand mixer. Measure 14 grams of fine sea salt, add it to the water, and stir until it's dissolved. Measure 1.2 grams (¼ plus ¹⁄₁₆ teaspoon) of instant dried yeast. Add the yeast to the water, let it rest there for a minute to hydrate, then swish it around until it's dissolved. Add 500 grams of high-protein bread flour to the mixing bowl.

2 Mix the Dough. Using the dough hook, mix for about 90 seconds on the slowest speed. Do not overmix or the dough will be too elastic and tough once baked. The target dough temperature at the end of the mix is 78° to 80°F (26° to 27°C). With a wet or floured hand, remove the dough from the mixer, lifting it from the bottom so you don't tear it. Place in a lightly oiled 6-quart dough tub and cover it with a tight-fitting lid. Alternatively, use a food processor fitted with the metal blade: add the ingredients in the same order and pulse only until the dough has come together. Or you can mix this dough by hand, with one adjustment: add 400 grams of flour and mix until you have thoroughly integrated the flour and water, then add the remaining 100 grams of flour in stages until it's all blended in and no dry flour remains. Use the pincer method (see page 86) to cut the dough in sections with your hand, alternating with folding the dough to develop it into a unified mass. It's a bit of work, but it's doable. Add a few drops of water if you have to.

3 Rise. A rise of 2 hours after mixing the dough is all you need for this recipe. The rest of the fermentation will happen in the dough balls. This dough will expand about 40 to 50 percent of its original volume in this 2-hour period.

4 Shape. After the first rise, divide the dough and shape it into balls. Moderately flour a work surface about 2 feet wide. With floured hands, gently ease the dough out of the tub. With your hands still floured, pick up the dough and ease it back down onto the work surface in a somewhat even shape. Dust the entire top of the dough with flour, then cut it into 3 equal-sized pieces. Shape each piece of dough into a medium-tight round following the instructions on pages 88 to 91, working gently and being careful not to tear the dough.

5 Second Fermentation. Put the dough balls on one or two lightly floured dinner plates, leaving space between them to allow for expansion. Lightly flour the tops, cover with plastic wrap, then put them into the refrigerator. These dough balls will hold for up to 3 days in the refrigerator. They should be best at 2 days.

6 Make Pizza. Give your dough balls 90 minutes or so out of the refrigerator before making pizza to let their gluten relax.

WILD YEAST (LEVAIN) CULTURE

Whether you call it sourdough, levain, or wild yeast culture, we're talking about the same thing. A wild yeast culture is created when yeast that are in the air (yup, pretty much everywhere) and in the flour combine to form a living culture that makes bread dough, pizza dough, and even pancakes rise. It's like the original bag of yeast, except you make it yourself! You can create your own by mixing flour and water daily for 7 days. It takes 5 minutes a day, including cleanup. Just take a quart-sized plastic deli container, pour in 100 grams of very warm water and 100 grams of whole wheat flour, stir with your hand until blended into a slurry, and let it sit for a day. Then, the next day, add another 100 grams of flour and 100 grams of water to the first day's mix, and stir and blend with your hand until all is integrated. On days 3 and 4, throw away half of the mixture before feeding with 100 grams each of flour and water. After a total of four days, it will be active, gassy, and alcoholic, and ready to convert into something you can use to make naturally leavened pizza dough (or bread, or pancakes!). Change the feeding to white flour on the sixth day, and it's ready to use: by day 8 you can have a very nice pizza coming out of your oven, with a natural leavening that you and nature put together effortlessly.

Start with 100 percent whole-wheat flour because, compared with white flour, it has much more of the natural flora we need to get the culture going. The outer layers of the wheat berry, the bran, and the interior wheat germ of whole wheat flour all contain the yeast and nutrition needed to kick-start the new culture. Once it's established, you can maintain your culture by feeding it with just white flour. If you keep it going with regular feedings every week (throw away all but 50 grams, add 100 grams each of flour and water), you only ever have to go through this startup process once.

After my first book was published, I realized a good, active wild yeast (aka natural levain) culture can be made up with less than half the flour I used the first time around, and on a simple 6-day schedule. Only about 1½ pounds of flour is needed to get it started, using the measurements here, and I've streamlined the storage and restoration process I described in my first book. Call this Levain 2.0.

Details follow, but here is a summary of how a wild yeast culture (levain) works in the context of pizza making. Once your levain is built—after a week of feeding it daily—there will be enough to make a pizza dough and to retain 200 or so grams of the master culture in a quart-size container in the refrigerator. Each time you want to make a new pizza dough, remove about 50 grams of master levain culture from the refrigerated container and use it to make up a fresh starter to leaven the pizza dough: mix the 50 grams of culture with 100 grams of water that's about 100°F (38°C) and 100 grams of the flour. Mix the starter in the evening, mix the final pizza dough in the morning, make up dough balls 2 hours later, and make pizza that night or

CONTINUED

WILD YEAST (LEVAIN) CULTURE, CONTINUED

the next day. Once you have done this a few times and learn the rhythm, you barely notice the amount of time it takes, because it's so little. And the result can be a very special pizza that will be very distinctly your own.

Here are step-by-step instructions.

MAKING THE LEVAIN

Start with one empty container with a lid that fits. I use a quart-sized deli container. Weigh the container and write down its empty weight on a piece of tape that you then attach to the outside of the container. You will need this later.

Day 1, any time of day: By hand, mix 100 grams of water (100°F/38°C) with 100 grams of room temperature whole wheat flour in your container. Leave it out at room temperature without its lid for a couple of hours, then put a lid on it.

Day 2, evening: Next, 24 to 36 hours after the first feeding of your new culture, add to it 100 grams of water (100°F/38°C), plus 100 grams of room temperature whole wheat flour. Mix by hand until integrated and let it sit out on the counter. Leave the lid off for a couple of hours to capture some of the natural yeast that's floating around in the air, then cover it.

Day 3, evening: Already, after just 48 hours from starting your new wild yeast culture, it should be gassy. It's alive! Remove about half of the mixture from the container (with a wet hand is easiest) and throw it away. Add to the remainder another 100 grams of water (100°F/38°C) plus 100 grams of room temperature whole wheat flour, and mix it all together by hand. Leave it out at room temperature, covered.

Day 4, evening: Remove about three-quarters of the bubbly mixture and throw that away, then once again add 100 grams of water, this time between 85° and 90°F (29° and 32°C), and 100 grams of room temperature whole wheat flour to your new culture. Mix by hand until integrated. Leave it out at room temperature, covered.

Day 5, evening: Using the weight of the empty container for reference, remove and dispose of all but 50 grams of the culture. Add 150 grams of water (85°F/29°C), plus 75 grams of room temperature whole wheat flour and 75 grams of room temperature all-purpose white flour. Mix by hand until integrated. Leave it out at room temperature, covered.

Day 6, evening: Your wild yeast culture is now almost ready to go. Remove and discard all but 50 grams of your culture and add 100 grams of water (85°F/29°C) and 100 grams of room temperature all-purpose white flour. Mix by hand until integrated and let sit out overnight, covered.

Day 7, morning: The culture should feel gassy and goopy and like there's life in there, and it will have a nice lactic, slightly alcoholic fragrance. Pop it in the fridge. Tonight you can mix a starter, and tomorrow morning a pizza dough for pizza tomorrow evening on day 8.

MAINTAINING THE LEVAIN

Once every week (to a week and a half), remove all but 25 grams of the levain from its container and discard. Add 100 grams of all-purpose white flour and 100 grams of 85°F (29°C) water, mix by hand, and let it sit out for 10 to 12 hours, then put it back in the fridge. Your culture should perform well for the next week and you should have enough to make four batches of this book's levain dough. If you need more than this, double the feeding: 50 grams of culture, 200 grams of white flour, and 200 grams of water at 85°F (29°C).

Every environment is different: if you are in wine country, for example, there is likely to be more ambient yeast in the air, especially during harvest season, than in other locales, and your levain culture will certainly be more active with less effort than if you live, in say, Arizona.

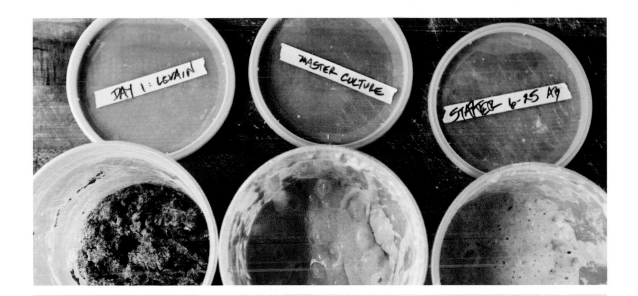

LEVAIN VOLUME CONVERSIONS

I highly encourage you to measure your levain ingredients by weight rather than volume; volume conversions are approximate.

100 GRAMS WHOLE WHEAT FLOUR = ¾ CUP + ½ TABLESPOON

100 GRAMS WATER = ⅓ CUP + 4 TEASPOONS

50 GRAMS LEVAIN = 2 TABLESPOONS + 1 TEASPOON

OVERNIGHT LEVAIN PIZZA DOUGH

I was never convinced that a pizza crust made with natural leavening from a wild yeast (aka sourdough) culture would make a better pizza than one made from a long-fermented dough based on commercial yeast. Different, yes, but better? Then I ate pizza made by the master, Franco Pepe, at Pepe in Grani. Franco's pizza crusts are really in a league of their own, with a delicate, incredibly light texture and flavors of ripe, lactic fermentation. His naturally leavened dough is mixed by hand and allowed to ferment overnight. There's magic in there, and it takes a *pizzaiolo* who is completely in touch with his pizza dough as a living thing to bring it out. I also think it takes the same person in the pizza kitchen every day. Anthony Mangieri of Una Pizza Napolitana in San Francisco is a notable American example of a *pizzaiolo* who is in touch with his natural-levain pizza in a way that is almost spiritual. Variations in temperature, humidity, and flour all require subtle adjustments, and ultimately it is the experienced eye and hand that guide you to know when a dough is ready. This means knowing the dough as a living thing. I'm not trying to scare you away from trying it—it's more that I want to express an appreciation for those who have mastered this delicate craft, which requires a little more judgment and a lot more experience than making pizza dough with a package of yeast.

Making pizza dough from a wild yeast culture that you create yourself (see page 127) is very satisfying. It takes a bit more time and planning, but once you get familiar with the routine, there's nothing difficult about it. With familiarity you can learn to appreciate the subtleties and rewards that go with the original method for making leavened dough. This is indeed the dough of days past, before one could go to the store to buy yeast. Note that the first time you make this dough, if you don't already have your levain built, you'll need to start building the levain 6 days before you start making your pizza dough—that is, 7 to 8 days before you bake the pizza.

MAKES 3 regular or 5 thin-crust dough balls

BUILD LEVAIN 6 days

MAKE LEVAIN STARTER 10 to 12 hours (overnight)

MIX FINAL DOUGH 10 minutes; knead 20 minutes later

BULK FERMENTATION 3 hours

DIVIDE, SHAPE, AND COVER DOUGH 10 minutes

SECOND FERMENTATION 5 to 6 hours at room temperature, with a hold time of 3 to 4 hours

SAMPLE SCHEDULE Mix your levain starter in the evening, mix the pizza dough the next morning at 9 a.m., shape into dough balls at noon, then make pizza between 5 p.m. and 9 p.m. Or refrigerate the dough balls at 4 p.m. and make pizza the next day, taking the dough out of the fridge 1 hour before you make pizza.

LEVAIN STARTER

INGREDIENT	QUANTITY	
Wild yeast (levain) culture (see pages 127 to 129)	50g	2 tbsp + 1 tsp
Water	100g	⅓ cup + 4 tsp
High-protein bread flour; okay to substitute all-purpose or 00 flour	100g	¾ cup + 2 tsp

FINAL DOUGH

INGREDIENT	QUANTITY (FINAL MIX)		BAKER'S % (TOTAL RECIPE)
Water	225g	Scant 1 cup	70%
Fine sea salt	14g	2½ tsp	2.8%
Levain starter	250g	All, above recipe	25%
White flour, preferably 00	375g	Scant 3 cups	100%

1 Measure and Combine the Starter Ingredients.
The evening of the day before you plan to make pizza, use your digital scale to measure 100 grams of 100°F (38°C) water into a quart-sized plastic container with a lid. Measure 50 grams from the container of wild yeast (levain) culture in your refrigerator right into the water and mix by hand. (Don't worry about completely dissolving the starter.) Measure 100 grams of bread flour into the levain mixture, and mix by hand until it all comes together in a semiliquid batter. Put the lid on it and let it sit out overnight at room temperature. (The warmer the location, the more lactic fermentation flavors will go into your crust, up to a point. Overdo it with the starter's fermentation and you will then get an excess of alcohol in the culture, producing more acetic acid flavors. If you live in a warm climate and have warm inside temperatures overnight, mix the levain with cooler water, for example at 75°F (24°C) instead of 100°F (38°C).

2 Measure and Combine the Dough Ingredients.
Ten to 12 hours after you mix the levain starter, it should be bubbly, goopy, and lively. Now make the dough. Measure 225 grams of 90° to 95°F (32° to 35°C) water at into a 6-quart dough tub. Sprinkle 14 grams of salt into the water and swirl around to dissolve. Add in all of the levain starter and blend it briefly by hand with the water and salt, using a pincer motion to cut it into chunks (don't worry about dissolving it completely; it won't). Add 375 grams of flour to the water-salt-starter mixture.

3 Mix the Dough. Mix by hand, first by stirring your hand around inside the dough tub to integrate the flour, water, salt, and yeast into a single mass of dough. Then use the pincer method (see page 86) to cut the dough in sections with your hand, alternating with folding the dough to develop it back into a unified mass. Continue for just 30 seconds to

CONTINUED

OVERNIGHT LEVAIN PIZZA DOUGH, CONTINUED

1 minute. The target dough temperature at the end of the mix is 80°F (27°C); use your probe thermometer to check it.

4 Knead and Rise. Let the dough rest for 20 minutes, then knead it on a work surface with a very light dusting of flour for about 30 seconds to 1 minute. The skin of the dough should be very smooth. Place the dough ball seam side down in the lightly oiled dough tub. Cover with a tight-fitting lid. Hold the dough for 3 hours at room temperature (assuming 70° to 74°F/21° to 23°C) for the first rise. This timeline is flexible, so if you need to shape after 2 hours, don't stress, just make up your dough balls a little early and add the difference in time to the next stage.

5 Shape. Divide the dough and shape it into dough balls. Moderately flour a work surface about 2 feet wide. With floured hands, gently ease the dough out of the tub. With your hands still floured, pick up the dough and ease it back down onto the work surface in a somewhat even shape. Dust the entire top of the dough with flour, then cut it into 3 or 5 equal-sized pieces, depending on the style of pizza. Use your scale to get evenly sized dough balls. Shape each piece of dough into a medium-tight round following the instructions on pages 88 to 91, working gently and being careful not to tear the dough.

6 Second Fermentation. Put the dough balls on lightly floured dinner plates or a baking sheet, leaving space between the balls to allow for expansion. Lightly flour the tops to prevent sticking, cover with plastic wrap, and let sit out at room temperature (I'm assuming 70°F/21°C) for about 5 hours. The dough balls should hold for 4 hours for making pizza. Or, refrigerate the dough balls 4 hours after shaping them, then use them to make pizza the next day.

7 Make Pizza. This dough is fantastic for any pizza.

Meatball Pizza, page 181

AL TAGLIO PIZZA DOUGH

If you want to make Roman-inspired Pizza Bianca or Pizza Rossa (page 173), this is your dough. The goal of this recipe is for you to make a bubbly, well-fermented dough—quite possibly even a little overfermented—that you will bake in a half sheet pan and have come out crisp and golden, not charred. In its best versions it is crisp on the outside and tender inside, and thin enough that you can fold a slice over itself and eat it like a sandwich, as if you were walking through the Campo de' Fiori marketplace in old Rome near where some of the best versions of this classic can be found.

The batch size of this dough is smaller than other recipes in this book, which are based on 500 grams of flour. It's sized to perfectly fit a half sheet pan with just the right thickness for the finished pizza bianca that is common at the best bakeries I've visited in Rome. Lining the sheet pan with parchment paper keeps the dough from sticking. Be sure to bake completely to medium brown so this pizza ends up crisp on the bottom but tender in the middle, not too chewy. Delicate, light, and crisp but not dry is the ideal.

MAKES enough for 1 Pizza Bianca or 1 Pizza Rossa in a half sheet pan

BULK FERMENTATION 12 to 14 hours

TRANSFER DOUGH TO AN OILED DINNER PLATE 5 minutes

SECOND FERMENTATION 3 hours

SAMPLE SCHEDULE Mix dough at 8 p.m., layer it onto an oiled dinner plate at 9 a.m., bake at noon.

1 Measure and Combine the Ingredients. Using your digital scale, measure 255 grams of 90° to 95°F (32° to 35°C) water into a 6-quart dough tub with a matching lid. Measure 10 grams of fine sea salt, add it to the water, and swish it around in the tub until the salt is dissolved. Measure 0.3 gram (¼ of ¼ teaspoon) of instant dried yeast. Add the yeast to the water, let it rest there for a minute to hydrate, then swish it around until it's dissolved. Add 355 grams of flour to the water-salt-yeast mixture and mix by hand until the flour has completely absorbed all of the water. A stirring motion with your hand is effective.

2 Mix the Dough. Once all the ingredients are combined into a single dough mass, mix by hand, wetting your working hand before mixing so the dough doesn't stick to you. Use the pincer method (see page 86) to cut the dough in sections with your hand, alternating with folding the dough to develop it into a unified mass. Continue for just 30 seconds to 1 minute. You can do this on the countertop, but

INGREDIENT	QUANTITY		BAKER'S %
Water	255g	1 cup + 1 tbsp	72%
Fine sea salt	10g	Scant 2 tsp	2.8%
Instant dried yeast	1.5g	¼ of ¼ tsp	0.07%
White flour, preferably 00	355g	2¾ cups + 1 tbsp	100%

working in the dough tub eliminates additional cleanup. The target dough temperature at the end of the mix is 80°F (27°C).

3 Knead and Rise. Let the dough rest for 20 minutes, then knead it on a work surface with a very light dusting of flour for about 30 seconds to 1 minute. The skin of the dough should be very smooth. Place the dough ball seam side down in the lightly oiled dough tub. Cover with a tight-fitting lid or plastic wrap. When the dough is double its original volume, about 12 to 14 hours after mixing, it will have spread out in the dough tub, with some bubbles on the top (this is a very small batch of dough, so it spreads out more than rises in the tub).

4 Shape. Moderately oil a full-sized (10- to 11-inch) dinner plate. Gently remove the dough from its tub and place it on the oiled plate, arranging the dough into a rectangular shape that covers most or all of the plate. Dust the top of the dough lightly with flour and cover it with plastic. Let it rest for 3 hours at room temperature. This is the equivalent of the dough ball stage for other pizzas. About 15 minutes before the dough is done resting, set a baking steel or stone on a middle rack of your oven. Preheat the oven to 550°F (290°C).

5 Transfer to a Sheet Pan. Use scissors to cut a piece of parchment paper equal to the size of the flat surface of a half sheet pan. Using a spray bottle, spritz a light film of plain water on the sheet pan—or just wipe a thin film of water onto the pan with your hand. Lay the parchment paper on the wet pan and smooth it out with your hands. It sticks! Moderately flour the entire top of the dough while it's still on the plate, then invert the plate of dough onto the middle of the sheet pan (the floured side will be face down, the oiled side face up). With floured hands, pick up the dough from each end, lift, and pull to stretch it to the edges of the pan. If the dough resists before it matches the dimensions of the pan, let it rest for 10 minutes, then finish. Work the dough into shape without compressing it, making an effort to get an even thickness throughout.

6 Make Pizza. It is now ready to dress as either Pizza Bianca or Pizza Rossa (page 173).

BAR PIZZA DOUGH

This recipe is adapted from one generously supplied by bar pizza aficionado Adam Kuban, and it works perfectly with Adam's "Love Supreme" Bar Pizza recipe on page 195. This dough is also great for a plain cheese or pepperoni pizza. It is thin, crisp, and classic. You'll need a stand mixer to make this dough, and ideally a nonstick deep-dish pizza pan with a 12-inch diameter. A seasoned 10-inch skillet can work too, in which case you should make smaller dough balls (160 grams instead of 190 grams each).

The dough recipe makes enough for four pizzas. Anything less and the stand mixer has a hard time picking up the dough for proper kneading. Extra dough balls will keep well wrapped in the freezer for a few weeks; just give them 8 to 10 hours to thaw at room temperature, or 24 hours in the fridge.

MAKES 4 dough balls for bar-style pizzas

BULK FERMENTATION 6 hours

DIVIDE, SHAPE, AND COVER DOUGH 10 minutes

SECOND FERMENTATION 24 to 72 hours

SAMPLE SCHEDULE Mix the dough at noon; shape into dough balls, cover, and refrigerate at 6 p.m.; and make pizza the next evening or the day after that.

INGREDIENT	QUANTITY		BAKER'S %
Water	280g	1 cup + 3 tbsp	60%
Fine sea salt	12g	Scant 2¼ tsp	2.5%
Instant dried yeast	0.8g	⅘ of ¼ tsp	0.17%
Canola or olive oil	9g	2 tsp	5%
All-purpose flour	465g	3¾ cups	100%

1 **Measure and Combine the Ingredients.** Using your digital scale, measure 280 grams of 90° to 95°F (32° to 35°C) water into the bowl of an electric stand mixer. Measure 12 grams of fine sea salt, add it to the water, and stir or swish around until dissolved. Measure 0.8 gram (⅘ of ¼ teaspoon) of instant dried yeast, add it to the water, and let it rest there for a minute to hydrate, then swish it around until dissolved. This takes a couple of minutes. Measure 9 grams of oil and add it to the water, and stir or swish it to incorporate. Measure 465 grams of flour and add it to the water-salt-yeast-oil mixture.

2 **Mix the Dough.** Using the dough hook attachment, knead the dough on medium speed until it starts to look smooth and a little shiny, about 2 minutes. At this point, you can cover the bowl tightly with plastic wrap or transfer the dough to a 4- or 6-quart plastic tub with a matching lid.

3 **Rise.** Let the dough stand at room temperature until it almost doubles in bulk, about 6 hours.

4 **Shape.** Moderately flour a work surface about 2 feet wide. With floured hands, gently ease the dough out of its container. With your hands still floured, pick up the dough and ease it back down onto the work surface in a somewhat even shape. Dust the entire top of the dough with flour, then cut it into 4 equal-sized pieces weighing 190 grams each. (Use your scale.) Shape each piece of dough into a medium-tight round following the instructions on pages 88 to 91, working gently and being careful not to tear the dough.

5 **Second Fermentation.** Put the dough balls on one or two lightly floured dinner plates, leaving space between them to allow for expansion. Lightly flour the tops, cover with plastic wrap, and put them into the refrigerator. They will hold for 48 to 72 hours.

6 **Make Pizza.** Check out the "Love Supreme" pizza recipe on page 195.

GLUTEN-FREE PIZZA DOUGH

Better and better quality gluten-free flour is coming to market. This is encouraging, and if you are on a gluten-free diet, you should keep your eyes open to new blends and brands. Dough made with gluten-free flour feels and acts differently from wheat flour, so you need to work it differently. You can still use yeast, and this recipe also includes baking soda to give the dough some lift. Since the dough lacks gluten, you can't stretch it the same way you do with traditional pizza doughs. Instead, it gets pressed into shape in a baking pan or a skillet.

The texture of this crust is more cakelike than pizza crust made from wheat flour. But if this is your only way to eat pizza, I think you will really enjoy this. Two gluten-free brands I can recommend are Cup4Cup and Caputo. Caputo's latest formulation, as of this writing, includes what they call "de-glutenated wheat," which is wheat starch with the gluten proteins removed, to give the flour the flavors of wheat it was missing. You may have to order online, and be prepared for the higher cost of gluten-free flour compared to wheat flour. I encourage you to try multiple brands of gluten-free flour to see which works best for you. The water absorption is going to vary a lot between one gluten-free flour and the next, depending on its grain and starch makeup. Hold back some of this recipe's water (about 20 percent of it) when mixing the dough, and slowly add it in until you get a cohesive mass of dough that is tacky, but not wetter or looser than that.

I like the crisper texture of this crust when it is parbaked for about 3 or 4 minutes before topping and baking. You can also top the raw dough with sauce and cheese—I've seen good pizzerias do it this way. It's up to you. An iron skillet is a good baking vessel for gluten-free pizza. If you want to make a 12-inch pizza in a pan with this dough, you will want dough balls that weigh about 370 grams, and you should finish the bake off the pan directly on a baking steel or stone to crisp it up.

MAKES 3 dough balls for 9- or 10-inch skillet pizzas

SAMPLE SCHEDULE Because there's no gluten to develop, the schedule is whatever you want it to be, but I like giving the dough time to rest before making dough balls, and then you can make pizza anytime. The dough balls will hold for at least 5 days, individually wrapped in the refrigerator.

INGREDIENT	QUANTITY		BAKER'S %
Water	365g	2¾ cups + 2 tbsp	73%
Fine sea salt	14g	2½ tsp	2.8%
Instant dried yeast	0.5g	⅛ tsp	0.1%
Baking soda	1.5g	⅓ tsp	0.3%
Extra-virgin olive oil	45g	3 tbsp + 1 tsp	0%
Gluten-free flour	500g	3⅔ cups	100%

1 Measure and Combine the Ingredients. Using your digital scale, measure 365 grams of water at 90° to 95°F (32° to 35°C) into a 6-quart dough tub with a matching lid. Measure 14 grams of fine sea salt, add it to the water, and stir until the salt is dissolved. Measure 0.5 gram (⅛ teaspoon) of instant dried yeast and 1.5 grams (⅓ teaspoon) of baking soda. Add the yeast to the water and stir until dissolved. This takes a couple of minutes—continuous stirring is not required. Then add 45 grams of olive oil and stir. Add 500 grams of gluten-free flour to the water mixture and mix by hand until the flour has completely absorbed all of the water. A stirring motion with your hand is effective. Slowly add the remaining 65 grams of water, using only as much is needed for the dough to come together and become tacky to the touch (you may not need all 65 grams).

2 Mix the Dough. Once all the ingredients are combined into a single dough mass, mix by hand, wetting your working hand before mixing so the dough doesn't stick to you. Use the pincer method (see page 86) to cut the dough in sections, alternating with folding the dough to develop it into a unified mass. Continue until all the ingredients are well integrated.

3 Rise. Let the dough rest for 30 minutes to 1 hour.

4 Shape. Moderately flour a work surface about 2 feet wide. With floured hands, gently ease the dough out of the tub. Cut it into 3 equal-sized pieces. Shape each piece of dough into a ball by folding the dough over itself several times on the floured surface.

5 Refrigerate. Wrap each dough ball in plastic wrap and store in the refrigerator for later use. These dough balls will last for at least 5 days, refrigerated.

6 Make Pizza. To make pizza from these dough balls, the most foolproof way for the home kitchen is to use a cast-iron skillet.

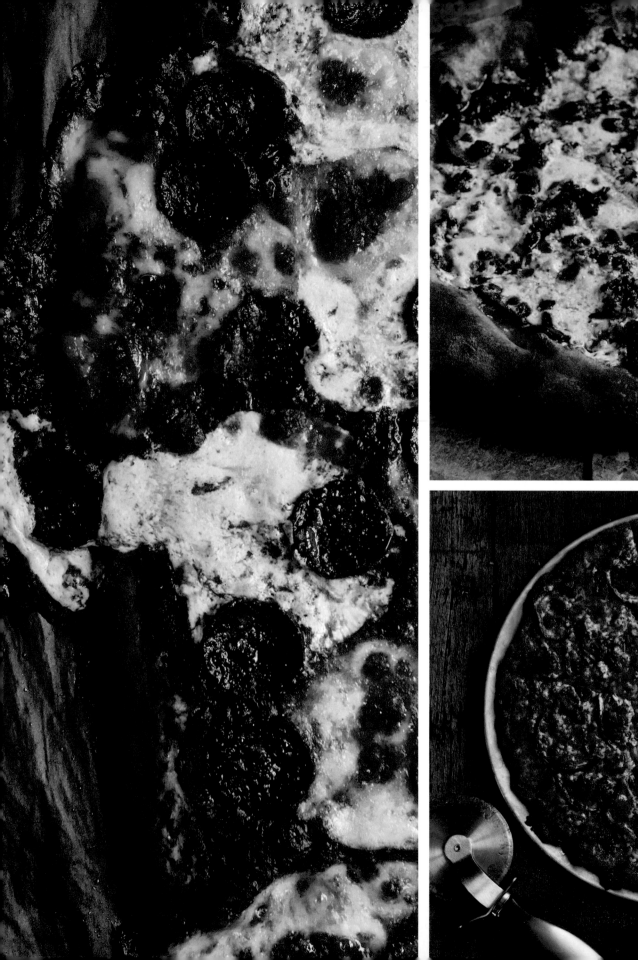

CHAPTER 7
PIZZA RECIPES

Much of the fun in writing this book was creating new recipes, both for pizza doughs and for composed pizzas. Some, like The Ferdinando (page 156), were my interpretation of something I'd read about, while others took a classic combination, like mortadella and pistachios or sausage and vodka sauce, and put it on pizza. Others—such as The White Owl (page 217), the Escarole Pizza (page 221), the Delicata Squash Pizza (page 223), the Tommy Habetz Pizza (page 233), and the Carbonara Pizza (page 171)—were all in-the-moment pizzas that made sense when I was staring at the ingredients. Others, like Brooklyn Hot Honey Pie (page 187) or A.J.'s Pie (page 183), were inspired by specific pizzas made by others that I've really enjoyed. Throw in a few classics, like Grandma Pie (page 192), Pizza Margherita (page 153), and Pizza Marinara (page 150); plus Ken's Artisan Pizza classics, a Tarte Flambée (page 211), and some flatbreads from my Trifecta Tavern, and you get a wide range of pizza recipes to inspire your pizza-baking adventures. Why three New York cheese pizzas? Because they are all different! And any New Yorker knows how much variety there is from one pizzeria to another, though all are making pizza with the same name.

Before we get into the recipes, please take note of some compositional aspects. Dry cheeses like grated Parmigiano-Reggiano, Grana Padano, and Pecorino Romano are frequently used in combination with mozzarella cheese, and the dry cheese usually goes down underneath the mozzarella. This keeps the dry cheese from scorching in the high heat of the oven. Similarly, to protect other ingredients from extreme heat, lay them under the cheese. For example, the escarole goes underneath its provolone and mozzarella; the mortadella mostly goes under its cheese, but I like some bits above the cheese to get crunchy. Other toppings, like sliced garlic or raw onions, get a thin coating of olive oil to keep them from scorching.

I use mozzarella frequently, but I didn't include a single pizza with smoked mozzarella. If you can find a good smoked mozz, please try it as a white pie and steal Chris Bianco's (of Pizzeria Bianco) idea to top it with fennel sausage and roasted onions (he calls it the Wiseguy). Mozzarella is my pizza cheese of choice, frequently paired with grated parm, grana, or pecorino underneath. But the many types of provolone work great, too.

I mentioned this already, but I want to quickly restate it here: to make good pizza, use good-quality ingredients. Some things, like mozzarella, have a big range, not just in terms of quality but also in baking characteristics—every cheese is different in the oven, as age and water content vary. Some brands of low-moisture mozzarella brown a lot faster than others do. And don't be discouraged if your first choice wasn't perfect. Mine wasn't either; it browned too fast, and I learned to look for brands whose color was whiter. Keep looking.

Most of the prep—even making the sauce—can happen while the oven is preheating, and a lot of the prep—roasting mushrooms, for example—takes place in the oven. Roasting butternut squash for an hour is probably the longest elapsed time step of any recipe, save for how long it takes for the dough to do its thing. Developing these recipes in my home kitchen was an excellent deterrent to creating recipes that involved a lot of work. Pizza doesn't demand extreme labor to be great anyway.

You can control the size of the *cornicione* (the rim of the pizza) when you shape the dough into a disk. If you like a large rim, leave a thicker portion of the disk of dough uncompressed when you stretch it out. For New York–style pizzas, leave a much thinner portion (½ at most) of the outer rim uncompressed. The larger the rim, the more it pushes the toppings toward the middle of the pizza as it bakes.

The pizza recipes are arranged by type, but you can make many pizza recipes in any style—pick your dough, pick your sauce, and go. For example, you can make the Artichoke and Bacon Pizza (page 227) in a Roman style, with a super-thin, crisp crust that you roll out with a pin, but you might want to go a tad lighter with toppings since it's a thinner crust.

There are many good things you can do to pizza immediately after it comes out of the oven. If you have a nice, aromatic olive oil, drizzle it on top of a margherita or marinara right after it comes out, then hover over the top and inhale deeply. Oh yeah. Many pizzas like a dose of grated cheese right then: a hard cheese like Parmigiano-Reggiano, Grana Padano, Pecorino Romano, or caciocavallo. Lemon zest, orange zest, or tangerine zest on a white pie can be nice. Cured anchovies should go on the pizza after it's baked, not before. Cured whole-muscle meats like prosciutto, *culatello*, coppa, speck, or bresaola should be sliced very thin and draped on the pizza right after it comes out of the oven; that way they just melt into the pie. We offer arugula (with a light toss in olive oil and sea salt) as a universal topping at Ken's Artisan Pizza. Finishing salts have never been more available than they are now, and I'm very fond of the big flake salt from my friends at Jacobsen Salt Co. here in Oregon. None of these things happened to the pepperoni pizza I grew up eating. I'm glad I grew up.

Of course, you are going to improvise your own toppings and put stuff you like on your pizza. Here are two suggestions to guide you. One: balance saltiness and moisture content in the toppings. If the toppings are salty, like prosciutto or salami, use a fresh cheese like unaged mozzarella. Use saltier cheeses like aged mozzarella or top the pizza with freshly grated pecorino if the toppings are not as salty.

Two: too much sauce with too much cheese will turn the top of your pizza into soup once it's all melted, so be careful. Moist cheese, like a brine-packed mozzarella, is likely to release moisture into the crust while it bakes, so you might lay it on the pizza halfway through the bake, as I recommend in the margherita recipe on page 153.

Most of all, have fun. Try to do it well. And stay with it, because the more you do it, the better you'll get.

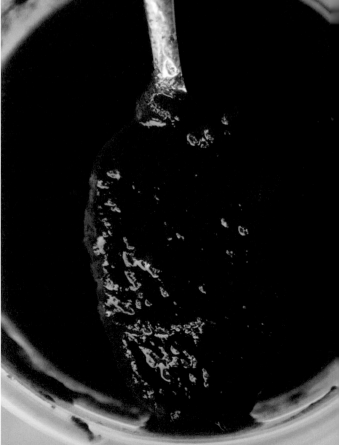

BASIC TOMATO SAUCE, TWO WAYS

This is the sauce I now use almost exclusively, the only variation being whether I use a food mill or a blender to make it, for different textures. It takes about two minutes to make.

MAKES about 750 grams (3 cups), enough sauce for seven 12-inch pizzas

1 can (800-gram/28-ounce) whole peeled tomatoes

8 grams (1½ teaspoons) fine sea salt

BLENDER METHOD

1   Pour the entire contents of the tomato can into the blender. Add the salt. Pulse on the lowest speed setting very, very briefly, just until the tomatoes are blended.

2   Pour the sauce into a sealable container. I use a quart-sized deli container with a lid. Label the container with the date and refrigerate what you don't use. It should keep for 1 week in the refrigerator.

FOOD MILL METHOD

1   Assemble your food mill with a large-hole die over a mixing bowl.

2   Pour half the contents of the tomato can into the food mill and crank it until all the tomatoes are ground up. Empty the mash that didn't make it through the holes into the mixing bowl. Repeat with the remaining tomatoes in the can. There should be nothing that you want to throw away. Add the salt to the tomatoes in the mixing bowl and mix with a large spoon.

3   Pour the sauce into a sealable container. I use a quart-sized deli container with a lid. Label the container with the date and refrigerate what you don't use. It should keep for 1 week in the refrigerator.

FWSY SAUCE

This recipe from *Flour Water Salt Yeast* was called Smooth Red Sauce, and it's flavored with olive oil, garlic, dried oregano, and chile flakes. I have adjusted that recipe here, removing the step of draining the tomatoes in a colander. The sauce will be thick enough provided you do not overmix it in the blender.

Use the best-quality dried oregano you can get; if you can find Calabrian oregano, all the better.

MAKES 750 grams (3 cups), enough sauce for five 12-inch pizzas

20 grams (1½ tablespoons) extra-virgin olive oil

1 clove garlic, chopped

8 grams (1½ teaspoons) fine sea salt

0.3 gram (¼ teaspoon) dried oregano

0.4 gram (¼ teaspoon) chile flakes

1 can (800-gram/28-ounce) whole peeled tomatoes

1 Put the olive oil, garlic, salt, oregano, and chile flakes in a blender. Add just a spoonful of tomatoes and blend briefly until the garlic and oil have emulsified. Then add the rest of the tomatoes and blend very quickly, with brief pulses only, until all the ingredients are combined. Overblending releases water from the tomato pulp and makes the sauce too thin.

2 Pour the sauce into a sealable container. I use a quart-sized deli container with a lid. Label the container with the date and refrigerate what you don't use. It should keep for 1 week in the refrigerator.

VODKA SAUCE

This sauce is designed for the Vodka Sauce and Sausage Pizza recipe on page 184, but it works well on a plain cheese pizza too, like the thin-crust vodka pizza at Rubirosa in New York City. Whether on pizza or pasta, this sauce goes nicely with shellfish, especially shrimp and lobster. The sauce needs to cook for quite some time for its flavors to blend and mellow. I think 30 minutes is fine, but you can go longer if you want; just keep an eye on it and add a few spoonfuls of water if you need to thin it out.

MAKES 825 grams (3⅓ cups), enough sauce for four 12-inch pizzas

75 grams (⅓ cup) vodka

50 grams (¼ cup) heavy cream

750 grams (3 cups) FWSY Sauce (page 146)

5 grams (1 tablespoon) grated Grana Padano or Parmigiano-Reggiano cheese

1   In a saucepan over medium-high heat, reduce the vodka until about 2 tablespoons remain, about 4 minutes. Pour in the cream and cook gently over low heat, stirring a few times, for 1 or 2 minutes.

2   Add the sauce and cheese. Raise the heat to high for a few minutes, just until it starts to boil, then reduce the heat to medium-low and simmer, uncovered, for 30 minutes, keeping an eye on the sauce to prevent it from boiling rapidly.

3   Set the sauce aside to cool, then pour it into a sealable container. I use a quart-sized deli container with a lid. Label the container with the date and refrigerate what you don't use. It should keep for 1 week in the refrigerator.

NEW YORK PIZZA SAUCE

This sauce is cooked and very lightly sweetened with sugar, similar to what a number of New York pizzerias use. It should be moderately thick when cooled; it's an easy adaptation of the FWSY Sauce (page 146), which is already flavored with oregano, garlic, and chile flakes.

MAKES 765 grams (3 cups), enough sauce for five 12-inch pizzas

750 grams (3 cups) FWSY Sauce (page 146)

15 grams (1 tablespoon) sugar

1   In a saucepan over medium-high heat, combine the sauce and the sugar and simmer for 15 to 20 minutes, stirring occasionally, until the sauce is only moderately reduced, still quite spreadable, and the sweetness and tomato flavors are lightly concentrated.

2   Set the sauce aside to cool, then pour it into a sealable container. I use a quart-sized deli container with a lid. Label the container with the date and refrigerate what you don't use. It should keep for 1 week in the refrigerator.

Pizza Marinara (page 150) with anchovies.

PIZZA MARINARA

The marinara pizza is underappreciated in the United States, where pizza without cheese seems like a sacrifice, but it remains very much appreciated in Naples and in my household. You might have it for a lunch or light meal, an appetizer, or a side dish. The marinara, which predates the margherita, began as a workman's meal in Naples in the 1700s. In its original version, it was tomato-free, topped with garlic, olive oil, and oregano. The following century, after tomatoes had been imported from America and were thriving at the foot of Mount Vesuvius, the marinara pizza took its current form. Before pizzerias offered seating, pizza was folded and eaten outdoors, or saved in its paper wrapping for later. The marinara got its name from the fishermen who would bring the pizza on board for their workday lunch at sea.

To be successful, this minimalist pizza demands a good crust and quality toppings: tomatoes—especially the tomatoes!—garlic, dried oregano, and olive oil. Saving the drizzle of olive oil until the pizza has finished baking preserves the aromatics of good-quality extra-virgin olive oil. One of my favorite pizzas is a marinara draped with three or four oil-packed anchovy fillets—Scalia brand anchovy fillets are delicious and can be found in a small, 2.8-ounce jar.

I like this very much as a snack on the lighter, Roman-style, super-thin crust, but the classic form is Neapolitan. Pick the dough and style you want. For Roman thin crust, use a small dough ball, about 150 grams in weight. For a Neapolitan-style version, go with a dough ball of about 260 to 270 grams.

MAKES one 12-inch regular or thin-crust pizza

1 dough ball

1 clove garlic

Extra-virgin olive oil

100 grams (⅓ cup + 1 tsp) Basic Tomato Sauce (page 145)

0.5 gram (¾ teaspoon) best-quality dried oregano, preferably Calabrian

Sea salt

3 or 4 anchovy fillets (optional)

1   If you use a dough recipe that calls for refrigeration, remove your dough ball from the refrigerator about 60 to 90 minutes before baking pizza. Put your pizza steel or stone on an upper rack in your oven no more than 8 inches below the broiler. Preheat the oven to 550°F (290°C) for 45 minutes.

2 Slice the garlic clove thinly, place it in a small bowl, and drizzle just enough olive oil over it to coat the slices. Use your fingers to ensure each slice is coated—this prevents the garlic from burning. Set aside. (Sliced garlic is traditional—but try it chopped, too, and see which way you prefer.)

3 Set up your pizza assembly station. Give yourself about 2 feet of width on the countertop. Moderately flour the work surface. Position your wooden peel next to the floured area and dust it lightly with flour. Have the sauce, garlic, and oregano prepared and at hand, plus a ladle or large spoon for the sauce. Switch the oven to broil 10 minutes before loading the pizza.

4 To shape the pizza, put the dough ball on the floured work surface, and flip to coat both sides moderately with white flour. Use one of the two shaping methods—Roman or Neapolitan—shown on pages 92 to 96. Transfer the disk of pizza dough (*il disco di pasta!*) to the flour-dusted wooden peel. Run your hands around the perimeter to relax it and work out the kinks.

5 Spread the tomato sauce over the dough to within ½ inch of the edge, smoothing and spreading it with the back of the spoon or ladle in a circular motion. Sprinkle the dried oregano evenly over the pizza. Evenly scatter the sliced garlic over the top of the pizza. Turn off the broiler, then gently slide the pizza onto the pizza steel or stone. Close the oven door and change the oven setting to bake at 550°F (290°C). Let the pizza bake for about 5 or 6 minutes, until the crust is golden with spots of dark brown. (Don't do a final broil step for this pizza, as it tends to scorch the garlic.) Use tongs or a fork to slide the pizza from the pizza steel or stone onto a large plate.

6 Drizzle a small amount of extra-virgin olive oil over the pizza and season with sea salt to taste. If you want to add anchovies, lay the fillets on the pizza now. Serve whole or sliced.

PIZZA MARGHERITA

This is the pizza that, like no other, defines "pizza" in hearts and minds. It was famously named for Queen Margherita after she visited Naples on June 9, 1889, and was served this pizza by the *pizzaiolo* Raffaele Esposito and his wife, Rosa Brandi.

Pizza Margherita is registered with the EU as a TSG (Traditional Specialties Guaranteed) product; this recipe uses the ingredients and the allowed measures as defined by the Associazione Verace Pizza Napoletana (AVPN). Still, there are differences: the texture of this pizza—baked in a home oven for about 7 minutes— is crisper than that of a true pizza margherita, which bakes in 60 to 90 seconds in a wood-fired oven at 905°F (485°C). That pizza is softer in the rim, and especially in the middle. Do not take this point of differentiation as an apology, though; this is a terrific pizza, and it's the one I make at home more often than any other. I love it in this version *and* in its true Neapolitan form.

The mozzarella cheese goes on the pizza after it has been in the oven for about 4 minutes; this is to keep the texture of the cheese consistent with what you would find at a pizzeria in Naples. If you bake with the mozzarella on the pizza for the entire baking time, the cheese will completely liquefy and it will be more like a New York cheese pizza with basil than a real Neapolitan margherita pizza.

Basil on the pizza after it is baked or before? It's traditional to put the basil leaves on the pizza before baking, and it bakes with the rest of the pizza. But Franco Pepe at Pepe in Grani puts fresh basil on his margherita after it is baked, and so do others I admire. I like it both ways.

If you can eat this pizza whole, or just cut in half, I think you get the best experience. Slicing it like an American pizza usually means some of the ooze in the middle goes on the cutting board. I want the ooze on my fork! A pair of kitchen scissors is a useful service addition to a knife and fork at the table if you want to cut pieces instead of slicing.

One note on the size of the dough ball: the AVPN specification for a Pizza Margherita indicates a dough ball weighing between 180 and 250 grams. One hundred eighty grams makes a very small pizza. Some well-known pizzerias in Naples, like Starita, use dough balls between 260 and 270 grams, and that larger size fits my recommendation for home baking. Choose your dough for this, but the Saturday Pizza Dough (page 108) is closest to the true AVPN version of Pizza Margherita.

CONTINUED

PIZZA MARGHERITA, CONTINUED

MAKES one 12-inch pizza

1 dough ball

60 to 80 grams (¼ to ⅓ cups) Basic Tomato Sauce (page 145)

Extra-virgin olive oil

10 to 15 grams (scant ¼ cup) grated Pecorino Romano or Parmigiano-Reggiano cheese

80 to 100 grams (3½ to 4 ounces) fresh whole-milk mozzarella cheese (*fior di latte*) or brine-packed *mozzarella di bufala*, sliced into short strips about ½ inch thick

3 to 5 fresh whole basil leaves

1   If you use a dough recipe that calls for refrigeration, remove your dough ball(s) from the refrigerator about 60 to 90 minutes before baking pizza. Put your pizza steel or stone on an upper rack in your oven no more than 8 inches below the broiler. Preheat the oven to 550°F (290°C) for 45 minutes.

2   Set up your pizza assembly station. Give yourself about 2 feet of width on the countertop. Moderately flour the work surface. Position your wooden peel next to the floured area and dust it lightly with flour. Have the sauce, oil, cheeses, and basil at hand, with a ladle or large spoon for the sauce. Switch the oven to broil 10 minutes before loading the pizza.

3   To shape the pizza, put the dough ball on the floured work surface and flip to coat both sides moderately with white flour. Use the shaping method shown on pages 92 to 95.

4   Transfer the disk of pizza dough to the peel and run your hands around the perimeter to relax it and work out the kinks.

5   Spread the tomato sauce over the dough to within ½ inch of the edge, smoothing it with the back of the spoon or ladle. Turn off the broiler, then gently slide the pizza onto the pizza stone or steel. Close the oven door and change the setting to bake at 550°F (290°C). Let the pizza bake for about 4 minutes, until the rim is just starting to turn golden. Use a pair of tongs to remove the pizza onto a plate. Drizzle a spoonful or so of olive oil on top of the pizza, then sprinkle the grated pecorino evenly over the sauce. Layer the mozzarella and basil leaves evenly over the pizza. Using your hands, place the pizza back onto the pizza steel or stone and continue baking for 1 to 2 minutes.

6   Change the oven setting from bake to broil and let the pizza bake until the cheese is softly melted and the crust is golden with spots of brown and a few small spots of char, about 2 minutes (check it after 1 minute to be safe). Use tongs or a fork to slide the pizza from the pizza steel or stone onto the plate. Drizzle a small amount of extra-virgin olive oil over the pizza and serve whole or sliced in half.

VARIATION Add sliced cherry tomatoes as soon as this pizza comes out of the oven for a margherita "extra."

Margherita "Extra" with cherry tomatoes.

THE FERDINANDO

Imagine yourself as the king of Naples in 1782. You want pizza, but you don't want your wife, Queen Maria Carolina, to find out. So you disguise yourself as a commoner, sneak out of the castle, and slink through the streets to a pizzeria called Ntuono (Tony's) to satisfy your craving. Pizza is for common folk, not for royalty like you; don't you know that? You order the same pizza everybody else orders, topped with olive oil, garlic, oregano, and salt, with a little bit of cheese sprinkled on after it is baked. DUDE, she's going to smell the garlic on your breath!

If it was good enough for Ferdinando to sneak out for, risking the wrath of his royal lady, then it must have been pretty tasty. And this historic pizza of Naples is also a delicious model of simplicity. Like all of the very simple pizzas, it demands an excellent crust.

To bake this pizza, you'll pass on the broil stage I recommend for most of the pizzas in this book, removing the pie after 5 minutes of baking. The oil and the garlic should be completely done at this point. Any extra baking, or finishing with a broil stage, will burn both the garlic and the bubbles in the crust.

MAKES one 12-inch pizza

1 dough ball

Extra-virgin olive oil

3 or 4 cloves garlic

0.5 gram (¾ teaspoon) dried oregano

Sea salt

15 grams (about ¼ cup) finely grated pecorino cheese

1   If you use a dough recipe that calls for refrigeration, remove your dough ball from the refrigerator about 60 to 90 minutes before baking pizza. Put your pizza steel or stone on an upper rack in your oven no more than 8 inches below the broiler. Preheat the oven to 550°F (290°C) for 45 minutes.

2   Slice the garlic thinly, place it in a small bowl, and drizzle just enough olive oil over it to coat the slices. Use your fingers to ensure each slice is coated—this prevents the garlic from burning. Set aside.

3   Set up your pizza assembly station. Give yourself about 2 feet of width on the countertop. Moderately flour the work surface. Position your peel next to the floured area and dust it lightly with flour. Have the olive oil, garlic, oregano, sea salt, and cheese at hand. Switch the oven to broil 10 minutes before loading the pizza.

4 To shape the pizza, put the dough ball on the floured work surface and flip to coat both sides moderately with white flour. Use the shaping method shown on pages 92 to 95. Transfer the disk of pizza dough to the peel. Run your hands around the perimeter to relax it and work out the kinks.

5 Drizzle about 20 grams (1½ tablespoons) of olive oil over the dough. Sprinkle the garlic and then the oregano evenly over the pizza. Sprinkle with sea salt. Turn off the broiler, then gently slide the pizza onto the pizza steel or stone. Close the oven door and change the oven setting to bake at 550°F (290°C). Let the pizza bake for about 5 minutes, until the crust is golden with spots of dark brown. The garlic color rules when to remove this pizza—don't let the garlic go beyond medium brown, and skip the broil step for this pizza, as it tends to scorch the garlic. Use tongs or a fork to slide the pizza from the pizza steel or stone onto a large plate.

6 Top the pizza with the grated cheese and drizzle a small amount of extra-virgin olive oil over it, and serve whole or sliced.

POMODORO ROYALE (WITH CHEESE)

This pizza is baked with nothing more than tomato sauce and basil, then it's topped with grated cheese *after* it has come out of the oven. If you can find cacio-cavallo, a stretched curd cheese from the south of Italy, give it a try—it comes from the milk of an unusual breed of cow, the Podolica, which are herded each spring up mountain slopes up to 1,000 meters high, where they graze on wild grasses, berries, and herbs. Parmigiano-Reggiano, Grana Padano, and aged pecorino are easier to find, and they also work well on this pizza.

This pizza works well as either a Roman-style thin-crust or as a Neapolitan-style pizza.

MAKES one 12-inch regular or thin-crust pizza

1 dough ball

100 grams (⅓ cup plus 1 teaspoon) Basic Tomato Sauce (page 145)

6 to 8 fresh basil leaves

Extra-virgin olive oil

20 to 30 grams (up to 1 ounce) caciocavallo or other firm cheese

1   If you use a dough recipe that calls for refrigeration, remove your dough ball from the refrigerator about 60 to 90 minutes before baking pizza. Put your pizza steel or stone on an upper rack in your oven no more than 8 inches below the broiler. Preheat the oven to 550°F (290°C) for 45 minutes.

2   Set up your pizza assembly station. Give yourself about 2 feet of width on the countertop. Moderately flour the work surface. Position your wooden peel next to the floured area and dust it lightly with flour. Have the sauce, basil, oil, and cheese at hand, plus a ladle or large spoon. Switch the oven to broil 10 minutes before loading the pizza.

3   To shape the pizza, put the dough ball on the floured work surface and flip to coat both sides moderately with flour. Use one of the two shaping methods (Neapolitan or Roman) shown on pages 92 to 96. Transfer the disk of pizza dough to the peel. Run your hands around the perimeter to relax it and work out the kinks.

4   Spread the tomato sauce over the dough to within ½ inch of the edge, smoothing it with the back of the spoon. Top with the basil leaves. Turn off the broiler, then gently slide the pizza onto the pizza stone. Close the oven door and change the oven setting to bake at 550°F (290°C). Bake for 5 minutes, until the rim is golden. While the pizza is baking, use a box grater or a Microplane to grate the cheese.

5   Change the oven setting from bake to broil and let the pizza cook until the crust is golden with spots of brown and a few small spots of char, about 2 minutes (check it after 1 minute to be safe). Use tongs or a fork to slide the pizza from the pizza steel or stone onto a large plate. Drizzle some olive oil over the pizza and use your fingers to evenly sprinkle the grated cheese over the pizza. Serve whole or sliced.

PROSCIUTTO AND BUFALA

This simple pizza features dollops of fresh buffalo-milk mozzarella and a layer of prosciutto laid on a pizza that is baked with just sauce and a drizzle of olive oil. The cheese goes on the pizza for the final 30 seconds of baking to soften it up. The hot crust and sauce should lightly melt the fresh cheese from underneath; the prosciutto layered over the cheese insulates it. In a perfect world, I would be able to bake the dough naked, without even the sauce, but what happens then is the dough bubbles up dramatically and gets overbaked in some spots. The sauce bakes into the dough and prevents this massive bubble effect, so you might say the sauce is used here more for structural impact than for flavor.

Simple is awesome when the crust is great and the toppings are of good quality. If you drape the prosciutto in folds across the pizza instead of layering it flat, you get a beautiful, dramatic visual effect. Serve this with a glass of Prosecco and a salad for a sweet weekend lunch. This pizza works fine with either a Neapolitan or a Roman-style pizza crust.

MAKES one 12-inch regular or thin-crust pizza

1 dough ball

50 grams (scant ¼ cup) Basic Tomato Sauce (page 145)

30 grams (1 ounce) fresh *mozzarella di bufala*, torn into bite-size pieces

Extra-virgin olive oil

55 grams (2 ounces) thinly sliced prosciutto (3 or 4 slices)

1 If you use a dough recipe that calls for refrigeration, remove your dough ball from the refrigerator about 60 to 90 minutes before baking pizza. Put your pizza steel or stone on an upper rack in your oven no more than 8 inches below the broiler. Preheat the oven to 550°F (290°C) for 45 minutes.

2 Set up your pizza assembly station. Give yourself about 2 feet of width on the countertop. Moderately flour the work surface. Position your wooden peel next to the floured area and dust it lightly with flour. Have the sauce, cheese, oil, and prosciutto on hand, plus a ladle or large spoon. Switch the oven to broil 10 minutes before loading the pizza.

3 To shape the pizza, put the dough ball on the floured work surface and flip to coat both sides moderately with flour. Use one of the two shaping methods—Neapolitan or Roman—shown on pages 92 to 96. Transfer the disk of pizza dough to the peel. Run your hands around the perimeter to relax it and work out the kinks.

CONTINUED

4 Spread the tomato sauce over the dough to within ½ inch of the edge, smoothing it with the back of the spoon or ladle in a circular motion. Turn off the broiler, then gently slide the pizza onto the pizza steel or stone. Close the oven door and change the oven setting to bake at 550°F (290°C). Bake for 4 minutes, until the rim is golden.

5 Change the oven setting from bake to broil and let the pizza bake until the body of the crust is pocked with lightly blackened bubbles, about 1 minute, but keep your eyes on it. Use tongs or a fork to slide the pizza from the pizza steel or stone onto a large plate. Distribute the cheese chunks evenly over the pizza, then return it to the oven for a final 30 seconds under the broiler (or a little longer if your broiler takes a while to heat up), to soften the cheese instead of melting it. Slide the pizza back onto the plate. Drizzle the top with olive oil and drape slices of prosciutto over the cheese, then drizzle with a little more olive oil to taste. Serve whole or sliced.

MORTADELLA AND PISTACHIO PIZZA

Sometimes a topping combination is so obvious it just begs you to try it on pizza. This pie is topped generously with pistachios and garlic; the mortadella goes mostly underneath the mozzarella so it warms up more than cooks. The edges of the mortadella that are directly exposed to the heat—since it is not completely covered by the cheese—get a nice crisp. The contrast of textures makes for good eating. While mortadella's hometown is Bologna in Italy, excellent American mortadellas are being made by Framani in Berkeley, California, and Olympia Provisions here in Portland. Go to your favorite deli counter and get a normal, sandwich-slice thickness of mortadella. If you want to try a different cheese than the *fior di latte* mozzarella, try a soft, unaged Asiago fresco.

This pie is more suitable for Neapolitan-style crust (although you can try New York–style, too) than thin-crust Roman because of the weight of the toppings.

MAKES one 12-inch pizza

1 dough ball

25 grams (3 tablespoons) shelled pistachios

1 large or 2 medium cloves garlic, chopped

Extra-virgin olive oil

10 to 15 grams (scant ¼ cup) grated Parmigiano-Reggiano or Grana Padano cheese

75 grams (2½ ounces) deli-sliced mortadella, cut into bite-size 1-inch strips

120 grams (4 ounces) fresh whole-milk mozzarella cheese or Asiago fresco, sliced

Freshly cracked black pepper (optional)

1 If you use a dough recipe that calls for refrigeration, remove your dough ball from the refrigerator about 60 to 90 minutes before baking pizza. Put your pizza steel or stone on an upper rack in your oven no more than 8 inches below the broiler. Preheat the oven to 550°F (290°C) for 45 minutes.

2 Crush the pistachios into chunks—not a powder—with a mortar and pestle (or with whatever crushing tool you have handy in your kitchen). In a small bowl, mix the pistachios with the chopped garlic and enough olive oil to coat and mix together by hand. Set aside.

CONTINUED

MORTADELLA AND PISTACHIO PIZZA, CONTINUED

3 Set up your pizza assembly station. Give yourself about 2 feet of width on the countertop. Moderately flour the work surface. Position your wooden peel next to the floured area and dust it lightly with flour. Have the olive oil, cheeses, mortadella, pistachio-garlic mixture, and pepper at hand. Switch the oven to broil 10 minutes before loading the pizza.

4 To shape the pizza, put the dough ball on the floured work surface and flip to coat both sides moderately with flour. Use the shaping method shown on pages 92 to 95. Transfer the disk of pizza dough to the peel. Run your hands around the perimeter to relax it and work out the kinks.

5 Drizzle about ½-tablespoon of olive oil over the disk of dough, then sprinkle on the grated Parmigiano-Reggiano. Cover the grated cheese with the mortadella strips, then with the mozzarella slices, and top it by spreading over the pistachio-garlic mixture with your fingers. Turn off the broiler, then gently slide the pizza onto the pizza stone. Close the oven door and change the oven setting to bake at 550°F (290°C). Bake for 5 minutes, until the rim is golden.

6 Change the oven setting from bake to broil and let the pizza cook until the cheese is softly melted and the crust is golden with spots of brown and a few small spots of char, about 2 minutes (check it after 1 minute to be safe). Use tongs or a fork to slide the pizza from the pizza steel or stone onto a large plate, then season with pepper. Serve whole or sliced.

ZUCCHINI BLOSSOM PIZZA

Throughout Italy, *fiori di zucca*, or zucchini blossoms, are plentiful on menus and at outdoor markets each spring and summer. You should buy yours at the farmers' market, too, and they will be best used the day you buy them. A Roman-style thin-crust pizza (so, use your 150-gram dough balls) topped with stuffed blossoms and a sprinkling of mint leaves needs no elaboration—just quiet enjoyment or conversation.

MAKES one 12-inch thin-crust pizza

1 (150-gram) dough ball

150 grams (½ cup) fresh ricotta cheese

15 grams (¼ cup) finely grated Pecorino Romano cheese

1 egg yolk

Zest of ¼ lemon

Sea salt

10 mint leaves, snipped or chopped

6 zucchini blossoms

Fragrant extra-virgin olive oil

75 grams (⅓ cup) Basic Tomato Sauce (page 145)

1   If you use a dough recipe that calls for refrigeration, remove your dough ball from the refrigerator about 60 to 90 minutes before baking pizza. Put your pizza steel or stone on an upper rack in your oven no more than 8 inches below the broiler. Preheat the oven to 550°F (290°C) for 45 minutes.

2   In a medium-sized bowl, mix the ricotta, Pecorino Romano, egg yolk, lemon zest, a pinch of salt, and half the mint leaves with a fork until completely blended. Cut off the zucchini blossom stems, cut open one side of each blossom, and use your fingers or your scissors to remove the pistil. Stuff each blossom with cheese mixture; figure about 1 tablespoon per blossom. Close the blossom back up and seal the petals with a twist. Set aside the remaining cheese stuffing to top the pizza. Gently rub the outside of each blossom with a thin film of olive oil; this will keep the petals from scorching.

3   Set up your pizza assembly station. Give yourself about 2 feet of width on the countertop. Moderately flour the work surface. Position your wooden peel next to the floured area and dust it lightly with flour. Have the sauce, stuffed blossoms, remaining cheese mixture, remaining mint, and olive oil at hand, plus a ladle or large spoon. Switch the oven to broil 10 minutes before loading the pizza.

4   To shape the pizza, put the dough ball on the floured work surface and flip to coat both sides moderately with flour. Use the Roman-style rolling-pin method on page 96. Transfer the disk of pizza dough to the peel. Run your hands around the perimeter to relax it and work out the kinks.

5 Turn off the broiler, then gently transfer the disk of rolled-out dough onto the preheated baking steel or stone. Close the oven door and change the oven setting to bake at 550°F (290°C). Bake for just 45 seconds, until slightly bubbly. This step gives the dough a little more structure to handle the amount of moisture about to go on top of it. Use tongs or a fork to slide the pizza from the pizza steel or stone onto a large plate.

6 Spread the tomato sauce over the crust to within ¼ inch of the edge, smoothing it with the back of the spoon or ladle in a circular motion. Arrange the stuffed zucchini blossoms on top of the pizza. Place 6 coin-sized chunks of the remaining cheese mixture between the blossoms on the pizza. Return the pizza to the pizza steel or stone, then bake for 5 minutes, until the rim is golden.

7 Change the oven setting from bake to broil and let the pizza cook until the crust is golden with spots of brown and a few small spots of char, about 2 minutes (check it after 1 minute to be safe). Be careful not to let the blossoms burn. Use tongs or a fork to slide the pizza from the pizza steel or stone onto a large plate. Evenly sprinkle the remaining mint leaves over the pizza and drizzle olive oil over the top. Serve whole or sliced in half.

RIVER PO PIZZA

The river Po runs east to west across Italy, through the heart of the Piedmont, Lombardy, and Emilia Romagna, one of Italy's most fertile and prosperous regions. There is a ridiculous abundance of great food here, from handmade pastas like *agnolini* and tortellini to DOP products like Prosciutto di Parma, Culatello di Zibello, Parmigiano-Reggiano cheese, and Aceto Balsamico di Modena. The pine nuts harvested from the pine woods of Ravenna are renowned. The red wines of the Piedmont—Barbaresco, Barolo, Barbera, and Dolcetto—are among my very favorites.

This pizza marries peppery arugula, a common green in this region, with Parmigiano-Reggiano and provolone cheeses, and it's topped with pine nuts and Felino salami. I'm a big fan of layering greens under cheese for the way the melted cheese wilts the greens. A very tiny spritz of lemon juice on the arugula provides just the right amount of acidity to balance the rich flavors of the cheese, salami, and pine nuts. Felino is a small town near Parma famous for this salami, made with peppercorns and white wine, following traditional methods of production. It's worth seeking out. If you cannot find Felino, substitute any not-spicy pork salami with peppercorns.

MAKES one 12-inch pizza

1 dough ball

35 grams (1¾ cups) arugula

10 grams (2¼ teaspoons) olive oil

70 grams (⅓ cup) Basic Tomato Sauce (page 145)

10 grams (3 tablespoons) grated Parmigiano-Reggiano cheese

1 small lemon wedge

110 grams (4 ounces) fresh provolone, thinly sliced into 5 or 6 pieces

7 grams (¼ ounce) pine nuts

24 grams (just under 1 ounce) Felino salami, thinly sliced into about 10 pieces

1   If you're using a dough recipe that calls for refrigeration, remove your dough ball from the refrigerator about 60 to 90 minutes before baking pizza. Put your pizza steel or stone on an upper rack in your oven about 8 inches below the broiler. Preheat the oven to 550°F (290°C) for 45 minutes.

2   In a small mixing bowl, toss the arugula in the olive oil.

3 Set up your pizza assembly station. Give yourself about 2 feet of width on the countertop. Moderately flour the work surface. Position your wooden peel next to the floured area and dust it lightly with flour. Have the tomato sauce, grated cheese, dressed arugula, lemon, provolone, pine nuts, and salami at hand, plus a ladle or large spoon. Switch the oven to broil 10 minutes before loading the pizza.

4 To shape the pizza, put the dough ball on the floured work surface and flip to coat both sides moderately with flour. Use the shaping method shown on pages 92 to 95. Transfer the disk of pizza dough to the peel. Run your hands around the perimeter to relax it and work out the kinks.

5 Spread the tomato sauce over the crust to within ½ inch of the edge, smoothing it with the back of the spoon or ladle in a circular motion. Sprinkle the Parmigiano-Reggiano cheese over the sauce, layer the dressed arugula over the pizza, and squeeze a very small spritz of lemon juice over the greens. Cover the greens with the provolone cheese slices and finish by topping the pizza with the pine nuts and salami.

6 Turn off the broiler, then gently slide the pizza onto the pizza steel or stone. Close the oven door and change the oven setting to bake at 550°F (290°C). Bake for 5 minutes, until the rim is golden.

7 Change the oven setting from bake to broil and let the pizza bake until the cheese is melted and the crust is golden with spots of brown and a few small spots of char, about 2 minutes (check it after 1 minute to be safe). Use tongs or a fork to slide the pizza from the pizza steel or stone onto a large plate. Pop open a bottle of Barbera and enjoy.

VARIATION This also works great as a folded pizza. Place the piping hot pizza on a large cutting board. Press the blade of a large chef's knife or mezzaluna across the middle of the pizza but do not cut through; just go far enough so that when you fold the pizza, this fold point is established. Fold the pizza in half along the perforation you just made to make a half-moon shape. Cut the folded pizza in half, perpendicular to the fold line, and serve immediately.

CARBONARA PIZZA

You made pizza on Saturday night, and now it's Sunday morning and you have an extra dough ball in the fridge. Don't wait in line for brunch—it's time for breakfast pizza.

Carbonara is a classic, simple Roman pasta dish with eggs, cured pork, cheese, and plenty of black pepper. This pizza is an obvious riff, and the trick is timing the egg to be baked all the way at the same moment the rest of the pizza is done. (Goldilocks inhabits my world frequently. You know you are going to time it just right, so somebody should make you a perfect Bloody Mary as a reward to go with this pizza.) Since your oven may not bake exactly like my oven does, you need to keep your eyes on it during the last couple of minutes. Crack the egg(s) into a bowl ahead of time. Then, after 4 to 5 minutes of baking, you pull the rack with the pizza steel or stone out from the oven far enough to carefully pour the egg(s) onto the middle of the pie. Bake until the egg is properly done with a runny yolk, and there's your sauce.

Although this recipe is Italian-inspired, I've never heard of anywhere in Italy serving pizza for breakfast. Welcome to America! This is a challenging pizza to slice because you'd lose the yolk on the cutting board if you cut through it, so use directional slicing that avoids the yolk. And use two eggs if you are sharing.

MAKES one 12-inch pizza

1 dough ball

75 grams (2½ ounces) uncooked bacon, cut into 1- to 2-inch slices, or substitute pancetta or guanciale

40 grams (¼ cup plus 2 tablespoons) grated Pecorino Romano

90 grams (3 ounces) *fior di latte* mozzarella

Freshly cracked black pepper

1 or 2 eggs, cracked into a small bowl, yolk intact

Extra-virgin olive oil

Zest of 1 lemon

CONTINUED

CARBONARA PIZZA, CONTINUED

1 If you use a dough recipe that calls for refrigeration, remove your dough ball from the refrigerator about 60 to 90 minutes before baking pizza. Put your pizza steel or stone on an upper rack in your oven no more than 8 inches below the broiler. Preheat the oven to 550°F (290°C) for 45 minutes.

2 In a skillet on a stovetop, sauté the bacon to medium doneness; drain and set aside.

3 Set up your pizza assembly station. Give yourself about 2 feet of width on the countertop. Moderately flour the work surface. Position your wooden peel next to the floured area and dust it lightly with flour. Have the cheeses, pepper, bacon, the bowl with the cracked egg(s), oil, and lemon zest at hand. Switch the oven to broil 10 minutes before loading the pizza.

4 To shape the pizza, put the dough ball on the floured work surface and flip to coat both sides moderately with flour. Use the shaping method shown on pages 92 to 96. Transfer the disk of pizza dough to the peel. Run your hands around the perimeter to relax it and work out the kinks.

5 Spread the grated cheese over the pizza, followed by the bacon pieces, then the sliced mozzarella. Finish with black pepper to taste. I prefer an aggressive amount of pepper. Turn off the broiler, then gently slide the pizza onto the pizza steel or stone. Close the oven door and change the oven setting to bake at 550°F (290°C). Bake for 4 minutes, until the rim is golden. Pull the oven rack holding the pizza steel or stone out toward you to give enough clearance, then tip the bowl to slide the egg(s) onto the pizza. Slide the rack back into place and close the oven door.

6 Change the oven setting from bake to broil and let the pizza finish until the egg is perfectly cooked, about 2 minutes (check it after 1 minute to be safe). The rest of the pizza should be finished, too. Use tongs or a fork to slide the pizza from the pizza steel or stone onto a large plate. Top with a drizzle of olive oil and the lemon zest. Serve, carefully slicing around the yolk.

PIZZA BIANCA AND PIZZA ROSSA

Pizza bianca is a thin, bubbly square slice of baked dough topped with olive oil and sea salt. Pizza rossa is the same, but baked with tomato sauce and dried oregano and dressed with a thin film of olive oil, or more tomato sauce, after it comes out of the oven. These two are staples of Roman bakeries, designed to be a quick grab-and-go snack or light lunch. You may have heard the term *pizza al metro*, or pizza by the meter—the pizzas bake in lengths up to about 2 meters long in deep-deck ovens. It's really fun to see these 5- or 6-foot pizzas go in and out of the ovens. At the counter you order a piece the size you desire; It's usually cut with a pair of scissors and wrapped in paper. They give you a slip that you take to the register to pay. If you've been to Rome but didn't do this, you need to go back.

MAKES one half-sheet pan pizza

FOR PIZZA BIANCA
Al Taglio Pizza Dough (page 134) shaped on a half sheet pan

30 grams (2 tablespoons) extra-virgin olive oil

Fine sea salt

FOR PIZZA ROSSA
Al Taglio Pizza Dough (page 134) shaped on a half sheet pan

30 grams (2 tablespoons) extra-virgin olive oil, plus more for brushing

200 grams (¾ cup plus 1 tablespoon) Basic Tomato Sauce (page 145)

Dried oregano, to taste

1 About 30 minutes before the dough is done resting, set a baking steel or stone on a middle rack of your oven. Preheat the oven to 550°F (290°C).

CONTINUED

TO MAKE PIZZA BIANCA

2 Cover the dough with a thin film of the extra-virgin olive oil, spreading it out evenly with your hand. Dimple (dock) the dough with your fingertips over its entire surface, as you would with focaccia. As a rough guideline, space the dock marks about ½ inch apart. Let the dough rest for 20 minutes.

3 Sprinkle fine sea salt to taste evenly over the entire surface of the dough. Place the pan on the preheated baking steel or stone and bake at 550°F (290°C) for about 15 minutes, until the bubbles of dough have a medium brown color and the rest is golden.

4 Check the bottom of the crust. It should have colored to a medium golden brown. If you want to further darken and crisp up the bottom, remove the entire pizza from the pan with a pair of tongs and slide it directly onto the surface of the pizza steel or stone for 2 to 3 minutes to finish baking (the parchment usually stays attached—this is fine). Let it cool for a couple of minutes, then use your hands to peel the parchment paper from the bottom of the crust. Serve warm, or later at room temperature.

TO MAKE PIZZA ROSSA

2 With your hand, evenly spread a very thin film of the olive oil over the top of the dough. Then spread the tomato sauce evenly over the surface of the dough, leaving just a thin ¼ inch or so at the rim uncoated. Let rest for 20 minutes.

3 Sprinkle dried oregano evenly over the entire surface. Place the pan on the preheated baking steel or stone and bake at 550°F (290°C) for about 15 minutes, until the crust is baked through and the rim is golden.

4 Check the bottom of the crust. It should have colored to a medium golden brown and be crisp on the bottom. In my oven, at this stage I remove the entire pizza from the pan (the parchment usually stays attached—this is fine) with a pair of tongs and slide it directly onto the surface of the pizza steel or stone for 3 to 4 minutes to finish baking until the bottom is golden. When it's done, use a pair of tongs to slide it back onto the pan.

5 Immediately after removing from the oven, use a pastry brush or a paintbrush and brush a very thin coating of olive oil over the entire pizza. (Some places in Rome paint the hot pizza rossa with a final thin coat of tomato sauce.) Let it cool for a couple of minutes, then use your hands to peel the parchment paper from the bottom of the crust. Serve warm, or later at room temperature.

NEW YORK CHEESE PIZZA

Think of this as the home kitchen version of a classic New York slice pizza. One of my favorites is at NY Pizza Suprema on 8th Avenue, just around the corner from Penn Station. A New York cheese pizza for slices is 18 inches in diameter or even a little larger—much too big to fit in a home oven. Our home kitchen version is about 12 inches. The good news is that we are baking at close to the same temperature as the real deal, and with a baking steel or stone, you can get a similar texture as well.

I have a specific dough for this pizza using high-protein bread flour and 64 percent hydration (see page 52)—most of the other dough recipes in this book are higher hydration and use 00 or all-purpose flours with moderate protein. This dough is easiest to make with a mixer instead of by hand. The stiffer dough gives a crisp crust that won't sag (unless you put too much sauce on the pie). New York–style tomato sauce is a little bit sweet, and it's precooked. This isn't how I usually like to make a pizza sauce—I like a fresh sauce that cooks while the pizza bakes in the oven—but it's characteristic of the style. Low-moisture, whole-milk mozzarella is an absolute must for this pizza to get the stretchy, stringy, semi-melted gooey cheese texture that holds its heat and integrity for a long time. Don't burn the roof of your mouth!

For a very crisp dough with zero tip-sag, bake this pizza, without using the broiler at the end of the cycle, for about 9 or 10 minutes, until the crust is golden brown with spots of dark brown. Or you can bake it the same as other pizzas in this book, with 5 minutes at 550°F (290°C) and then 2 minutes on broil, and get a crust that is still crisp but a little softer in the middle and easier to fold.

MAKES one 12-inch pizza

1 dough ball from 48- to 72-Hour New York Pizza Dough (page 124)

100 grams (⅓ cup plus 1 teaspoon) New York Pizza Sauce (page 148)

10 to 15 grams (scant ¼ cup) grated Pecorino Romano or Grana Padano cheese

110 grams (3½ ounces) low-moisture mozzarella cheese, sliced or shredded with a box grater

Chile flakes (optional)

Dried oregano (optional)

1   Remove your dough ball from the refrigerator about 60 to 90 minutes before baking pizza. Put your pizza steel or stone on an upper rack in your oven no more than 8 inches below the broiler. Preheat the oven to 550°F (290°C) for 45 minutes.

CONTINUED

NEW YORK CHEESE PIZZA, CONTINUED

2 Set up your pizza assembly station. Give yourself about 2 feet of width on the countertop. Moderately flour the work surface. Position your wooden peel next to the floured area and dust it lightly with flour. Have the sauce and cheeses at hand, plus a ladle or large spoon for the sauce. Switch the oven to broil 5 minutes before loading the pizza.

3 To shape the pizza, put the dough ball on the floured work surface and flip to coat both sides moderately with flour. Use the shaping method for New York–style pizza shown on pages 92 to 95; create a narrower rim of the dough than for Neapolitan pizza.

Transfer the disk of pizza dough to a lightly flour-dusted wooden peel. Run your hands around the perimeter to relax it and work out the kinks.

4 Spread the tomato sauce over the dough to within ¼ inch of the edge, smoothing and spreading it with the back of the spoon or ladle. Sprinkle the grated pecorino evenly over the sauce. Layer the grated mozzarella evenly over the pizza.

5 Turn off the broiler, then gently slide the pizza onto the pizza stone. Close the oven door and change the oven setting to bake at 550°F (287°C). Bake for 9 or 10 minutes, until the rim is golden brown. Serve sliced into quarters. Have dried oregano and chile flakes on hand for topping, if desired.

SIMPLE TOMATO PIE

There is something fun about pizza made from a very thin crust, simply because you get to eat more slices before you fill up. More is better, right?! This sheet-pan pie resembles bar pizza, except it's rectangular instead of round, and like Trenton tomato pies and many Grandma pies, the dough is topped first with cheese and then tomato sauce.

Feel free to make up your own cheese combination for this pie. I like a blend of grated low-moisture whole-milk mozzarella with slices of fresh mozzarella, with some grated hard cheese underneath as usual. The flavor of the blended mozzarellas is creamy yet savory, and it has a nice string-cheese stretchiness when you pull a slice away from the pie.

Use a rolling pin for this pizza dough and form it to fit a half sheet pan, or most of it. To keep the dough from sticking to the pan, you need to give the pan a light coating of olive oil or other fat first, or line the pan with parchment paper. This recipe uses the same dough balls that are used to make Neapolitan or New York–style pizzas. Use plenty of flour on both sides of the dough when rolling it out so it doesn't stick to the rolling pin or the countertop.

MAKES one half sheet pan pizza

1 dough ball

20 grams (⅓ cup) grated Pecorino Romano or Grana Padano cheese

75 grams (2½ ounces) low-moisture mozzarella, grated through a box grater's large holes

125 grams (4½ ounces) *fior di latte* fresh mozzarella, thinly sliced

225 grams (¾ cup plus 4 teaspoons) tomato sauce

Chile flakes

1   If you use a dough recipe that calls for refrigeration, remove your dough ball from the refrigerator about 60 to 90 minutes before baking pizza. Put your pizza steel or stone on an upper rack in your oven, about 8 inches below the broiler. Preheat the oven to 550°F (290°C) for at least 45 minutes.

2   Use your hand to apply a thin film of olive oil evenly on the bottom and inside rims of a half sheet pan, or line it with parchment paper (but not both). Moderately flour an expanse of smooth countertop surface and, with a rolling pin, roll the dough out in a rectangular shape that approximates the shape of the sheet pan (be generous with the flour). Do this in two stages, first running the pin over the dough's edges and working it outward until it resists further stretching. Let it rest for 5 to 10 minutes. Then lightly

CONTINUED

SIMPLE TOMATO PIE, CONTINUED

dust both sides of the dough and finish rolling it out to a more exact sheet-pan shape. You can pick up the dough and use your fists to stretch it as you would a round Neapolitan or New York–style pizza, except in the shape of a rectangular pan. Don't stress about fitting the pan exactly. Some doughs, like the New York dough, are naturally stiffer and resistant to rolling out completely to the dimensions of the pan. Switch the oven to broil 10 minutes before loading the pizza.

3 Pick up the rolled-out dough and place it on the oiled or parchment-lined pan. Smooth out the dough, spreading it to the shape of the pan. Spread the grated Pecorino Romano evenly over the pizza, then top with the two mozzarellas, then with the sauce.

4 Turn off the broiler and place the pizza on the preheated pizza steel or stone. Change the oven setting to bake at 550°F (290°C) and bake the tomato pie for about 12 to 14 minutes. Check progress at 8 to 10 minutes and rotate your pan if one side is baking faster than the other. Slice into squares and serve, passing the chile flakes at the table. Put a quarter in the juke, select James Brown's "I Feel Good," and pour yourself a sudsy glass of beer.

MEATBALL PIZZA

I like a garlicky, moist meatball that can handle extended cooking or baking without drying out. A standard trick to keep them moist is to add bread crumbs soaked in milk to the mix, along with eggs as a binder. Parmigiano-Reggiano cheese and chopped garlic are typical as well, and I've added a fistful of chopped parsley both for the green contrast and because it tastes good.

If you're going to go to the trouble to make meatballs, it seems a shame to make up a small batch. My base meatball recipe makes twenty-six to twenty-eight 2-inch meatballs, but sometimes my enthusiasm goes wild and they become comically large for a pizza. And that's just fine with me. You only need four meatballs, cut in half, for one pizza of the size we make in the home kitchen oven, so you might want to halve this recipe. Better yet, invite a crowd and make pizza *and* spaghetti and meatballs. Pour lots of red wine. You can also use the meatballs for a Grandma pie on a half sheet pan, which would use up about twelve halved meatballs.

For meatball pizza, bake the meatballs in an ovenproof skillet (I can fit fourteen in one 9-inch skillet) while the oven is warming up. Then, after they have cooled slightly, slice them in half. Placing meatballs cut side down is essential to making sure they hold their position and don't roll around when you scooch the pizza into your oven. Round meatballs have poor directional sense.

MAKES one 12-inch pizza

1 dough ball

4 meatballs (recipe follows), sliced in half

90 grams (⅓ cup) tomato sauce

15 grams (¼ cup) grated Pecorino Romano or Grana Padano cheese

90 grams (3 ounces) low-moisture mozzarella, grated through a box grater's large holes, or fresh mozzarella, thinly sliced

1   If you use a dough recipe that calls for refrigeration, remove your dough ball from the refrigerator about 60 to 90 minutes before baking pizza. Put your pizza steel or stone on an upper rack in your oven no more than 8 inches below the broiler. Preheat the oven to 550°F (290°C) for 45 minutes.

2   Put the meatballs in a skillet and place on a lower oven rack beneath the preheating pizza steel or stone, after the oven has reached temperature. Remove after 10 minutes. The meatballs should be cooked almost completely through. Slice in half once cooled and set aside.

3   Set up your pizza assembly station. Give yourself about 2 feet of width on the countertop. Moderately flour the work surface. Position your wooden peel next to the floured area and dust it lightly with flour. Have the sauce, cheeses, and sliced meatballs at hand, plus a ladle or large spoon for the sauce. Switch the oven to broil 10 minutes before loading the pizza.

CONTINUED

4 To shape the pizza, put the dough ball on the floured work surface and flip to coat both sides moderately with flour. Use one of the shaping methods (New York or Neapolitan) shown on pages 92 to 95. Transfer the disk of pizza dough to the peel. Run your hands around the perimeter to relax it and work out the kinks.

5 Spread the tomato sauce over the dough to within ¼ inch of the edge, smoothing it with the back of the spoon or ladle. Place the 8 meatball halves cut side down on top of the sauce. Sprinkle the grated pecorino cheese evenly over the meatballs and sauce. Spread the grated mozzarella evenly over the pizza.

6 Turn off the broiler, then gently slide the pizza onto the pizza steel or stone. Close the oven door and change the oven setting to bake at 550°F (290°C). Bake for 5 minutes, until the rim is golden. Change the oven setting from bake to broil and let the pizza finish until the cheese is melted and the crust is golden with spots of brown and a few small spots of char, about 2 minutes (check it after 1 minute to be safe). Use tongs or a fork to slide the pizza from the pizza steel or stone onto a large plate. Serve halved or sliced.

MEATBALLS

MAKES 26 to 28 (60-gram/2-ounce) meatballs

110 grams (1 cup) bread crumbs

185 grams (¾ cup) whole milk

450 grams (1 pound) ground pork

450 grams (1 pound) ground beef
(burger grind, not lean)

2 eggs

5 large cloves garlic (about 25 grams), chopped

40 grams (1 cup) chopped parsley

50 grams (½ cup) grated Parmigiano-Reggiano
or Grana Padano cheese

6 grams (1 teaspoon) fine sea salt

Cracked black pepper

1 Soak the bread crumbs in the milk for 10 minutes, then drain off any excess milk. In a large mixing bowl, combine all the ingredients and mix by hand (you can use vinyl kitchen gloves if you have them) until completely combined, but do not overmix.

2 Shape the meatballs by scooping 60 grams of the meat mixture into the cup of your nondominant hand. Use the palm of your dominant hand to shape each meatball, going in a circular motion and pressing down slightly. The meatballs will have a diameter of approximately 2 inches. Cook as desired, or freeze for longer storage.

A.J.'S PIE

Rubirosa on Mulberry Street in Manhattan's SoHo makes one of my favorite New York pizzas, on a very thin, crisp crust reminiscent of those at Roman pizzerias. My first pizza at Rubirosa, "The Classic," hooked me for good. It is just tomato sauce and cheese. The crust is so thin that I can eat a whole pie without feeling completely stuffed, and usually the more bites of pizza I can eat, the happier I am. I was going to meet the owner, A.J. Pappalardo, for a beer on a subsequent visit, but tragically he passed suddenly the week before I returned to New York. This is for you, A.J. I hope it does you proud.

This thin-crust pizza is smaller—about 12 inches in diameter—than the pizza at Rubirosa (which is about 18 inches) so it will fit in the home kitchen oven.

MAKES one 12-inch thin-crust pizza

1 (150-gram) dough ball

110 grams (⅓ cup plus 2 teaspoons) tomato sauce

80 grams (3 ounces) fresh mozzarella, thinly sliced and cut into 1-inch squares

15 grams (¼ cup) Grana Padano cheese, grated

Extra-virgin olive oil

Dried oregano (optional)

Chile flakes (optional)

1 If you use a dough recipe that calls for refrigeration, remove your dough ball from the refrigerator about 60 to 90 minutes before baking pizza. Put your pizza steel or stone on an upper rack in your oven no more than 8 inches below the broiler. Preheat the oven to 550°F (290°C) for 45 minutes.

2 Set up your pizza assembly station. Give yourself about 2 feet of width on the countertop. Moderately flour the work surface. Position your wooden peel next to the floured area and dust it lightly with flour. Have the sauce and cheeses at hand, plus a ladle or large spoon. Switch the oven to broil 10 minutes before loading the pizza.

3 To shape the pizza, put the dough ball on the floured work surface and flip to coat both sides moderately with white flour. Use the Roman-style rolling-pin method on page 96. Transfer the disk of pizza dough to the peel. Run your hands around the perimeter to relax it and work out the kinks.

4 Spread the tomato sauce over the dough almost all the way to the edge, smoothing it with the back of the spoon or ladle. Top with the slices of mozzarella, spacing them evenly around the pizza to form concentric circles. With your fingers, sprinkle the Grana Padano cheese in circles around the mozzarella.

5 Turn off the broiler, then gently slide the pizza onto the pizza steel or stone. Close the oven door and change the oven setting to bake at 550°F (290°C). Bake for 5 minutes, until the rim is golden. Change the oven setting from bake to broil and let the pizza bake until the crust is golden with spots of brown and a few small spots of char, about 1 to 2 minutes (check it after 1 minute to be safe). Use tongs or a fork to slide the pizza from the pizza steel or stone onto a large plate. Drizzle a small amount of aromatic olive oil over the pizza. Serve, sliced into 4 pieces, on a round pizza pan if you have one. Have dried oregano and chile flakes on hand for topping, if desired.

VODKA SAUCE AND SAUSAGE PIZZA

Call it a 1970s throwback if you will, but this works so well on pizza that every time I look at this recipe, I want to drop everything and make it (and sneak a shot of vodka into my diet). Top it with fresh mozzarella (the kind you find wrapped in plastic, not brine-packed *fior di latte*), fennel sausage, and tomato sauce that's blended with vodka and cream; any leftover sauce is great for pasta.

MAKES one 12-inch pizza

1 dough ball

150 grams (5 ounces) link fennel sausage or Italian sausage

90 grams (⅓ cup) Vodka Sauce (page 147)

110 grams (4 ounces) fresh whole-milk mozzarella, thinly sliced

4 or 5 basil leaves

1   If you use a dough recipe that calls for refrigeration, remove your dough ball from the refrigerator about 60 to 90 minutes before baking pizza. Put your pizza steel or stone on an upper rack in your oven no more than 8 inches below the broiler. Preheat the oven to 550°F (290°C).

2   Cut the link sausage at an angle into ½-inch slices. Place the slices in an ovenproof skillet and, while the oven is preheating, partially cook them for 2 to 3 minutes (they will finish cooking on the pizza).

3   Set up your pizza assembly station. Give yourself about 2 feet of width on the countertop. Moderately flour the work surface. Position your wooden peel next to the floured area and dust it lightly with flour. Have the sauce, cheese, and sausage at hand, plus a ladle or large spoon for the sauce. Switch the oven to broil 10 minutes before loading the pizza.

4   To shape the pizza, put the dough ball on the floured work surface and flip to coat both sides with flour. Use one of the shaping methods (New York or Neapolitan) on pages 92 to 95. Transfer the disk of pizza dough to the peel. Run your hands around the perimeter to relax it and work out the kinks.

5   Spread the tomato sauce over the dough to within ¼ inch of the edge, smoothing it with the back of the spoon or ladle. Place the sausage link pieces cut side down on top of the sauce. Layer the sliced mozzarella over the pizza, draping some of it over the sausage.

6   Turn off the broiler, then gently slide the pizza onto the pizza steel or stone. Close the oven door and change the oven setting to bake at 550°F (290°C). Bake for 5 minutes, until the rim is golden. Change the oven setting from bake to broil and let the pizza cook until the cheese is melted and the crust is golden with spots of brown and a few small spots of char, about 2 minutes (check it after 1 minute to be safe). Use tongs or a fork to slide the pizza from the pizza steel or stone onto a large plate. Use scissors to cut the basil leaves over the top of the pizza and serve immediately, halved or sliced.

BROOKLYN HOT HONEY PIE

Paulie Gee's pizzeria in the Greenpoint neighborhood of Brooklyn, New York, has a beautiful Stefano Ferrara wood-fired oven turning out fantastic pizzas every night. Paulie's ingredient combinations are sometimes classic and sometimes unique, with clever names like "Feel Like Bacon Love." Paulie uses Mike's Hot Honey on his "Hellboy" pizza, which inspired this recipe: a simple tomato-cheese pizza topped with coppa and a drizzle of honey (don't go overboard) after it comes out of the oven. If you have pickled onions handy, slice them and bake them on top of the cheese. The onions, the chile flakes, and the honey turn this otherwise conventional pizza into disco night. The trick when using these assertive flavors is to moderate and keep them in balance.

MAKES one 12-inch pizza

1 dough ball

90 grams (3 ounces) low-moisture whole-milk mozzarella

15 to 20 grams (¼ to ⅓ cup) Pecorino Romano cheese

100 grams (⅓ cup plus 1 teaspoon) tomato sauce

20 grams (⅔ ounce) Quick Pickled Onions (recipe follows; optional)

35 grams (1¼ ounces) coppa or prosciutto, thinly sliced

A drizzle of honey

Chile flakes

1   If you use a dough recipe that calls for refrigeration, remove your dough ball from the refrigerator about 60 to 90 minutes before baking pizza. Put your pizza stone on an upper rack in your oven no more than 8 inches below the broiler. Preheat the oven to 550°F (290°C) for 45 minutes.

2   Use a box grater's large holes to grate the mozzarella. Use the grater's smaller holes to grate the Pecorino Romano cheese.

3   Set up your pizza assembly station. Give yourself about 2 feet of width on the countertop. Moderately flour the work surface. Position your wooden peel next to the floured area and dust it lightly with flour. Have the sauce, cheese, onions, coppa, and honey at hand. Switch the oven to broil 10 minutes before loading the pizza.

4   To shape the pizza, put the dough ball on the floured work surface and flip to coat both sides moderately with white flour. Use one of the shaping methods (New York or Neapolitan) shown on pages 92 to 95. Transfer the disk of pizza dough to the peel. Run your hands around the perimeter to relax it and work out the kinks.

5   Top the pizza dough with the tomato sauce, then the grated pecorino, followed by the grated mozzarella. Layer the pickled onions evenly over the mozzarella. Turn off the broiler, then gently slide the pizza onto the pizza stone. Close the oven door and

CONTINUED

change the oven setting to bake at 550°F (290°C). Bake for 5 minutes, until the rim is golden. Change the oven setting from bake to broil and let the pizza cook until the cheese is melted and the crust is golden with spots of brown and a few small spots of char, about 1 more minute. Use tongs or a fork to slide the pizza from the pizza steel or stone onto a large plate. Top the hot pizza with a layering of the coppa and then drizzle lightly with honey. Serve whole or sliced with chile flakes as a condiment.

QUICK PICKLED ONIONS

MAKES enough for 4 to 5 pizzas

1½ red, yellow, or white onions, thinly sliced

240 grams (1 cup) vinegar

235 grams (1 cup) water

1½ cloves garlic

1 gram (½ teaspoon) mustard seed

½ dried hot chile

1 gram (½ teaspoon) dill seed

35 grams (2 tablespoons) salt

1   Pack the sliced onions into one 16-ounce glass jar. Combine the remaining ingredients in a pot and bring to a boil over high heat. Pour the hot brine over the onions, covering them completely.

2   Refrigerate overnight before using; this will hold in the fridge for several weeks.

PEPPERONI, MUSHROOM, AND ONION PIZZA

You really don't need me to tell you to put pepperoni on a pizza, but I'm going to throw down this one—a much better home version of the pizza you might have ordered for delivery had you not bought this book. Once you make this pizza, you're going to start keeping a stash of pizza shells ("shell" is industry speak for parbaked crust) in your freezer. (See the dough recipes for the answer to the question, "Why make three dough balls when I want just one pizza?")

Pizzas made with a parbaked crust have their own reason for existence beyond giving you something useful to do with unbaked dough balls. They are crisper and crunchier than the standard pizza dough that is sauced and topped raw; you might enjoy it just for its texture. I love the crunch of the rim when my mezzaluna or pizza wheel slices through this crust.

This is totally a Sunday football pizza. (Or a Tuesday night baseball game pizza, for that matter.) And, of course, you can put olives, pickled jalapeño peppers, red bell peppers, or sausage on it and turn it into Uncle Louie's Final Feast pizza, if that's what thrills you. The parbaked crust, even though it is light, has more structure to handle a heavier hand with sauce and toppings.

You can parbake the crust and immediately top it while it's still warm, then bake it to finish; you can parbake an hour ahead of time; or you can parbake unused dough balls, then wrap and freeze for later use. The frozen shell can thaw while your oven is preheating.

MAKES one 12-inch pizza

1 dough ball

15 grams (1 tablespoon) extra-virgin olive oil

4 medium button mushrooms, thinly sliced and lightly coated in 1 tablespoon olive oil

1 clove garlic, chopped

Fine sea salt

110 grams (⅓ cup plus 2 teaspoons) tomato sauce

10 to 15 grams (scant ¼ cup) Pecorino Romano or Parmigiano-Reggiano cheese, grated

110 grams (3½ ounces) fresh mozzarella, thinly sliced, or low-moisture whole-milk mozzarella cheese, shredded with a box grater

16 thin slices pepperoni

¼ red onion, thinly sliced and tossed in olive oil

Chile flakes (optional)

Dried oregano (optional)

1 If you use a dough recipe that calls for refrigeration, remove your dough ball from the refrigerator about 60 to 90 minutes before baking pizza. Put your pizza steel or stone on an upper rack in your oven no more than 8 inches below the broiler. Preheat the oven to 550°F (290°C) for 45 minutes.

2 In a sauté pan over medium heat, heat 1 tablespoon of the olive oil and sauté the mushrooms and garlic with a pinch of salt until the garlic is translucent, not browned.

CONTINUED

PEPPERONI, MUSHROOM, AND ONION PIZZA, CONTINUED

3 Set up your pizza assembly station. Give yourself about 2 feet of width on the countertop. Moderately flour the work surface. Position your wooden peel next to the floured area and dust it lightly with flour. Have the sauce, cheeses, and toppings at hand, plus a ladle or large spoon for the sauce. Switch the oven to broil 5 minutes before loading the pizza.

4 To shape the pizza, put the dough ball on the floured work surface and flip to coat both sides moderately with white flour. Use one of the shaping methods (Neapolitan or New York) shown on pages 92 to 95. Transfer the disk of pizza dough to the peel. Run your hands around the perimeter to relax it and work out the kinks.

5 To parbake the pizza crust, top the pizza dough with about half of the tomato sauce. Turn off the broiler, then gently slide the pizza onto the pizza steel or stone. Close the oven door and change the oven setting to bake at 550°F (290°C). Bake for 3 minutes, change the oven setting to broil, and remove the parbaked crust after 1 minute more. Keep the oven on broil if you are going to make pizza right away.

6 Spread the remaining half of the tomato sauce over the dough to within ¼ inch of the edge, smoothing it with the back of the spoon or ladle. Sprinkle the grated pecorino cheese evenly over the sauce. Layer the mozzarella evenly over the pizza. Top with the sautéed mushrooms, pepperoni, and onions. Turn off the broiler, then gently place the pizza onto the pizza steel or stone (with parbaked pizza you can place it with your hands). Close the oven door and change the oven setting to bake at 550°F (290°C). Bake for 4 minutes, until the cheese is partially melted and the crust is golden.

7 Change the oven setting from bake to broil and let the pizza bake until the cheese is fully melted and the crust is golden with spots of brown and a few small spots of char, about 2 minutes (check it after 1 minute to be safe). Use tongs or a fork to slide the pizza from the pizza steel or stone onto a large plate. Serve sliced, with chile flakes and dried oregano on hand.

GRANDMA PIE

This recipe uses parbaking, a two-stage process that bakes tomato sauce and olive oil into the dough in the first stage, then adds more sauce and cheese for the second-stage bake. Some people like sauce on top of the cheese, others like the cheese on top. I like it both ways. Buddy's pizza in Detroit puts cheese, then sauce, then cheese again on their pies. Yahtzee! Start with the Saturday Pan Pizza Dough on page 116, then segue into this recipe.

I got the idea for the two-stage bake after talking with Brandon Pettit of Seattle's Delancey. He told me about how he would use a double baking process for a thickish crust pan pizza—it works well in a short-order cooking situation, late night at a bar. I like it for how it allows for easy final assembly and baking. I also think the caramelized tomato sauce from the first-stage bake adds another deep dimension of tomato flavor. Thanks, Brandon!

The tomato and olive oil from the first bake soak into the dough; the simplest version of this pie is to do the final bake with just another layer of tomato, a sprinkling of dried oregano and sea salt, and finished with a brush of olive oil (this would be a Tomato Pie in Pennsylvania).

This pizza is easy and extremely delicious. Serve it with some simple vegetables and red wine. Consider this a platform for wherever your inspiration leads you: go crazy with toppings of your choice or go basic and top each slice with a nice basil leaf after it has baked. My no-brainer is to load it with medium-thick slices of salami—the kind where each slice turns into little cups when it bakes. In summer, I try cherry tomatoes with garlic and summer squash or zucchini (all tossed in oil) and some crispy diced salami. In Maryland I might use blue crab and tomato sauce with fresh corn, then season it with Old Bay and bake a few claws on the pie 'cause why not. Or I can easily imagine a version of eggplant Parmesan on the pizza, with thin slices of grilled eggplant with fresh mozzarella, tomato sauce, and basil, and maybe some Calabrian chiles for flavor, heat, and color.

MAKES one half sheet pan pizza

Saturday Pan Pizza Dough, page 116, parbaked

150 grams (½ cup) tomato sauce

50 grams (½ cup) Parmigiano-Reggiano or Grana Padano cheese, grated

150 grams (5 ounces) low-moisture mozzarella, grated

125 grams (4 ounces) fresh mozzarella, thinly sliced

30 grams (2 tablespoons) olive oil

10 to 12 fresh basil leaves

Other toppings of your choice (optional)

1   Put your pizza steel or stone on a middle rack in your oven. Preheat the oven to 550°F (290°C) for at least 45 minutes. Switch the oven to broil 5 minutes before loading the pizza.

2   Place the parbaked dough on a dry or very lightly oiled half sheet pan. Spread the sauce over the pizza

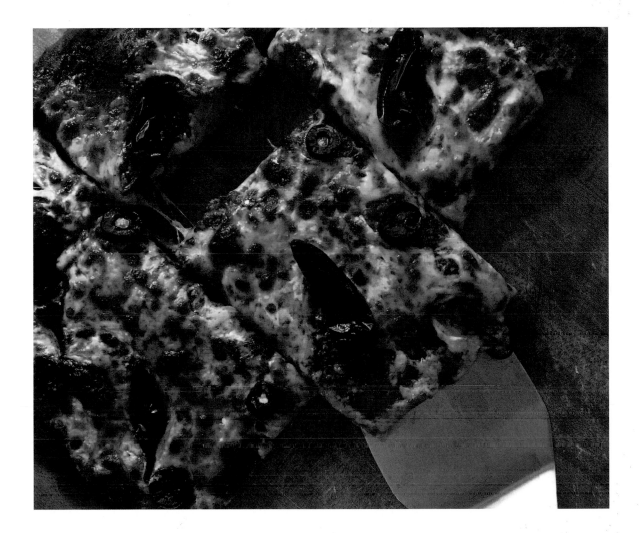

with the back of a spoon, then top with the grated hard cheese followed by the grated mozzarella. Top with the sliced mozzarella and any other toppings you choose.

3 Turn off the broiler. Place the pizza pan on the pre-heated pizza steel or stone. Change the oven setting to bake at 550°F (290°C), and bake for 10 minutes. Change the oven setting from bake to broil and let the pizza finish baking until the cheese is melted and the crust is golden with spots of brown and a few small spots of dark brown, about 2 minutes (check it after 1 minute to be safe). Top with the olive oil and fresh basil, slice into squares, and serve.

ADAM KUBAN'S "LOVE SUPREME" BAR PIZZA

A bar-style pizza bakes in a pan, which gives it its signature perfectly circular shape and cheesy edges. Adam uses Lloyd Pans' preseasoned nonstick 12-inch nesting deep-dish pizza pans, which can be found online. The pans that have perforated bottoms are cool because they allow the crust to get especially crispy, and don't require you to finish directly on the baking steel—a sometimes smoky proposition if the cheese on the rim leaks down the side. (But man, that cheese on the rim gets crisp and packs a punch of baked-cheese flavor that is essential to the goodness of this pie.) If you don't have a deep-dish pan, try a 10-inch cast-iron skillet; you'll have to reduce the weight of the dough ball to closer to 160 grams, though.

A bar pizza is decidedly old-school in style, so the toppings here are similarly iconic, what Adam thinks of as the "supreme pizza" combo—green pepper, red onion, and fennel sausage.

MAKES one 12-inch bar pizza

1 dough ball from Bar Pizza Dough (page 136)

90 grams (⅓ cup) tomato sauce

25 grams (⅓ cup) Pecorino Romano, finely grated

55 grams (2 ounces) mild white cheddar, coarsely grated

135 grams (4½ ounces) low-moisture whole-milk mozzarella, coarsely grated

½ small green bell pepper, diced

½ small red onion, sliced into thin semicircles

60 grams (2 ounces) loose Italian sausage

1 Remove your dough ball from the refrigerator about 60 to 90 minutes before baking pizza. Put your pizza steel or stone on the middle rack of your oven (not the top rack). Preheat the oven to 550°F (290°C) for 45 minutes.

2 When the dough ball reaches room temperature, remove the plastic wrap and flour both sides of the dough ball and your countertop where you will roll it out. Working to maintain the dough's circular shape, flatten it with your hand until it's about ½ inch thick. Sprinkle more flour on top and roll out with a rolling pin. Add more flour to the work surface and dough as needed to keep it from sticking. Occasionally flip the dough and rotate a quarter turn to help maintain the circular shape. When the dough resists, you will need to let it relax for 5 to 10 minutes.

3 Lift the dough from the work surface and drape it over the backs of the knuckles of both hands, passing it from hand to hand in a clockwise motion. This has the added benefit of helping shed any excess flour. Don't worry if you end up stretching the dough a little too big for the pan; if you stretch it just right, it will snap back to the correct size. If it's too small, let it rest in the pan until it relaxes, about 5 minutes, then press it out to the edges.

4 Set up your pizza assembly station. Give yourself about 2 feet of width on the countertop. Moderately flour the work surface. Have the sauce, cheeses,

CONTINUED

ADAM KUBAN'S "LOVE SUPREME" BAR PIZZA, CONTINUED

pepper, onion, and sausage prepared and at hand, plus a ladle or large spoon for the sauce.

5   Spread the tomato sauce over the dough to within ½ inch of the edge, smoothing and spreading it with the back of the spoon or ladle in a circular motion from the center out. Sprinkle the pecorino over the bare dough along the edge of the pan as well as across the sauce. Line the outer edge of the pan with the shredded white cheddar. Cover the sauce with the shredded mozzarella. Top with the diced green pepper, onion, and sausage. Place the pan on the preheated steel or stone in your oven. Bake at 550°F (290°C) until the cheese is bubbling and beginning to turn golden brown and the edges of the pizza have pulled away from the pan, about 9 minutes.

6   At this point you have two options: bake 1 to 2 minutes more in the pan, until the bottom is golden brown with some darker spots. Or, alternatively, you can finish the pizza directly on the pizza steel or stone to get an added degree of crispness (but beware, it might smoke a bit). To do this, run a spatula (a fish turner is ideal) along the inner edge of the pan to dislodge any cheese, and then gently lift the pizza and slide it onto a pizza peel. Transfer the pizza from the peel back onto the baking steel or stone. Cook until the bottom is golden brown with some darker spots and crisp, 1 to 2 minutes. Use a pair of tongs or a peel to remove the pizza from the steel or stone onto a round pizza tray. Slice into 6 pieces and serve.

MARGHERITA AND ARUGULA, TWO WAYS

The three most popular pizzas on the menu at Ken's Artisan Pizza (KAP) since we opened in 2006 have been Margherita, Margherita with Arugula, and Soppressata pizzas. For the Margherita with Arugula, we dress about 2 ounces of fresh arugula with a very thin coating of olive oil and a light sprinkling of sea salt, then top the pizza with the greens right after it comes out of the oven. The arugula has a peppery, slightly nutty, fresh green flavor and first-timers always raise their eyebrows at the big pile of greens on top of their pie (and I can read their thought bubble: "WTF, salad on my pizza?"). We offer arugula as an add-on to any one of the KAP pies, and in time the Soppressata pizza with added arugula has become a frequent insiders' choice. Many people have been coming for years and order this every single time. We love these folks.

I like it best when I fold a slice of this pizza, enveloping the arugula. But you could have way more fun than that if you fold the *entire* pizza after dressing it with the arugula. Folding the pizza in half utterly changes the whole thing. The heat wilts the arugula and the pie stays hot for a long time, insulated by crust on both the top and the bottom. Folding it requires a large chef's knife or a mezzaluna to set the fold point across the middle of the crust, much like the perforation on a piece of paper. This recipe gives you the option of making either the straight-up Margherita with Arugula or the Soppressata version, folded or flat.

This one has *fior di latte* mozzarella on the pizza for the entire bake, giving it a molten-lava effect, which wilts the arugula beautifully. It's a good way for you to see the difference in how cheese melts with a longer baking time compared with the alternative method of baking without the cheese for several minutes, then adding the cheese for the end of the bake (see Pizza Margherita recipe, page 153).

MAKES one 12-inch pizza

1 dough ball

90 grams (⅓ cup) tomato sauce

10 to 15 grams (scant ¼ cup) grated Pecorino Romano or Parmigiano-Reggiano cheese

110 grams (3½ ounces) fresh mozzarella cheese (*fior di latte*), cut into pieces ¼ to ½ inch thick, or thin strips

15 to 18 thin slices *soppressata*, about 2 inches in diameter (optional)

60 grams (2 ounces) arugula

Extra-virgin olive oil

1 lemon wedge (optional)

Fine sea salt

1 If you use a dough recipe that calls for refrigeration, remove your dough ball from the refrigerator about 60 to 90 minutes before baking pizza. Put your pizza steel or stone on an upper rack in your oven no more than 8 inches below the broiler. Preheat the oven to 550°F (290°C) for 45 minutes.

CONTINUED

MARGHERITA AND ARUGULA, TWO WAYS, CONTINUED

2 Set up your pizza assembly station. Give yourself about 2 feet of width on the countertop. Moderately flour the work surface. Position your wooden peel next to the floured area and dust it lightly with flour. Have the sauce, cheeses, *soppressata* (if desired), and arugula at hand, with a ladle or large spoon for the sauce. Switch the oven to broil 10 minutes before loading the pizza.

3 To shape the pizza, put the dough ball on the floured work surface, and flip to coat both sides moderately with flour. Use one of the shaping methods (Neapolitan or New York) shown on pages 92 to 95. Transfer the disk of pizza dough to the peel. Run your hands around the perimeter to relax it and work out the kinks.

4 Spread the tomato sauce over the dough to within ½ inch of the edge, smoothing it with the back of the spoon or ladle. Sprinkle the grated hard cheese evenly over the sauce. Layer the sliced mozzarella evenly over the pizza. If you're using the *soppressata*, evenly spread the slices over the cheese. Turn off the broiler, then gently slide the pizza onto the pizza stone. Close the oven door and change the oven setting to bake at 550°F (290°C). Bake for 5 minutes, until the rim is golden.

5 While the pizza is baking, toss the arugula by hand in a mixing bowl with just enough olive oil to coat, a spritz of lemon if you like, and a light sprinkling of salt.

6 Change the oven setting from bake to broil and let the pizza finish until the cheese is melted and the crust is golden with spots of brown and a few small spots of char, about 2 minutes (check it after 1 minute to be sure). Use tongs or a fork to slide the pizza from the pizza steel or stone onto a large plate. Immediately after the pizza is removed from the oven, top it with the arugula. Serve sliced into quarters.

VARIATION To fold the pizza, top it with the dressed arugula and place it on a large cutting board. Set the fold point across the middle of the pizza with a large chef's knife or mezzaluna. Press the blade into the pizza, but do not cut all the way through; just go far enough so that when you fold the pizza, this fold point is established. Fold the pizza in half along the perforation you just made to make a half-moon shape. Cut the folded pizza in half, perpendicular to the fold line, and serve immediately.

ARRABIATA PIZZA

My professional pizza life began in 2005 at Ken's Artisan Bakery, when we opened up the bakery's cafe for pizza one night each week and called it Monday Night Pizza. We baked pizzas in our bread oven at about 525°F (275°C) and served Caesar salad, beer, and wine, with ice cream for dessert. One night that summer, careless planning on my part led to our just having a few pizzas on the menu. Needing at least one more pie on the list, I looked around, found a jar of hot peppers that belonged to our dishwasher, and thought, "*arrabiata pizza*." Ten years later, at Ken's Artisan Pizza, we are still serving this spicy bomb of a pie, and it remains one of my favorites.

You can channel your inner Calabrese here using Calabrian chile peppers—which we like for both their heat and their flavor—or you can substitute any other hot pepper you enjoy. We use Tutto Calabria brand "Hot Long Chili Peppers," which come packed in oil, vinegar, and salt. Fresh, hot chile peppers are a great alternative in their late summer to autumn season. When you handle them, don't touch your eyes or other body parts until you wash the oils off your fingers! Enjoy this pizza with any rustic red wine from the south of Italy or with ice-cold beer like Tecate. (Yes, Mexican beer with spicy-hot pizza is a great match.)

MAKES one 12-inch pizza

1 dough ball

90 grams (⅓ cup) tomato sauce

10 to 15 grams (scant ¼ cup) Pecorino Romano or Grana Padano cheese, grated

90 grams (3½ ounces) fresh whole-milk mozzarella cheese (*fior di latte*), cut into ¼-inch-thick pieces or thin strips

10 grams (⅓ ounce) jarred whole chile peppers, stemmed, seeded, and sliced

4 or 5 whole basil leaves

Extra-virgin olive oil

1   If you use a dough recipe that calls for refrigeration, remove your dough ball from the refrigerator about 60 to 90 minutes before baking pizza. Put your pizza steel or stone on an upper rack in your oven no more than 8 inches below the broiler. Preheat the oven to 550°F (290°C) for 45 minutes.

2   Set up your pizza assembly station. Give yourself about 2 feet of width on the countertop. Moderately flour the work surface. Position your wooden peel next to the floured area and dust it lightly with flour. Have the sauce, cheeses, peppers, and basil at hand, with a ladle or large spoon for the sauce. Switch the oven to broil 10 minutes before loading the pizza.

3   To shape the pizza, put the dough ball on the floured work surface and flip to coat both sides moderately with flour. Use one of the shaping methods (Neapolitan or New York) shown on pages 92 to 95. Transfer the disk of pizza dough to the peel. Run your hands around the perimeter to relax it and work out the kinks.

4   Spread the tomato sauce over the dough to within ½ inch of the edge, smoothing it with the back of the spoon or ladle. Sprinkle the grated hard cheese evenly over the sauce. Layer the sliced mozzarella evenly over the pizza. Top with the chiles and basil leaves and drizzle olive oil in a few stripes over the pizza.

5   Turn off the broiler, then gently slide the pizza onto the pizza steel or stone. Close the oven door and change the oven setting to bake at 550°F (290°C). Bake for 5 minutes, until the rim is golden. Change the oven setting from bake to broil and let the pizza finish until the cheese is melted and the crust is golden with spots of brown and a few small spots of char, about 2 minutes (check it after 1 minute to be sure). Use tongs or a fork to slide the pizza from the pizza steel or stone onto a large plate. Serve sliced.

PROSCIUTTO PIZZA

This pizza is the favorite of Alan Maniscalco, our chef at Ken's Artisan Pizza. It features Prosciutto di San Daniele, from the town of San Daniele in the steep hill country just south of the Dolomites in northern Italy. I toured one of the San Daniele ham-curing facilities in 2008 and learned that the hams hang and cure for 12 to 24 months in a mix of air from the sea and the mountains, which helps create a very special product. Humidity and temperature controls are set to very specific levels; this particular facility's production manager often sleeps in the curing facility when the weather is changing in order to make overnight adjustments to the flow of outside air. The hams are tested with a narrow piece of horse bone inserted into one of the exposed ham veins, to make sure there is no spoilage. It's a smell test. Literally. If the bone comes out smelling putrid, the ham gets tossed. The cure itself is nothing but pure white coarse sea salt from Sicily, and time.

These carefully tended hams from San Daniele have a beautifully sweet ham flavor. We slice the prosciutto very thin, as is the custom. We lay down about six slices to completely cover the tomato-cheese pizza, then slice the pie and run it quickly to the table. The heat from the just-baked pizza almost melts the prosciutto. It's a wonderful thing. Feel free to substitute *culatello*, Prosciutto di Parma, Serrano ham, *pata negra*, or a good-quality American cured ham.

MAKES one 12-inch pizza

1 dough ball

90 grams (⅓ cup) tomato sauce

110 grams (3½ ounces) fresh whole-milk mozzarella cheese (*fior di latte*), cut into ¼-inch-thick pieces or thin strips

4 or 5 whole leaves fresh basil

55 grams (2 ounces) prosciutto, about 6 very thin slices

Extra-virgin olive oil

1 If you use a dough recipe that calls for refrigeration, remove your dough ball(s) from the refrigerator about 60 to 90 minutes before baking pizza. Put your pizza steel or stone on an upper rack in your oven no more than 8 inches below the broiler. Preheat the oven to 550°F (290°C) for 45 minutes.

2 Set up your pizza assembly station. Give yourself about 2 feet of width on the countertop. Moderately flour the work surface. Position your wooden peel next to the floured area and dust it lightly with flour. Have the sauce, cheese, basil, and sliced prosciutto prepared and at hand, plus a ladle or large spoon for the sauce. Switch the oven to broil 10 minutes before loading the pizza.

3 To shape the pizza, put the dough ball on the floured work surface and flip to coat both sides moderately with flour. Use one of the shaping methods (Neapolitan or New York) shown on pages 92 to 95.

Transfer the disk of pizza dough to the peel. Run your hands around the perimeter to relax it and work out the kinks.

4 Spread the tomato sauce over the dough to within ½ inch of the edge, smoothing it with the back of the spoon or ladle. Layer the sliced mozzarella evenly over the pizza. Top with the basil.

5 Turn off the broiler, then gently slide the pizza onto the pizza stone. Close the oven door and change the oven setting to bake at 550°F (290°C). Bake for 5 minutes, until the rim is golden. Change the oven

setting from bake to broil and let the pizza finish until the cheese is melted and the crust is golden with spots of brown and a few small spots of char, about 2 minutes (check it after 1 minute to be sure). Use tongs or a fork to slide the pizza from the pizza steel or stone onto a large plate. Immediately after the pizza is removed from the oven, top it with the prosciutto, covering the other toppings with prosciutto slices. Serve right away, sliced into quarters.

FENNEL SAUSAGE AND ONION PIZZA

This pie has been on the menu at Ken's Artisan Pizza since we opened. Some like it spicy (me!) and some don't (*what?*), so we offer it with Calabrian chiles as an option for the spice-inclined (yay!).

Making your own loose sausage is so easy. Make up a spice mix (see page 205) and mix 25 grams (about 1 ounce) of it with 450 grams (1 pound) of ground pork. (Note that you'll need only 150 grams/5 ounces for this pizza—eat any leftover loose sausage you make for breakfast!) If you're feeling less ambitious, buy loose sausage at the store, or you can even buy cased sausage (just slice it and use it instead of loose). If you are using fresh chile peppers here rather than jarred, coat the slices in oil to prevent them from scorching in the oven (and don't touch your eyes!).

MAKES one 12-inch pizza

1 dough ball

½ medium yellow onion, thinly sliced

½ tablespoon butter

3 to 4 grams (½ teaspoon) salt

150 grams (5 ounces) loose fennel sausage (see headnote)

90 grams (⅓ cup) tomato sauce

90 grams (3½ ounces) fresh whole-milk mozzarella cheese (*fior di latte),* cut into ¼-inch-thick pieces or thin strips

10 grams (approximately 3) whole jarred chile peppers, stemmed, seeded, and sliced (optional)

6 or 7 whole basil leaves

Extra-virgin olive oil

1   If you use a dough recipe that calls for refrigeration, remove your dough ball from the refrigerator about 60 to 90 minutes before baking pizza.

2   In a skillet over medium-high heat, sauté the onions, butter, and salt, stirring often to prevent sticking. After 5 minutes, reduce the heat to low. Cook for another 20 to 25 minutes, stirring occasionally, making sure to scrape up any dark bits that stick to your pan. Once the onions are soft and completely brown, turn off the heat and set aside.

3   Put your pizza steel or stone on an upper rack in your oven no more than 8 inches below the broiler. Preheat the oven to 550°F (290°C) for 45 minutes.

4 In a 9- or 10-inch skillet over medium heat, cook the sausage until completely cooked, about 5 minutes. (You could also do this in the oven; it will take about 7 or 8 minutes if the oven is at 550°F [290°C].) Let cool and then crumble with your hands.

5 Set up your pizza assembly station. Give yourself about 2 feet of width on the countertop. Moderately flour the work surface. Position your wooden peel next to the floured area and dust it lightly with flour. Have the sauce, cheese, sausage, onions, peppers, and basil prepared and at hand, with a ladle or large spoon for the sauce. Switch the oven to broil 10 minutes before loading the pizza.

6 To shape the pizza, put the dough ball on the floured work surface and flip to coat both sides moderately with flour. Use one of the shaping methods (Neapolitan or New York) shown on pages 92 to 95. Transfer the disk of pizza dough to the peel. Run your hands around the perimeter to relax it and work out the kinks.

7 Spread the tomato sauce over the dough to within ½ inch of the edge, smoothing it with the back of the spoon or ladle. Layer the sliced mozzarella evenly over the pizza. Top with the sausage, caramelized onion, chiles, and basil leaves, and drizzle olive oil in a few stripes over the pizza.

8 Turn off the broiler, then gently slide the pizza onto the pizza stone. Close the oven door and change the oven setting to bake at 550°F (290°C). Bake for 5 minutes, until the rim is golden. Change the oven setting from bake to broil and let the pizza finish until the cheese is melted and the crust is golden with spots of brown and a few small spots of char, about 2 minutes (check it after 1 minute to be sure). Use tongs or a fork to slide the pizza from the pizza steel or stone onto a large plate. Serve sliced.

FENNEL SAUSAGE SPICE MIX

MAKES 110 grams (4 ounces)

40 grams (½ cup) ground fennel seed

30 grams (2 tablespoons) fine sea salt

20 grams (3 tablespoons) ground black pepper

15 grams (1 tablespoon) sugar

5 grams (2 teaspoons) pimentón or ground red pepper

Combine the ingredients in a jar with a lid, stir or shake to combine, and store until ready to use. To make sausage, combine 25 grams (about 1 ounce) of the spice blend with 450 grams (1 pound) of pork. Cook the sausage immediately or store in an airtight container in the refrigerator for a day or two.

SPRING ONION PIZZA

Spring never, ever comes too soon, and we have many regular patrons and staff at Ken's Artisan Pizza who celebrate the arrival of warmer, sunnier weather heralded by this pizza—one of our first harbingers of the new season.

I asked Sheldon Marcuvitz, co-owner of Your Kitchen Garden (a great local farm in Canby, Oregon, that grows vegetables for restaurants), for some help describing just what a spring onion is.

"It is definitely not a bunching onion, which is the same as a scallion; that is, no bulbs," he explained. "[Spring onion] bulbs can be formed to any extent, from barely swelling to full-sized, as long as the top is still attached and green. The barely formed ones are usually quite strong and vegetal tasting, we find; not really sweet and oniony. The flavor develops a lot as the bulb gets close to being fully formed: the water content drops and the sugars build. So, I would say their season is April or May through June and into July."

Spring onions are best found at your local farmers' market, when they will be fresh from the soil. The spring onions we use at my pizzeria still have their dirty roots attached when they are delivered. I love that.

This is a white pizza—that is, with no tomato sauce—and it gets a drape of several very thin slices of prosciutto just after the pizza has come out of the oven. If you want to go meat-free, this pizza works great without prosciutto. In that case, you might want to kick up the spice with some chiles. Note, however, that hot peppers and prosciutto don't make the best pairing. The Spring Onion Pizza with Prosciutto is a staff favorite at my pizzeria.

MAKES one 12-inch pizza

1 dough ball

3 spring onions, including their green stalks

Extra-virgin olive oil

Fine sea salt

90 grams (3½ ounces) fresh whole-milk mozzarella cheese (*fior di latte*), cut into ¼-inch-thick pieces or thin strips

15 grams (¼ cup) Grana Padano cheese, shaved with a peeler

55 grams (2 ounces) prosciutto, in 6 thin slices (optional)

1 If you use a dough recipe that calls for refrigeration, remove your dough ball from the refrigerator about 60 to 90 minutes before baking pizza. Put your pizza steel or stone on an upper rack in your oven no more than 8 inches below the broiler. Preheat the oven to 550°F (290°C) for 45 minutes.

2 Cut the onions about halfway up the stalks, right where they start to turn dark green, and discard the tops. Chop the remaining green stalks into ⅛-inch-thick pieces and set aside. Slice the bulb ends of the onions lengthwise into 4 to 6 slices each. Coat these long onion slices in olive oil, season with a sprinkling of sea salt, and place in a skillet. Sauté over medium heat (or roast in the preheating oven—use an oven-proof skillet) until they just lose their crunch, about 4 to 5 minutes. Remove from the heat and mix with the chopped slices from the stalks. Set aside.

3 Set up your pizza assembly station. Give yourself about 2 feet of width on the countertop. Moderately flour the work surface. Position your wooden peel next to the floured area and dust it lightly with flour. Have the cheeses, onions, and prosciutto (if desired) prepared and at hand. Switch the oven to broil 10 minutes before loading the pizza.

4 To shape the pizza, put the dough ball on the floured work surface and flip to coat both sides moderately with flour. Use one of the shaping methods (Neapolitan or New York) shown on pages 92 to 95. Transfer the disk of pizza dough to the peel. Run your hands around the perimeter to relax it and work out the kinks.

5 Layer the sliced mozzarella evenly over the pizza and cover with the shaved Grana Padano cheese. Top with the onions and drizzle olive oil in a few stripes over the pizza.

6 Turn off the broiler, then gently slide the pizza onto the pizza steel or stone. Close the oven door and change the oven setting to bake at 550°F (290°C). Bake for 5 minutes, until the rim is golden. Change the oven setting from bake to broil and let the pizza finish until the cheese is melted and the crust is golden with spots of brown and a few small spots of char, about 2 minutes (check it after 1 minute to be sure). Use tongs or a fork to slide the pizza from the pizza steel or stone onto a large plate. Immediately after the pizza is removed from the oven, lay the prosciutto slices over the other toppings. Serve right away, sliced.

OREGON BASIL PESTO AND BURRATA FLATBREAD

In addition to Tarte Flambée (page 211), the menu at Trifecta Tavern offers a frequently changing flatbread topped with a rotation of seasonal items, and pestos (not always from basil) often form the base of those toppings. Here in Oregon we like to substitute hazelnuts for the pine nuts used in more traditional pesto.

Trifecta flatbreads are super-thin-crusted snacks more than full meals, intended to be one shared plate among several at a table. Use a pin to roll out the dough and bake like Roman-style pizzas (see page 96). We bake this in our Mugnaini wood-fired oven around 800°F (it works great in the home oven at 550°F (290°C).

It is easiest to parbake this flatbread, as pesto spreads out easier on lightly baked rather than raw dough—we use the back of a large soup spoon to spread the pesto. It also prevents the pesto from becoming overbaked. For the same reason, this flatbread and the Nettle Pesto Flatbread on page 217 are baked for a shorter time than other flatbreads, so you'll have a softer crust, delicate and pliable and bubbly from its parbake.

Burrata is a fresh-milk mozzarella with cream and strings of mozzarella folded into the middle. It comes in a ball that's about baseball-sized or maybe a little smaller, and it's very moist. You want to use it fresh at room temperature (unbaked), and top it on the pizza after it comes out of the oven. It has a very short shelf life, but a good *burrata* is memorable, especially when it comes from water buffalo milk. Some cheese shops carry *burrata* that comes in weekly, fresh from Italy. Gioia Cheese Company in California makes a decent American *burrata*, but it's not really the same as the Italian version. If you can't find *burrata* but you do have a very fresh mozzarella that you like, substitute the mozz. You could also substitute a fresh, soft goat cheese and be happy with this recipe.

Make the pesto while the oven is preheating. The recipe makes more than you will use for a single flatbread: I suggest baking two additional Roman-style flatbreads naked before you parbake the dressed flatbread; they'll each need about 2 minutes on the pizza stone or steel at 550°F (290°C). They will puff up like pita bread, and you can use them as dippers for the remaining pesto. Be happy.

MAKES one 12-inch flatbread

1 (150-gram) dough ball
60 grams (¼ cup) pesto (recipe follows)
1 ball *burrata* cheese
Freshly cracked black pepper

CONTINUED

TARTE FLAMBÉE, CONTINUED

3 Set up your pizza assembly station. Give yourself about 2 feet of width on the countertop. Moderately flour the work surface. Position your wooden peel next to the floured area and dust it lightly with flour. Have the cheese, onions, lardons, and chopped parsley prepared and at hand.

4 To shape the pizza, put the dough ball on the floured work surface and flip to coat both sides moderately with flour. Use the Roman-style rolling-pin method on page 96. Transfer the disk of pizza dough to the peel. Run your hands around the perimeter to relax it and work out the kinks.

5 To parbake the pizza dough, turn off the broiler, then gently slide the pizza onto the pizza steel or stone. Close the oven door and change the oven setting to bake at 550°F (290°C). Bake for just about 45 seconds until the dough is set (and bubbly!) and remove it from the oven.

6 Place blobs of the prepared *fromage blanc* over the parbaked crust and spread it evenly in swipes with the back of a large spoon. Sprinkle the sweated onions and then the lardons over the cheese, and crack a moderate amount of black pepper over the top.

7 Return the pizza to the pizza steel or stone and bake for 5 minutes, until the rim is golden. Change the oven setting from bake to broil and let the pizza finish until the cheese is melted and bubbling and the crust is golden with spots of brown and a few small spots of char, about 2 minutes (check it after 1 minute to be sure). Use tongs or a fork to slide the pizza from the pizza steel or stone onto a large plate. Top with the chopped parsley and serve whole or sliced.

NETTLE PESTO FLATBREAD WITH MOREL MUSHROOMS

In the springtime, stinging nettle grows wild in woods and forests throughout the U.S. and in Europe. At Trifecta Tavern, we buy our nettles from foragers who also bring us wild mushrooms, fiddlehead ferns, and herbs. The nettles need to be handled with gloves to prevent stings from their tiny, needlelike hairs. Blanching them in boiling water very briefly removes the sting, and the nettle becomes a favorite springtime ingredient used in soups, pastas (nettle gnocchi!), and here in a pesto. It has a green, woodsy, nutty character. Nettle is a little grassier tasting than basil, and we prefer to blend nettles with walnuts as opposed to pine nuts or hazelnuts.

Nettles and morel mushrooms have similar seasons. If you can find morels at the farmers' market, or even if you can forage your own, you really should try adding them to this flatbread. If you can't find morels, try chanterelle mushrooms, lightly sautéed with garlic and butter.

This recipe has a little bit of prep to blanch the nettles and make up the nettle pesto and prepare the morels, but it's so worth it. Like the other Trifecta flatbreads, make this in the Roman pizza style with a small dough ball rolled out very thin with a pin. If you can't find nettles, this flatbread would also be delicious with a basil pesto.

Make the pesto and prep the mushrooms while the oven is preheating. The pesto recipe makes more than you will use for a single flatbread. I suggest baking two additional Roman-style flatbreads naked before you parbake the dressed flatbread; they'll each need about 2 minutes on the pizza stone or steel at 550°F (290°C). They will puff up like pita bread, and you can use them as dippers for the remaining pesto. (You could also use the pesto for toasts or bruschetta.)

MAKES one 12-inch flatbread

1 (150-gram) dough ball
60 grams (¼ cup) nettle pesto (recipe follows)
Roasted morel mushrooms (recipe follows)
About 1 tablespoon aromatic olive oil

1   If you use a dough recipe that calls for refrigeration, remove your dough ball from the refrigerator about 60 to 90 minutes before baking flatbread. Put your pizza steel or stone on an upper rack in your oven no more than 8 inches below the broiler. Preheat the oven to 550°F (290°C) for 45 minutes. Switch the oven to broil 10 minutes before loading the flatbread.

2   Set up your flatbread assembly station. Give yourself about 2 feet of width on the countertop. Moderately flour the work surface. Position your wooden peel next to the floured area and dust it lightly with flour. Have the pesto and mushrooms prepared and at hand.

3 To shape the flatbread, put the dough ball on the floured work surface and flip to coat both sides moderately with flour. Use the Roman-style shaping method with a rolling pin on page 96. Transfer the disk of dough to the peel. Run your hands around the perimeter to relax it and work out the kinks.

4 To parbake the dough, turn off the broiler, then gently slide the flatbread onto the pizza steel or stone. Close the oven door and change the oven setting to bake at 550°F (290°C). Bake for just about 45 seconds until the dough is set (and bubbly!) and remove it from the oven.

5 To top the flatbread, use a spoon to place 5 or 6 blobs of the pesto over the parbaked crust; spread it evenly in swipes to cover the entire disk, save for the last ½ inch of the perimeter. Top with the prepared mushrooms.

6 Bake on the pizza steel or stone until the rim is golden with splotches of brown, 3 to 4 minutes. Change the oven setting from bake to broil and let the pizza finish for about 30 seconds until the crust is golden with spots of brown. Use tongs or a fork to slide the pizza from the pizza steel or stone onto a large plate. Drizzle with aromatic olive oil and serve sliced.

CONTINUED

NETTLE PESTO

MAKES 245 grams (1 cup) pesto

225 grams (8 ounces) fresh nettles, with stems on

90 grams (½ bunch) Italian parsley, leaves and small stems only

30 grams (¼ cup) untoasted walnuts

1 or 2 cloves garlic

1 gram (½ teaspoon) cracked black pepper

45 grams (½ cup) Grana Padano, Parmigiano-Reggiano, or Pecorino Romano cheese, grated

Pinch of fine sea salt

120 grams extra-virgin olive oil

1   To blanch the nettles, bring a large pot of water to a rolling boil. Without touching them with your hands, submerge the nettles with stems on for 15 seconds, then shock them in ice water (preferred) or put them in a colander and run cold water in a heavy stream over them for a couple of minutes to stop the cooking. Drain the nettles, remove the leaves from the stems, wring them out to remove any excess water (they're safe to touch now), and lay out on a towel.

2   In a large mixing bowl, combine the nettle leaves, parsley, walnuts, garlic, black pepper, cheese, and salt. Mix by hand, then put into a food processor fitted with a chopping blade. Drizzle in the olive oil while pulsing until it all comes together.

ROASTED MOREL MUSHROOMS

MAKES enough for 1 flatbread

90 grams (3 ounces) fresh morel mushrooms

15 grams (1 tablespoon) olive oil

2 cloves garlic, chopped

Fine sea salt

1   Wash the mushrooms (if they're wormy, soak them in salt water for 5 minutes) and drain. Slice the mushrooms into halves or quarters lengthwise, toss them in the olive oil with the garlic, season with sea salt, and roast in an ovenproof skillet in the preheating oven for 4 or 5 minutes.

THE WHITE OWL

Celery root and baby turnips? Sounds funky. Looks cool. Tastes really good. I'm always on the hunt for a combination of winter veg that works on a pizza, and one night at Trifecta Tavern this combo disappeared about 30 seconds after I brought it in with a couple more traditional pizzas for the staff meal. A layer of grated low-moisture mozzarella underneath shredded celery root and sliced white baby turnips gives the whole pie just enough gooeyness to balance the purity of the roots. It's super tasty, and the texture of the toppings—white on white on white—comes out just right. Chile flakes give it a nice bit of zip. Slices of Calabrian or another spicy red pepper on top would be a nice, colorful alternative to the chile flakes.

MAKES one 12-inch pizza

1 dough ball

125 grams (4½ ounces, about ⅓ of a whole) celery root

Extra-virgin olive oil

Sea salt

Chile flakes

2 baby white turnips (each about 2 inches in diameter)

90 grams (3 ounces) low-moisture mozzarella cheese

1　If you use a dough recipe that calls for refrigeration, remove your dough ball from the refrigerator about 60 to 90 minutes before baking pizza. Put your pizza steel or stone on an upper rack in your oven no more than 8 inches below the broiler. Preheat the oven to 550°F (290°C) for 45 minutes.

2　Prep the celery root, baby turnips, and cheese. Cut the base off the celery root and place it cut side down. Cutting vertically with a sharp knife, remove about ⅛ inch of the outer layer of the celery root to reveal the edible interior. Grate through the large holes on a box grater until you have 125 grams (4½ ounces)—it will be about a third of the root. (If you shred the rest, it's good mixed with whisked eggs, salt, and a little nutmeg and fried over medium-high heat like a pancake.) Put the shredded celery root in a medium-sized mixing bowl and toss it with about 15 grams (1 tablespoon) of olive oil and sea salt and chile flakes to taste. (One tablespoon of chile flakes will be pretty spicy, but that's how I like it.) Thinly slice the baby turnips (15 to 20 turnip slices is enough for topping the pizza) and toss them with your fingers in enough olive oil to coat each slice. Use a box grater's large holes to grate the mozzarella.

CONTINUED

217

THE WHITE OWL, CONTINUED

3   Set up your pizza assembly station. Give yourself about 2 feet of width on the countertop. Moderately flour the work surface. Position your wooden peel next to the floured area and dust it lightly with flour. Have the prepared celery root, turnips, and cheese at hand. Switch the oven to broil 10 minutes before loading the pizza.

4   To shape the pizza, put the dough ball on the floured work surface and flip to coat both sides moderately with flour. Use one of the shaping methods (Neapolitan or New York) shown on pages 92 to 95. Transfer the disk of pizza dough to the peel. Run your hands around the perimeter to relax it and work out the kinks.

5   Top the pizza dough with a drizzle of olive oil, then all of the shredded mozzarella. Next, use your fingers to spread the grated celery root evenly over the pizza, and finally, top with the slices of baby turnips as if they were pepperoni.

6   Turn off the broiler, then gently slide the pizza onto the pizza stone or steel. Close the oven door and change the oven setting to bake at 550°F (290°C). Bake for 5 minutes, until the rim is golden. Change the oven setting from bake to broil and let the pizza finish until the cheese is melted, the celery root and turnips have nice browning on the edges, and the crust is golden with spots of brown and a few small spots of char, about 2 minutes (check it after 1 minute to be sure). Use tongs or a fork to slide the pizza from the pizza steel or stone onto a large plate. Serve sliced.

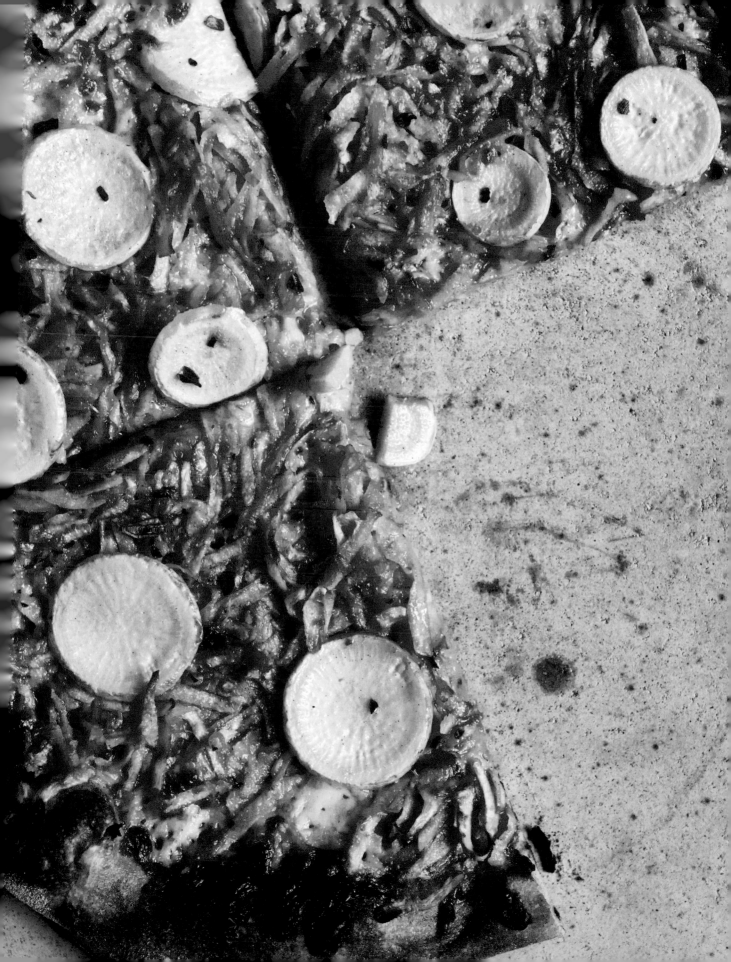

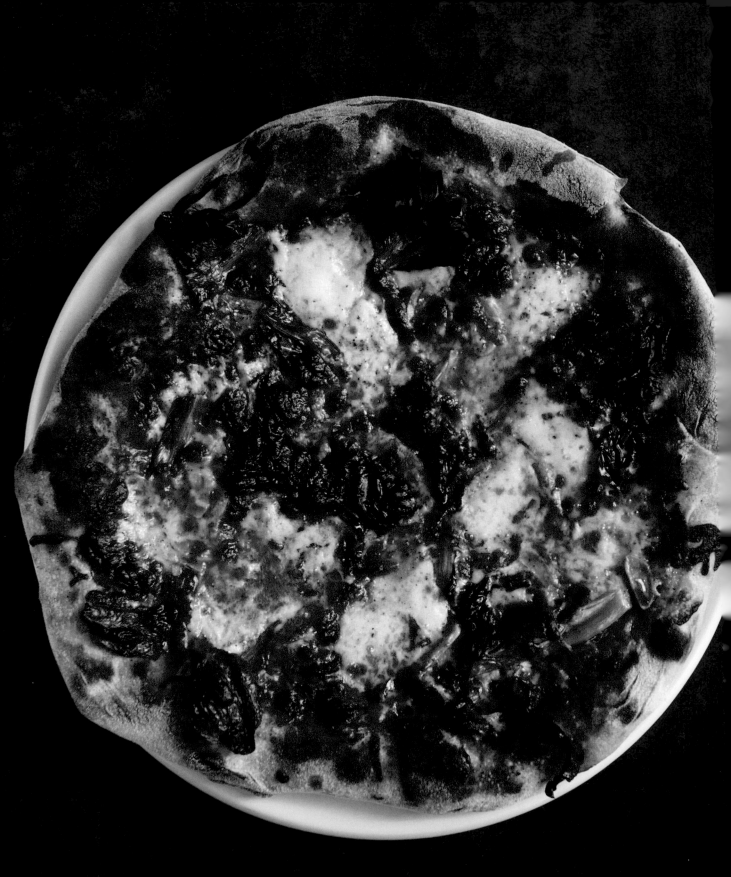

ESCAROLE PIZZA

I first had an escarole pizza at Pepe in Grani. Franco Pepe presented it as a folded pizza, which served the purpose of wilting the escarole via the hot crust and melted cheese. Escarole is in the chicory family, and it is quite tender for a hearty green, with just a slight hint of bitterness. In Oregon's Willamette Valley, escarole is harvested from June through November. You're more likely to find it at the farmers' market than at Safeway. Pizza's hot cheese will wilt the escarole and leave it with a tender but satisfying crunch when you eat it. Garlic, lemon, cured meats, and even dried fruits like cherries or raisins are terrific partners. For this pizza, dress the dough with a film of tomato sauce, then layer bite-size pieces of fresh escarole that have been tossed lightly in olive oil. Squeeze a little fresh lemon juice over the escarole and top with sliced garlic, then cover with grated provolone, sliced fresh mozzarella, and finally, cracked black pepper over the top. The escarole bits that are exposed directly to the heat get a nice crispy crunch when baked. Escarole also works on a white pie. Try this: top the escarole with garlic, then crumbled bacon, then cheese, and top with dried cherries or raisins that have been soaked to rehydrate (I soak them in Earl Grey tea).

Try this pizza with a minerally white wine, like a Falanghina from Campania, or any white wine from Friuli. An Oregon Pinot Gris would also be an excellent choice.

MAKES one 12-inch pizza

1 dough ball

3 or 4 escarole leaves

Extra-virgin olive oil

60 grams (2 ounces) provolone

60 grams (2 ounces) fresh mozzarella

2 or 3 cloves garlic

60 grams (¼ cup) tomato sauce

1 lemon wedge

Black pepper

1   If you use a dough recipe that calls for refrigeration, remove your dough ball from the refrigerator about 60 to 90 minutes before baking pizza. Put your pizza steel or stone on an upper rack in your oven no more than 8 inches below the broiler. Preheat the oven to 550°F (290°C) for 45 minutes.

2   Prep the escarole, cheese, and garlic. Rinse the escarole and pat dry, then tear or cut it into bite-size pieces and toss with olive oil to coat lightly. Grate the provolone using the large holes of a box grater and slice the mozzarella into 4 or 5 wedges. Slice the garlic thinly and coat lightly with olive oil.

3   Set up your pizza assembly station. Give yourself about 2 feet of width on the countertop. Moderately flour the work surface. Position your wooden peel next to the floured area and lightly dust it with flour. Have the tomato sauce, escarole, cheeses,

CONTINUED

ESCAROLE PIZZA, CONTINUED

garlic, lemon, and pepper on hand, with a ladle or large spoon for the sauce. Switch the oven to broil 10 minutes before loading the pizza.

4   To shape the pizza, put the dough ball on the floured work surface and flip to coat both sides moderately with flour. Use one of the shaping methods (Neapolitan or New York) shown on pages 92 to 95. Transfer the disk of pizza dough to the peel. Run your hands around the perimeter to relax it and work out the kinks.

5   Top the pizza dough with a thin coating of tomato sauce. Layer the escarole over the sauce to cover the pizza, and squeeze a small spritz of lemon juice over the greens. Cover the greens with the shredded provolone and then the garlic slices. Finish by topping the pizza with the slices of fresh mozzarella and grind black pepper over it to taste.

6   Turn off the broiler, then gently slide the pizza onto the pizza stone. Close the oven door and change the oven setting to bake at 550°F (290°C). Bake for 5 minutes, until the rim is golden. Change the oven setting from bake to broil and let the pizza finish until the cheese is softly melted and the crust is golden with spots of brown and a few small spots of char, about 2 minutes (check it after 1 minute to be sure). Use tongs or a fork to slide the pizza from the pizza steel or stone onto a large plate. Serve whole or sliced.

VARIATION To fold the pizza, place it on a large cutting board. Press the blade of a large chef's knife or mezzaluna across the middle of the pizza, but do not cut all the way through; just go far enough to facilitate folding. Fold the pizza in half along the perforation you just made to make a half-moon shape. Cut the folded pizza in half, perpendicular to the fold line, and serve immediately.

DELICATA SQUASH PIZZA

What I love about the appropriately named delicata squash is that it looks cool, it's delicious, and you can eat the skin once it's cooked. Wash it, cut it in half, scoop out the guts, and roast or sauté it without worrying about the challenge that other winter squashes present: working around an inedible skin. The delicata roasts quickly, giving this pizza an easy timeline, and it also happens to be beautiful. It makes a lovely decoration in your kitchen until used. It's one of many things I look forward to eating in the autumn and winter.

I like this pizza as a Roman-style, super-thin, crisp-crust pizza: delicata squash meets delicate pizza crust. The key as always is maintaining balance: you don't want to overwhelm the squash with too much cheese or sauce on the Roman pie. To finish this pizza, bunch up a handful of basil leaves and, using scissors, cut them over the top of the pizza. Spread the pieces out by hand, top with a drizzling of olive oil, and let the aromatics of the basil jump up your nostrils and into your dreams.

MAKES one 12-inch thin-crust pizza

1 (150-gram) dough ball

1 delicata squash

Extra-virgin olive oil

100 grams (⅓ cup plus 1 teaspoon) tomato sauce

40 grams (1½ ounces) fontina cheese, grated

80 grams (about 3 ounces) fresh mozzarella, sliced

Sea salt

Chile flakes

8 to 10 basil leaves

1   If you use a dough recipe that calls for refrigeration, remove your dough ball from the refrigerator about 60 to 90 minutes before baking pizza. Put your pizza steel or stone on an upper rack in your oven no more than 8 inches below the broiler. Preheat the oven to 550°F (290°C) for 45 minutes.

2   While the oven is heating, prep and roast the squash. Rinse the squash and very carefully cut it in half lengthwise. Use a spoon to scrape out the pulp and seeds in the hollow of the squash. With your hand, spread a light film of olive oil over the surface of the squash, and then over the outer skin. Place cut side up on an ovenproof skillet, and roast in your oven once it has reached 550°F (290°C) for 18 to 20 minutes, or until tender all the way through (a paring knife should slide easily through the squash). Remove from the oven and set aside to cool.

CONTINUED

DELICATA SQUASH PIZZA, CONTINUED

3 Place each squash half cut side down and slice into half-moons about ⅛ inch thick. Reserve 140 grams (5 ounces) of the squash for topping the pizza (serve the rest warmed with a drizzle of oil as a side dish, or snack on it while the pizza is baking).

4 Set up your pizza assembly station. Give yourself about 2 feet of width on the countertop. Moderately flour the work surface. Position your wooden peel next to the floured area and dust it lightly with flour. Have the tomato sauce, squash, cheeses, salt, and chile flakes at hand, and a ladle or large spoon for the sauce. Switch the oven to broil 10 minutes before loading the pizza.

5 To shape the pizza, put the dough ball on the floured work surface and flip to coat both sides moderately with flour. Use the Roman-style rolling-pin method on page 96. Transfer the disk of pizza dough to the peel. Run your hands around the perimeter to relax it and work out the kinks.

6 Spread the tomato sauce over the dough, smoothing it with the back of the spoon or ladle, then layer the slices of squash evenly around the pizza. Next, sprinkle the grated fontina cheese and finish with the mozzarella. Season with sea salt and chile flakes.

7 Turn off the broiler, then gently slide the pizza onto the pizza stone. Close the oven door and change the oven setting to bake at 550°F (290°C). Bake for 5 minutes, until the rim is golden. Change the oven setting from bake to broil and let the pizza finish until the cheese is softly melted and the crust is golden with spots of brown and a few small spots of char, about 2 minutes (check it after 1 minute to be sure). Use tongs or a fork to slide the pizza from the pizza steel or stone onto a large plate. Bunch up the basil leaves in one hand and, using a pair of scissors, snip a generous amount over the hot pizza. Use your hands to spread out the basil evenly, drizzle olive oil generously over the whole pizza, and serve whole or sliced.

BUTTERNUT SQUASH PIZZA

This autumn-and-winter pizza reminds me of the steady snare drumbeat throughout Ravel's *Bolero*, each bite adding emphasis to the thrill of the bite before. Roasted squash, crispy sage leaves, and bacon underneath pecorino and mozzarella cheeses make beautiful pizza music on top of a tender yet crisp and well-baked crust.

The butternut squash takes about an hour to roast at 400°F (205°C): halve it, scoop out the seeds and pulp, coat it lightly with olive oil and sprinkle with salt, and place cut side up in a roasting pan or ovenproof skillet. It's done when a paring knife slides easily into the flesh. You can do this a day or two before making pizza, or while the oven preheats. Once the squash is tender and then cooled, scoop out the flesh with a spoon and cut the bigger chunks into walnut-sized pieces or smaller for sprinkling over the pizza.

MAKES one 12-inch pizza

1 dough ball

115 grams (4 ounces) uncooked bacon, sliced into 1- to 2-inch lengths

4 or 5 sage leaves

15 grams (½ ounce) Pecorino Romano cheese

120 grams (4 ounces) *mozzarella di bufala* or *fior di latte* mozzarella, cut into ¼-inch to ½-inch-thick slices

Extra-virgin olive oil

140 grams (5 ounces) roasted butternut squash, in walnut-sized chunks

1   If you use a dough recipe that calls for refrigeration, remove your dough ball from the refrigerator about 60 to 90 minutes before baking pizza. Put your pizza steel or stone on an upper rack in your oven no more than 8 inches below the broiler. Preheat the oven to 550°F (290°C).

2   Prep the toppings. Spread the bacon pieces evenly in a 9- or 10-inch skillet set over medium-high heat and sauté to medium doneness. It will cook further and crisp up while the pizza is baking. Drain on paper towels. Remove all but about 2 spoonfuls of the bacon fat from the pan and set it over medium-high heat, until it bubbles when you drop in a sage leaf. Fry the sage leaves until crisp, about 1 minute, and set aside on a paper towel to drain. Use the medium-fine holes on a box grater to grate the pecorino cheese. If you are using *mozzarella di bufala*, pat the slices with a paper towel to remove some of their liquid.

3   Set up your pizza assembly station. Give yourself about 2 feet of width on the countertop. Moderately flour the work surface. Position your wooden peel next to the floured area and dust it lightly with flour. Crumble the sage leaves and have them and the bacon, cheeses, olive oil and squash at hand. Switch the oven to broil 10 minutes before loading the pizza.

CONTINUED

BUTTERNUT SQUASH PIZZA, CONTINUED

4   To shape the pizza, put the dough ball on the floured work surface and flip to coat both sides moderately with flour. Use one of the shaping methods (Neapolitan or New York) shown on pages 92 to 95. Transfer the disk of pizza dough to the peel. Run your hands around the perimeter to relax it and work out the kinks.

5   To top the pizza, drizzle 4 or 5 light stripes of olive oil over the dough and then top in this order: half the bacon, the chunks of squash, crumbled sage leaves, grated pecorino, and remaining bacon. Reserve the mozzarella for halfway into the bake. Turn off the broiler, then gently slide the pizza onto the pizza stone. Close the oven door and change the oven setting to bake at 550°F (290°C). Let the pizza bake for about 4 minutes, until the rim is just starting to turn golden. Use a pair of tongs to remove the pizza onto a plate.

6   Layer the mozzarella evenly over the pizza. Using your hands, place the pizza back onto the pizza steel or stone and continue baking for 1 to 2 minutes. Change the oven setting from bake to broil and let the pizza finish until the cheese is melted and the crust is golden with spots of brown and a few small spots of char, about 2 minutes (check it after 1 minute to be sure). Use tongs or a fork to slide the pizza from the pizza steel or stone onto a large plate. Serve whole or sliced.

ARTICHOKE AND BACON PIZZA

If you lived in Rome or Venice or many other Italian cities you would go to the outdoor market, buy some hand-turned artichoke hearts at a reasonable price, and take them home to cook. In the United States, you are much more likely to buy artichokes whole. If you want to take the time to turn your own, you can slice and sauté the hearts in olive oil and then layer them onto this pizza. For many people, buying marinated artichoke hearts is more economical and approachable, laborwise, than turning their own chokes. I will confess right here and now to really liking jarred marinated artichokes. Either way, this combination of artichoke hearts with two cheeses, lemon zest, and bacon makes for a delicious pizza.

MAKES one 12-inch pizza

1 dough ball

75 grams (2½ ounces) uncooked bacon, cut into 1- to 2-inch slices

15 grams (1 tablespoon) extra-virgin olive oil

1 lemon

55 grams (2 ounces) provolone cheese, grated

4 marinated artichoke hearts, sliced into quarters

55 grams (2 ounces) fresh goat cheese

Freshly cracked black pepper

1 If you use a dough recipe that calls for refrigeration, remove your dough ball from the refrigerator about 60 to 90 minutes before baking pizza. Put your pizza steel or stone on an upper rack in your oven no more than 8 inches below the broiler. Preheat the oven to 550°F (290°C) for 45 minutes.

2 Spread the bacon pieces evenly in a 9- or 10-inch skillet set over medium-high heat and sauté to medium doneness. It will cook further and crisp up while the pizza is baking. Drain on paper towels.

3 Set up your pizza assembly station. Give yourself about 2 feet of width on the countertop. Moderately flour the work surface. Position your wooden peel next to the floured area and dust it lightly with flour. Have the olive oil, lemon, cheeses, and sliced artichoke hearts at hand. Switch the oven to broil 10 minutes before loading the pizza.

4 To shape the pizza, put the dough ball on the floured work surface and flip to coat both sides moderately with flour. Use one of the shaping methods (Neapolitan or New York) shown on pages 92 to 95. Transfer the disk of pizza dough to the peel. Run your hands around the perimeter to relax it and work out the kinks.

5 Drizzle some of the olive oil over the dough in stripes. Zest half of the lemon directly over the pizza to cover the dough evenly, reserving the other

CONTINUED

ARTICHOKE AND BACON PIZZA, CONTINUED

half to top the pizza after baking. Spread the grated provolone over the pizza, followed by the quartered artichoke hearts, the bacon pieces, and then the goat cheese in 6 to 8 dollops (use a spoon and your fingers). Finish with black pepper to taste.

6 Turn off the broiler, then gently slide the pizza onto the pizza steel or stone. Close the oven door and change the oven setting to bake at 550°F (290°C). Bake for 5 minutes, until the rim is golden. Change the oven setting from bake to broil and let the pizza finish until the cheese is melted and the crust is golden with spots of brown and a few small spots of char, about 2 minutes (check it after 1 minute to be sure). Use tongs or a fork to slide the pizza from the pizza steel or stone onto a large plate. Drizzle the remaining olive oil in stripes over the pizze and grate the remaining lemon zest over the entire pizza. Serve whole or sliced.

CHANTERELLE AND GARLIC PIZZA

Shortly after the autumn rainy season begins, usually in early October, mushroom guys show up on our doorsteps at Ken's Artisan Pizza and Trifecta Tavern & Bakery. They forage chanterelles from the nearby forests and woods, and the 'shrooms show up on a lot of menus around town. I remember my late friend and occasional mentor, Robert Reynolds, quoting *his* mentor, Josephine Araldo, who said that cooking mushrooms without garlic "isn't worth a rabbit's fart." I couldn't find it in his treasure of a book, *An Excuse to Be Together,* but I'm holding onto the attribution because if he didn't write it, I'm sure he (and she) said it. Point memorably made: I always use garlic when I'm cooking mushrooms, and in this case I use garlic generously.

The tang of fresh goat cheese is a great foil to the meatiness of mushrooms and the bite of garlic. The pecorino adds some savory saltiness and the thyme is pretty and bright. This pizza is great with Champagne or a good pilsner, and its flavors linger beautifully.

MAKES one 12-inch pizza

1 dough ball

225 grams (8 ounces) fresh chanterelle mushrooms, shredded by hand into ¼-inch-thick strands

3 cloves garlic, chopped

50 grams (scant ¼ cup) extra-virgin olive oil

Fine sea salt

6 to 8 sprigs fresh thyme (lime thyme if you can find it), half picked, half left whole

70 grams (3½ ounces) fresh goat cheese

8 grams (2 tablespoons) grated Pecorino Romano cheese

Fresh cracked black pepper

1   If you use a dough recipe that calls for refrigeration, remove your dough ball from the refrigerator about 60 to 90 minutes before baking pizza. Put your pizza steel or stone on an upper rack in your oven no more than 8 inches below the broiler. Preheat the oven to 550°F (290°C) for at least 45 minutes.

2   Put the chanterelles and the chopped garlic into a mixing bowl with the olive oil and toss with your hand. You want enough oil to coat all the mushrooms, but not more. Sprinkle with sea salt to taste and toss to integrate. Put the prepared mushrooms and garlic into a cast-iron pan with the whole thyme sprigs and put into the preheated oven for 8 to 10 minutes, checking at 5 minutes, since the oven is very hot. Once the mushrooms are cooked through, remove from the oven and set aside.

3 Set up your pizza assembly station. Give yourself about 2 feet of width on the countertop. Moderately flour the work surface. Position your wooden peel next to the floured area and lightly dust it with flour. Have the the prepped mushrooms, cheeses, pepper, and fresh thyme leaves at hand. Switch the oven to broil 10 minutes before loading the pizza.

4 To shape the pizza, put the dough ball on the floured work surface and flip to coat both sides moderately with flour. Use one of the shaping methods (Neapolitan or New York) shown on pages 92 to 95. Transfer the disk of pizza dough to the peel. Run your hands around the perimeter to relax it and work out the kinks.

5 Top the pizza dough with grape-sized chunks of the fresh goat cheese distributed evenly all over the top. Sprinkle the grated pecorino evenly over the top, then distribute the mushrooms and garlic and grind cracked pepper over.

6 Turn off the broiler, then gently slide the pizza onto the pizza steel or stone. Close the oven door and change the oven setting to bake at 550°F (290°C). Bake for 5 minutes, until the rim is golden. Change the oven setting from bake to broil and let the pizza finish until the cheese is melted and the crust is golden with spots of brown and a few small spots of char, about 2 minutes (check it after 1 minute to be sure). Use tongs or a fork to slide the pizza from the pizza steel or stone onto a large plate. Serve whole or sliced with a sprinkling of the fresh thyme leaves.

THE TOMMY HABETZ PIZZA

Today Tommy Habetz is the co-owner and co-founder of Bunk Sandwiches and Bunk Bar in Portland, Oregon, along with his friends and business partners Nick Wood and Matt Brown. Tommy's career goes back to New York, where he worked as a cook at Bobby Flay's Mesa Grill, sous chef at Mario Batali's Po, and then co-sous chef of Lupa in Greenwich Village.

Tommy and I were in my kitchen on an August evening drinking Brunello and talking pizza, and together we came up with this summery pie based on dressed cherry tomatoes, lightly cooked sweet onions, and *soppressata* from Portland's Chop Butchery & Charcuterie. The cheese was mostly *mozzarella di bufala*, but a very light sprinkling of freshly grated Pecorino Romano was the bomb that sent this pie to another planet. It took Tommy's deft touch for this pie to hit the stratosphere, and as usual, it's the kind of touch that comes from many years of cooking great food. I am humbly representing this great pizza, with permission, and naming it after my friend Tommy Habetz.

MAKES one 12-inch pizza

1 dough ball

12 ripe cherry tomatoes

Extra-virgin olive oil

A very short splash (about ¼ teaspoon) red wine vinegar or another tasty vinegar

½ sweet onion, cut in half and sliced vertically

60 grams (2 ounces) stick salami, such as *soppressata*, thinly sliced into 12 to 15 pieces

115 grams (4 ounces) fresh *mozzarella di bufala* or whole-milk mozzarella (*fior di latte*), cut into ½-inch-thick pieces

7 grams (¼ ounce) Pecorino Romano cheese, grated

1   If you use a dough recipe that calls for refrigeration, remove your dough ball from the refrigerator about 60 to 90 minutes before baking pizza. Put your pizza steel or stone on an upper rack in your oven no more than 8 inches below the broiler. Preheat the oven to 550°F (290°C) for at least 45 minutes.

2   Prep the tomatoes and onions. Slice the cherry tomatoes in half and put them in a mixing bowl. Add 30 grams (2 tablespoons) of the olive oil and the vinegar. Toss by hand and set aside. Cook the onion very lightly—not to translucent—over moderate heat with just enough oil to keep the onions from sticking to the pan. Set aside in a small bowl. (If you like, soak the onion slices in cold water for 10 minutes before sweating to remove the oniony bite.)

CONTINUED

3 Set up your pizza assembly station. Give yourself about 2 feet of width on the countertop. Moderately flour the work surface. Position your wooden peel next to the floured area and lightly dust it with flour. Have the prepped cherry tomatoes, onions, sliced salami, and cheeses at hand. Switch the oven to broil 10 minutes before loading the pizza.

4 To shape the pizza, put the dough ball on the floured work surface and flip to coat both sides moderately with flour. Use one of the shaping methods (Neapolitan or New York) shown on pages 92 to 95. Transfer the disk of pizza dough to the peel. Run your hands around the perimeter to relax it and work out the kinks.

5 Drizzle a small amount of extra-virgin olive oil over the top of the pizza, and top it with the cherry tomatoes, onions, sliced salami, and shredded pieces of mozzarella, in that order. Then sprinkle the grated pecorino over the top before baking.

6 Turn off the broiler, then gently slide the pizza onto the pizza steel or stone. Close the oven door and change the oven setting to bake at 550°F (290°C). Bake for 5 minutes, until the rim is golden. Change the oven setting from bake to broil and let the pizza finish until the cheese is melted and the crust is golden with spots of brown and a few small spots of char, about 2 minutes (check it after 1 minute to be sure). Use tongs or a fork to slide the pizza from the pizza steel or stone onto a large plate. Serve sliced.

THE PIE HOLE SKILLET PIZZA

This ultra-simple, easy-to-make pizza in a cast-iron skillet is one of my favorites—simplicity like this demands the best quality of dough, tomatoes, and olive oil. Heavy with tomato sauce and topped with dried oregano and one or two slices of fresh mozzarella in the middle, it gets a generous dousing of good olive oil immediately after it comes out of the oven. The aromatics are seductive. I love the white hole—the pie hole—of molten mozzarella in the middle of the pie. Feel free to top the pizza with a few anchovies after it comes out of the oven.

If you're using a 275-gram dough ball, a 10-inch skillet is ideal. If you have a 9-inch skillet, use a 220-gram dough ball. Making more than one? Two skillets can fit side-by-side on a standard-size pizza steel or stone. If your skillet is reasonably seasoned, there's no need to oil it before laying the dough in it. The crust will be crisper if you bake this pizza on top of a preheated pizza steel or stone than if you bake it on an open oven rack. If you don't have a pizza steel or stone, bake it on a rack position low in the oven and check the bottom of the crust with a pair of tongs after 10 minutes of baking.

MAKES one 10-inch skillet pizza

1 (275-gram) dough ball

115 grams (⅓ cup plus 2 teaspoons) tomato sauce

2 grams (1 teaspoon) dried oregano

50 grams (2 ounces) fresh whole-milk mozzarella cheese (*fior dl latte*) or *mozzarella di bufala*, packed in brine

Extra-virgin olive oil

Sea salt

Chile flakes

1 If you use a dough recipe that calls for refrigeration, remove your dough ball(s) from the refrigerator about 60 to 90 minutes before baking pizza. Put your pizza steel or stone on an upper rack in your oven no more than 8 inches below the broiler. Preheat the oven to 550°F (290°C) for 45 minutes. Switch the oven to broil 10 minutes before loading the pizza.

2 Set up your pizza assembly station. Give yourself about 2 feet of width on the countertop. Moderately flour the work surface. Have the tomato sauce, oregano, cheese, and olive oil on hand, and a ladle or large spoon for the sauce.

3 To shape the pizza, put the dough ball on the floured work surface and flip to coat both sides moderately with flour. Use the shaping method shown on pages 92 to 95. Shape this round a little bit smaller than for baking on the hearth, to 10 inches in diameter, or 9 inches if that is the size of your skillet. Transfer the disk of pizza dough to a cast-iron skillet. The

CONTINUED

235

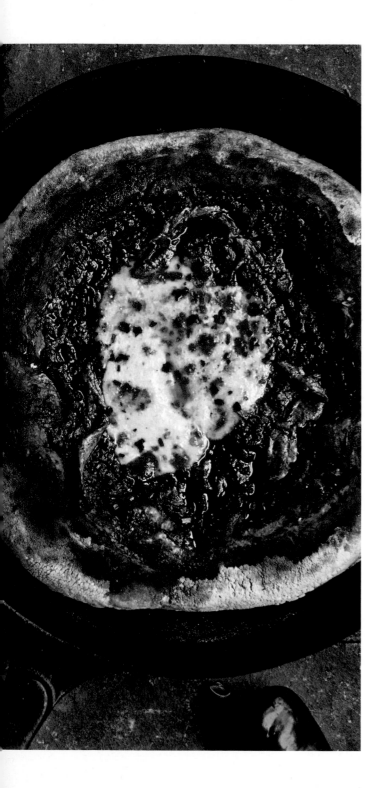

THE PIE HOLE SKILLET PIZZA, CONTINUED

edges of the dough should extend just to the sides; do not press the dough up the sides of the skillet, as that makes the perimeter of the pizza too doughy.

4 Spread the tomato sauce over the dough, smoothing it with the back of the ladle or spoon. Sprinkle the dried oregano evenly over the sauce and place the mozzarella in the middle. Very lightly drizzle olive oil around the outer edge of the sauce.

5 Place the skillet on the preheated pizza steel or stone. Close the oven door and change the oven setting to bake at 550°F (290°C). Let the pizza bake for about 15 minutes, checking it at 10 to 12 minutes.

6 Tilt the skillet over a work surface and use a pair of tongs to pull the pizza out of the skillet. The pizza should slide right out of the pan without sticking. Remove it to a plate to serve whole, or slice and serve and then drizzle olive oil generously over the entire pizza and sprinkle with sea salt and chile flakes. This is a fun one to cut with a pair of kitchen shears.

HAWAIIAN PIZZA

On the mainland, most of the pineapples you'll find were grown in Costa Rica or Mexico, yet the pineapple remains a symbolic fruit of the Hawaiian Islands, where the Dole Pineapple company onced turned the island of Lanai into a pineapple plantation. The Hawaiian pizza is a modern-day classic piece of Americana. I have always enjoyed the combination of ham and sweet fruit on a pizza, pepped up with chile flakes and balanced with savory roasted onions. I like to wipe a few dollops of bacon fat on the dough before saucing it to add another layer of flavor. This pizza is not as cheesy as some others, since I don't want it to become too heavy.

Pre-roast the diced pineapple to concentrate its flavor and release some moisture before adding it to the pizza. You can do this while you preheat the pizza stone, after the oven has come to temperature. This pizza is terrific with a glass of Alsatian Riesling, by the way.

MAKES one 12-inch pizza

1 dough ball

1 whole pineapple

¼ to ½ sweet onion, preferably torpedo or Maui, or substitute Vidalia or Walla Walla

15 grams (1 tablespoon) extra-virgin olive oil

Fine sea salt

Chile flakes

15 grams (1 tablespoon) or less rendered bacon fat (optional)

90 grams (⅓ cup) tomato sauce

15 grams (¼ cup) Pecorino Romano cheese, finely grated

50 grams (about 2 ounces) cooked (deli-counter) ham, sliced medium-thick in 2- to 3-inch lengths

40 grams (1½ ounces) low-moisture, whole-milk mozzarella cheese, coarsely grated

1   If you use a dough recipe that calls for refrigeration, remove your dough ball from the refrigerator about 60 to 90 minutes before baking pizza. Put your pizza steel or stone on an upper rack in your oven no more than 8 inches below the broiler. Preheat the oven to 550°F (290°C) for 45 minutes.

2   While the oven is heating, prep and roast the pineapple and onion. Peel the pineapple with a sharp knife, then cut the fruit away from its core. Cut the fruit into ½-inch squares. Slice the onion vertically into ½-inch lengths. In a mixing bowl, toss the pineapple and onion in the olive oil with a sprinkling of fine sea salt and chile flakes to taste. Pour

CONTINUED

into a cast-iron pan and roast at 550°F (290°C) for 10 minutes. The pineapple should be nicely caramelized where it was in contact with the pan. Reserve 100 grams (3½ ounces) of the roasted pineapple and onion mixture for topping the pizza. Snack on the rest.

3 Set up your pizza assembly station. Give yourself about 2 feet of width on the countertop. Moderately flour the work surface. Position your wooden peel next to the floured area and lightly dust it with flour. Have the bacon fat, tomato sauce, pecorino, ham, roasted pineapple and onion, and mozzarella at hand, and a ladle or spoon for the sauce. Switch the oven to broil 10 minutes before loading the pizza.

4 To shape the pizza, put the dough ball on the floured work surface and flip to coat both sides moderately with flour. Use one of the shaping methods (Neapolitan or New York) shown on pages 92 to 95. Transfer the disk of pizza dough to the peel. Run your hands around the perimeter to relax it and work out the kinks.

5 Dab bacon fat evenly around the dough, then spread the dough with the tomato sauce, smoothed with the back of the ladle or spoon. Add the toppings in this order: pecorino, ham, roasted pineapple and onion, and mozzarella.

6 Turn off the broiler, then gently slide the pizza onto the pizza stone. Close the oven door and change the oven setting to bake at 550°F (290°C). Bake for 5 minutes, then take a quick look at the pizza to judge its progress. Turn on the broiler again, and finish the pizza until the cheese is completely melted and the crust is golden with spots of brown and a few small spots of char, about 2 minutes. Use tongs or a fork to slide the pizza from the pizza steel or stone onto a large plate. Serve.

RACLETTE PIZZA

I should have known, when I asked Steve Jones what his favorite pizza was from his series of weekly pizza nights at Portland's Cheese Bar, that he would answer on the opposite side of the cheese universe from fresh, milky mozzarella. Steve likes cheese with distinctive personality and a little bit of funk. Enter, stage left, Raclette Pizza. But this isn't just a goofy cheese lover's pizza: it makes culinary sense, with its blend of beer-braised leeks and roasted potatoes and an optional finish of any cured pork product. A good portion of your house will smell like a Swiss chalet when you pull this belly-warmer out of the oven.

MAKES one 12-inch pizza

1 dough ball

1 large leek or 2 medium leeks

15 grams (1 tablespoon) butter

250 grams (1 cup) nonhoppy beer, such as farmhouse ale or Saison Dupont

35 grams (1½ ounces) pork belly lardons or pancetta, sliced into 1-inch pieces (optional)

1 medium yellow potato, roasted and crumbled

125 grams (4½ ounces) raclette cheese, grated

1 If you use a dough recipe that calls for refrigeration, remove your dough ball from the refrigerator about 60 to 90 minutes before baking pizza. Put your pizza steel or stone on an upper rack in your oven no more than 8 inches below the broiler. Preheat the oven to 550°F (290°C) for 45 minutes.

2 Cut the leek into ½-inch slices and sauté with the butter over medium heat until they get a little color. Add the beer and carefully cook it down until there's just a film of beer left, about 5 to 10 minutes, then cover and cook over very low heat until the leeks are nearly spreadable in texture, another 20 minutes. Cook the lardons over medium-high heat until they are about halfway done, about 3 minutes. They will finish cooking in the oven.

3 Set up your pizza assembly station. Give yourself about 2 feet of width on the countertop. Moderately flour the work surface. Position your wooden peel next to the floured area and dust it lightly with flour. Have the braised leeks, lardons, potato, and cheese at hand. Switch the oven to broil 10 minutes before loading the pizza.

4 To shape the pizza, put the dough ball on the floured work surface and flip to coat both sides moderately with flour. Use one of the shaping methods (Neapolitan or New York) shown on pages 92 to 95. Transfer the disk of pizza dough to the peel. Run your hands around the perimeter to relax it and work out the kinks.

5 Spread the braised leeks evenly over the top of the pizza, followed by the crumbled potato, and then the cheese. If you are using lardons, sprinkle them over the cheese. Turn off the broiler, then gently slide the pizza onto the pizza stone. Close the oven door and change the oven setting to bake at 550°F (290°C). Bake for 5 minutes, until the rim is golden. Change the oven setting from bake to broil and let the pizza finish until the crust is golden with spots of brown and a few small spots of char, about 2 minutes (check it after 1 minute to be sure). Use tongs or a fork to slide the pizza from the pizza steel or stone onto a large plate. Serve sliced.

MEASUREMENT CONVERSION CHARTS

VOLUME

Formulas

1 teaspoon = 4.93 milliliters

1 tablespoon = 14.79 milliliters/3 teaspoons

1 cup = 236.59 milliliters/16 tablespoons

1 liter = 202.88 teaspoons/67.63 tablespoons/4.23 cups

U.S.	IMPERIAL	METRIC
1 tablespoon	½ fl oz	15 ml
2 tablespoons	1 fl oz	30 ml
¼ cup	2 fl oz	60 ml
⅓ cup	3 fl oz	90 ml
½ cup	4 fl oz	120 ml
⅔ cup	5 fl oz (¼ pint)	150 ml
¾ cup	6 fl oz	180 ml
1 cup	8 fl oz (⅓ pint)	240 ml
1¼ cups	10 fl oz (½ pint)	300 ml
2 cups (1 pint)	16 fl oz (⅔ pint)	480 ml
2½ cups	20 fl oz (1 pint)	600 ml
1 quart	32 fl oz (1⅔ pints)	1 l

WEIGHT

Formulas

1 ounce = 28.35 grams

1 pound = 453.59 grams/16 ounces

1 kilogram = 2.2 pounds

U.S./IMPERIAL	METRIC
½ oz	15 g
1 oz	30 g
2 oz	60 g
¼ lb	115 g
⅓ lb	150 g
½ lb	225 g
¾ lb	350 g
1 lb	450 g

LENGTH

Formulas

---

1 inch = 2.54 cm
1 foot = 0.3 m/12 inches
1 cm = 0.39 inch
1 m = 3.28 feet/39.37 inches

INCH	METRIC
¼ inch	6 mm
½ inch	1.25 cm
¾ inch	2 cm
1 inch	2.5 cm
6 inches (½ foot)	15 cm
12 inches (1 foot)	30 cm

TEMPERATURE

Formulas

$\frac{9}{5} C + 32 = F$
$(F - 32) \times \frac{5}{9} = C$

FAHRENHEIT	CELSIUS/GAS MARK
250°F	120°C/gas mark ½
275°F	135°C/gas mark 1
300°F	150°C/gas mark 2
325°F	160°C/gas mark 3
350°F	175° or 180°C/gas mark 4
375°F	190°C/gas mark 5
400°F	200°C/gas mark 6
425°F	220°C/gas mark 7
450°F	230°C/gas mark 8
475°F	245°C/gas mark 9
500°F	260°C

ACKNOWLEDGMENTS

Three short months after opening Trifecta Tavern, I was crazy enough to decide to write this book. There is no way I could have completed this project without the excellent work—every day—of my staff at Trifecta, Ken's Artisan Bakery, and Ken's Artisan Pizza, where pride of place and product drive my talented teams. A very heartfelt thank-you to you all.

The greatest joy for me came from the people who welcomed me into their worlds—who generously taught me about their approach to pizza, their tomatoes, their water buffalo cheese, or their flour. A special thank-you to Fred Mortati of Orlando Foods and John Magazino of Chef's Warehouse, for making the introductions to producers in Italy and opening doors to the land of Campania, where I found the true soul of pizza. Likewise, heartfelt thanks go out to Costantino Cutolo of Compagnia Mercantile D'Oltremare, Bernardino De Vita of Agricola Casearia Lupara, and Mauro and Antimo Caputo of Antico Molino Caputo in Naples.

Two of Italy's greatest pizzaiolos, Enzo Coccia and Franco Pepe, gave me a strong sense of pizza's place in Campania; they have devoted their lives to advancing the craft that is not only theirs, but also their fathers' and their grandfathers' *professione*. The pride, professionalism, artistry, and just plain magnificence of their pizzas touched me deeply.

Alan Weiner took so many great photos for this book that we were greatly challenged deciding what to place and which shots needed a separate gallery of their own. A giant thanks to Alan, a photojournalist extraordinaire.

First level editing and recipe testing from Kat Merck was indispensable.

Finally, a very special thanks to the team at Ten Speed Press. I am very proud to be one of your authors. Designer Kara Plikaitis put text and photos into a beautifully designed book, and copyeditor Clancy Drake kept my words on the straight and true. Most of all, senior editor Emily Timberlake has the magic to inspire and guide, encourage, and even laugh at my marginal jokes.

Much love to all. Especially Gomez, who never has a bad day.

INDEX

Published in the United States by Ten Speed Press, an imprint of the
Crown Publishing Group, a division of Penguin Random House LLC, New York.
www.crownpublishing.com
www.tenspeed.com

Ten Speed Press and the Ten Speed Press colophon are registered trademarks
of Penguin Random House LLC.

Library of Congress Cataloging-in-Publication Data
Forkish, Ken, author.
The elements of pizza : unlocking the secrets to world-class pies at home / Ken Forkish ;
photography by Alan Weiner.
     pages cm
Includes bibliographical references and index.
1. Pizza. I. Weiner, Alan (Alan S.), photographer. II. Title.
TX770.P58.F675 2016
641.82'48—dc23

                          2015032247

Hardcover ISBN: 978-1-60774-838-0
eBook ISBN: 978-1-60774-839-7

Printed in China

Design by Kara Plikaitis

13

First Edition